UNDERSTANDING LITERACY DEVELOPMENT

LITERACY DEVELOPMENT

A Global View

UNDERSTANDING LITERACY DEVELOPMENT

A Global View

Edited by

Anne McKeough
University of Calgary

Linda M. Phillips
University of Alberta

Vianne Timmons
University of Prince Edward Island

Judy Lee Lupart
University of Alberta

LAWRENCE ERLBAUM ASSOCIATES, PUBLISHERS
2006   Mahwah, New Jersey   London

KH

Lawrence Erlbaum Associates, Inc., Publishers
10 Industrial Avenue
Mahwah, New Jersey 07430
www.erlbaum.com

Cover design by Kathryn Houghtaling Lacey

Library of Congress Cataloging-in-Publication Data

Understanding literacy development : a global view / edited by Anne McKeough ... [et al.].
    p. cm.
    Includes bibliographical references and index.
ISBN 0-8058-5115-1 (cloth : alk. paper)
ISBN 0-8058-5116-X (pbk. : alk. paper)
1. Reading—Cross-cultural studies. 2. Literacy—Cross-cultural studies.
   I. McKeough, Anne.
LB1050.2.U54   2005
302.2'244—dc22
                                       2005062481
                                        CIP

Books published by Lawrence Erlbaum Associates are printed on acid-free paper, and their bindings are chosen for strength and durability.

Printed in the United States of America
10 9 8 7 6 5 4 3 2 1

12/21/06

To our mothers,
Carmelita McKeough, Elizabeth Ennis Phillips,
Georgetta Timmons, and *Doris Leone Harris,*
who were our first and most committed teachers.

Contents

Preface

The development of literacy is a pressing concern for governments, business communities, educational professionals, and the general public around the globe. The United Nations Educational, Scientific, and Cultural Organization's 2002 illiteracy figures range from 7% to 14% for developed countries and are as high as 48% in least developed countries. The cost of not reading well can be disastrous in terms of lost human potential and productivity and a general failure to access many of life's opportunities. Children who experience literacy challenges are at high risk for school failure in their youth and chronic unemployment and poor health in adulthood and, consequently, for perpetuating the cycle of poverty and low literacy in the next generation. Limited literacy affects what happens in and beyond schools. As such, literacy development is a high-stakes endeavor. Social institutions and individuals have invested hugely, in terms of material and human capital, yet daily we hear disappointing statistics outlining the costs of low literacy. Reforms clearly are required. But what directions and approaches are best? What aspects of literacy development are most critical? What is the best of what we know concerning how to support literacy development? Are we using the knowledge we have across learning contexts and across the life span?

To address these questions, we have assembled leading literacy experts from around the world, thus providing a global view of literacy development across cultures, countries, and circumstances. Taken together, our contributors target a wide and comprehensive set of critical literacy issues.

They offer an exhaustive exploration of the complexities of literacy development—issues related to early literacy, school instruction (e.g., phonological awareness, reading comprehension, and metalinguistic awareness), family literacy (low income, low educational levels, and second languages), adolescent and adult literacy (e.g., role of the media and technology, purposes of literacy, and diverse ways to engage in literacy), and teacher development (e.g., diagnostic teaching, teacher attitudes and change, and professional learning communities).

To help organize these many threads, the book is organized into three parts. In Part I, the contributors address key elements that affect young children's acquisition of literacy skills and strategies. In the second part, the authors extend the discussion to literacy development outside of the school walls, providing important insights into how literacy can be supported in multiple contexts from early infancy to adulthood. In the book's final section, Part III, the authors consider teacher development, recognizing frontline educators as a key component to improving literacy development.

Across this comprehensive analysis of literacy development are some important commonalities that link the many critical aspects of literacy development. Chief among them is the call for reform. Authors in Part I call for changes in instructional practices based on the best of what research has determined literacy development involves, Part II authors call for foundational changes in how we conceive of literacy development and who should be involved in its support, and Part III authors outline what needs to change in teacher development if teachers are to be maximally effective. A second theme running through all of the book's chapters is diversity. In every chapter of the volume, the authors address a common concern: how to address their clientele's diversity. Literacy learners differ in many ways, including in cultural background, neurophysiology, material resources, experience with language, and developmental level. Thus, the need for customizing instruction is critical. Together, the authors mount a convincing argument that, to meet the unique needs of diverse literacy learners, support must be tailored to those needs. The third common theme is a reliance on research to point the way to best practice. Research, the authors argue, is often underutilized, and this has led to learners being offered less than the best. Finally, a fourth theme is the need for a balanced and integrated approach to supporting literacy development, including the integration of multiple reading skills, multiple literacy contexts, and multiple aspects of professional development.

At a time when education is burdened by increasing economic pressure to do more with less, it is imperative that educators and decisionmakers at all levels have access to current, broad-ranging, and in-depth information and evidence to inform their choices. This volume, which compiles critical research on a wide spectrum of literacy concerns, is an invaluable tool. The audience we are addressing with this book includes a broad range of professionals who engage in educational practice, research, and policymaking. As such, the book will be of interest to (a) university faculty and students in departments of curriculum and instruction, teacher education, educational psychology, and early childhood; (b) employees of school boards (e.g., administrators, supervisors of curriculum development and program delivery, psychologists, student services consultants and clinicians, and both regular classroom and special education teachers); (c) employees of other social institutions, such as government ministries responsible for designing and implementing school curricula and health; (d) social scientists interested in the role of literacy education; and (e) academic societies (e.g., International Reading Association, Society for the Scientific Study of Reading, Canadian Society for the Study of Education, National Reading Conference, and the American Educational Research Association).

Literacy is currently a hot topic. A review of the listings of just two major academic publishers revealed approximately 125 titles related to the topic published since 2000. When we consider how many publishing houses take up the topic, the number of books devoted to literacy is quite staggering. Why, then, do we believe that this volume will be of interest? Put simply, because no other publication aims to address a *global* view of literacy. This volume is unique in that it offers a new platform on which researchers, educators, and students of literacy can stand to gain a novel perspective— one that lets them see simultaneously the multiple faces of literacy, the multiple contexts in which literacy takes place, and the multiple paths to its development.

ACKNOWLEDGMENTS

We acknowledge gratefully the support of the our cosponsors at the University of Alberta (Edmonton Catholic School Board; Edmonton Public School Board; and Elk Island School Division and Office of the Vice President, Research), the University of Calgary (Calgary Board of Education, Calgary Catholic Schools, Calgary Regional Consortium, Canadian Rockies Regional School Division, Golden Hills School Division, and Rocky View School Division), and the University of Prince Edward Island (Eastern School Board, Kiwanis, New Brunswick Department of Education, and Prince Edward Island Department of Education), the faculties of education at the three institutions, the Canadian Language and Literacy Research Network, and the National Literacy Secretariat. We are grateful to the following individuals for their excellent work interviewing the contributors: Heather Blair, Christine Gordon, Christa Fox, Sue Humphry, Carol Leroy, Margaret Mackey, Barbara MacNutt, Jill McClay, and Joanne Steinmann. Cherie Geering, Canadian Center for Research on Literacy at the University of Alberta, helped tremendously with the author and subject indexes and we are most appreciative. We also thank Sarah McCarthey (University of Illinois, Urbana–Champaign), Kathleen Hinchman (Syracuse University), and Marilyn J. Chambliss (University of Maryland College Park) for their thoughtful reviews of the manuscript. A final word of appreciation goes to our editor, Naomi Silverman, for her timely support and guidance.

1

Developing Literacy:
Themes and Issues

Anne McKeough
Marya Jarvey
University of Calgary

Until fairly recently, most volumes on literacy development focused primarily on techniques and strategies aimed at fostering students' skills in academic contexts, and although this focus remains an extremely important one, more current work has evidenced a broadening in what is seen as central to literacy development (Kamil, Mosenthal, Pearson, & Barr, 2000). The range of questions now being addressed includes the following: What literacy instruction practices have strong research evidence to support them (Slavin, 2002)? What role do teacher knowledge and beliefs play in the type of literacy instruction offered (Olson, 2002; Olson & Torrance, 2001), and how can teacher development best be supported (DuFour & Eaker, 1998)? What is the role of culture in literacy development (Bruner, 1990)? How do families interface with schools' efforts to develop early literacy (Dunst, 2002), and how might elements of popular culture influence literacy development (Storey, 1996)? What do we know about the nature of language processes, in particular, about written languages across cultures that might inform teachers of literacy (Ingram Willis, Garcia, Barrera, & Harris, (2003)? Finally, what are the particular challenges faced by diverse groups of learners and their teachers (Allington, 2002; Kamil, Manning, & Walberg, 2002; Taylor & Pearson, 2002)?

In this book, we bring together the seminal work of scholars who have contributed to and indeed shaped this new view of literacy development. Taken together, their insights into literacy offer a global view of this centrally important domain, one that is thorough and comprehensive. As such, the volume offers a combined focus on content knowledge: what the field has come to know about understanding literacy development (e.g., phonemic awareness and phonics, cross-linguistic requirements, and comprehension) and on participants in the literacy enterprise (i.e., children, parents, teachers, and the culture at large). To assemble such a wide-ranging picture, it was necessary to include scholars who live and work outside of North America to show how literacy issues have been approached in other national and cultural contexts, the commonalities and unique features of efforts being made to understand and support literacy development around the world, and the reforms that are called for. Thus, the title of this volume, *Understanding Literacy Development: A Global View*, is meant to convey two things: (a) that the volume provides a broad and encompassing look at current issues and questions under study in the field of literacy development and (b) that the list of contributors is international, providing views of literacy theory, research, and practice from around the world.

Such an array of issues and perspectives on literacy development requires a framework to organize the work. Although the topic of literacy development could be parsed in a number of ways, in this book we have chosen to explore three main thrusts: In Part I, *"Improving School-Based Literacy Development,"* we present research-based practices that promote literacy in early life, from preschool to the early school years. In the second part, *"Literacy Development Beyond the School Walls,"* broader cultural contexts for literacy development—non-school-based literacy environments that influence preschool and school-aged children, struggling adolescent readers, and adult learners—are addressed. In the final part of the book, *"Changing Literacy Practices,"* the focus turns to an often-ignored component of supporting literacy: teacher professional development. In each of these sections, the volume's contributors shed light on literacy development across ages, backgrounds, and societal beliefs and circumstances.

IMPROVING SCHOOL-BASED LITERACY DEVELOPMENT

How do we make sense of the competing ideas and the myriad instructional programs and teaching resources? How do we sift out the best of what we know about supporting literacy development in the early years and at school? The authors of the chapters in Part I approach these questions from a research base. Each calls for reforms in the way we think about and approach literacy development, either at the level of understanding students' learning or at the level of understanding teachers' effective practice.

Ingvar Lundberg begins this first section with a call for a balanced approach to literacy development, arguing for attention to what he refers to as the *two tracks to literacy*—decoding and comprehension—and highlighting challenges to literacy development, viewed from the perspective of these two tracks. Decoding difficulties, he proposes, which can originate in infancy from deleterious social, physical, and environmental factors (e.g., second-hand smoke and poor medical treatment), influence infants' hearing and hence their perception of the patterns in speech sounds. The precise quality of phonological representations is subsequently linked to phonological awareness. Robust European and North American research findings point to a link between limited phonological awareness and risk for reading failure. Improving chances for successful literacy development, then, means addressing the factors contributing to infant health. Moreover, because the quantity and quality of language interactions in children's home environments influence vocabulary acquisition and, in turn, reading comprehension, Lundberg also calls for increased awareness of the impact of children's social environment. He cites Swedish research to demonstrate that helping children to attend explicitly to these aspects of language at the preschool age reduces later literacy development challenges. Thus, further reform advocated by Lundberg involves developing early child care training programs and broadening our notion of where and by whom such instruction should be offered. Parent education programs, community literacy resource centers, home visits by literacy specialists, and cooperative parent support networks are his alternatives to more traditional preschool environments.

The next three chapters address literacy development as the child enters school. Tom Nicholson and Richard C. Anderson and Wenling Li focus primarily on decoding, and Michael Pressley and Katie Hilden focus on comprehension.

Nicholson endorses the centrality of phonemic awareness and phonics to literacy development, targeting the problem of not using the best of what research has uncovered and calling for reform in what literacy students learn and how they are taught. He builds a strong case for the need to build phonological awareness and phonetic components into reading programs to balance the current focus on text comprehension and interpretation. Drawing on research from New Zealand, Australia, and the United States, Nicholson documents how and why neglecting to offer explicit instruction in phonological coding skills results in a failure to meet the literacy development needs of a significant number of children. He further calls for changes in how and where reading programs are delivered, sympathizing with resource-strapped families who may not be able to provide children with the skilled adult attention or material supports necessary to help their children at home and advocating that society has a responsibility to help these children. Besides providing appropriate in-school programming to assist struggling students, he advocates using resources beyond the school, services such as family literacy centers, after-school programs, and summer schools.

In chapter 4, Pressley and Hilden echo Nicholson's call to use the best of what we know about understanding and supporting literacy development, but here the emphasis is largely on reading comprehension strategy instruction. Their view is that a balanced literacy instruction program needs to reflect research that has shown the importance of precisely teaching specific reading strategies, along with building fluency through decoding instruction and building word knowledge through vocabulary work. They cite 30 years of research that has shown that explicitly teaching cognitive comprehension strategies (e.g., predicting, questioning, seeking clarifications, summarizing, attending to elements of story structure, constructing mental images, and connecting to prior knowledge) leads to improved reading comprehension. And again like Nicholson, these authors go on to call for reform in society's role in supporting literacy development. Whereas schools can and must use what has been shown by research to be effective instruction, other social institutions (e.g., libraries, booksellers, and children's television program planners, as well as local and national governments) need to play an active role in supporting students' literacy development by providing them with improved access to world knowledge, another proven factor in the literacy equation.

In chapter 5, Richard Anderson and Wenling Li use a cross-linguistic lens to highlight what they consider critical elements in the reading process—elements that demand instructional attention. Their discussion of universals in reading Chinese and English, languages with very different literacy demands, underscores the centrality of metalinguistic awareness to literacy development. They first focus on the role of phonological awareness in decoding written text and argue that, although aspects of phonology are weighted differently in each language (e.g., in English, phoneme-level awareness is critical in correlating speech to text, whereas in Chinese, syllable awareness is far more important, as Chinese characters are pronounced with a single syllable), it plays a critical role in both languages. Anderson and Li identify a second metalinguistic component, morphological awareness (i.e., the ability to identify, consider, and manipulate word parts that hold meaning) that is similarly central to literacy development. Morphology has received less attention in literacy circles than has phonology, and the research presented in chapter 5 is recent and seminal. The authors demonstrate that although Chinese morphology is more transparent than its English counterpart (i.e., in Chinese, each syllable represents one morpheme and corresponds to one character, whereas in English the relations are more complex), research findings point to a strong relationship between morphological awareness and reading proficiency in both languages. Their convincing argument for the universality of these two metalinguistic factors, and hence instructional focus on them, provides a clear direction for understanding and supporting literacy development.

In Part I of this book, then, the authors offer concrete suggestions for reform. Across three continents, calls are issued to attend to those aspects of literacy development that research has shown to be important during the early and middle years of childhood and to offer appropriate learning supports in school and community contexts. In Part II, this second context, the broader community/cultural context, becomes the focus as authors explore its influence on literacy development and suggest reforms that extend beyond the school walls.

LITERACY DEVELOPMENT BEYOND SCHOOL WALLS

In chapter 6, Donna E. Alvermann extends the analysis of the cultural impact on literacy development. She examines traditional school culture, with its promotion of certain normative ways of reading texts, arguing that privileging school literacy over other forms of literacy is likely not in the best interests of struggling readers. She calls for reform in the degree of emphasis placed on these normative ways of reading because their usefulness is waning as new media and interactive communication technologies emerge. To replace these outmoded approaches, Alvermann advocates teaching for critical awareness using media and technology. Arguing that developing adolescents' critical awareness of how all types of texts (e.g., print, visual, oral, or Internet mediated) positions them as readers and viewers within their cultural, social, and historical contexts, she calls on all who are engaged in the literacy enterprise to reexamine their beliefs and practices, challenging us to analyze our assumptions about what it means to be literate in the 21st century and what literacy development should entail.

Heather Sample Gosse and Linda M. Phillips also examine links between cultural contexts and literacy development, in chapter 7. They discuss the influence of home environments on infant development and see the family as a social system that is foundational to literacy development. How society values (or undervalues) the home environment, the way in which families are supported through social policies, and the attention given to the home by the culture at large all have implications for the quality of literacy development that goes on there. A research-based rationale for *family as foundational* convincingly positions Sample Gosse and Phillips to argue for the necessity of facing current challenges to literacy development that arise from diverse demographics. Paramount among these challenges is effectively supporting families to socialize their children into literacy, given the difficulties faced by families of visible minorities, families of lower socioeconomic status, and families whose mother tongue is not English. Such support involves knowing the underlying beliefs, attitudes, values, and expectations that families hold about literacy, methods used to assess them, and diverse ways of enhancing literacy development. Sample Gosse and Phillips maintain, however, that if teaching emergent literacy skills in the home and the community is divorced from what is taught in formal educational settings, children may experience a setback or discontinuity in their literacy development. In fact, it is often the explicit wish of families that the two curricula interface. This latter point takes up and expands on the call made in Part I for increased societal involvement in the literacy development of children.

In chapter 8, Mary Hamilton, like Sample Gosse and Phillips, argues that understanding literacy learners' social contexts is a prerequisite to providing them with appropriate literacy support. Her look outside the school walls extends to adult learners who use literacy for a wide range of self-determined purposes (e.g., writing minutes of meetings, compiling family histories, and completing welfare benefit entitlement forms). Within this broader view that she advocates, the focus shifts from a deficit model of literacy development to one that encompasses the diverse ways people engage in literacy activities and how these are differentially valued by society. Citing European and North American research, Hamilton argues for a major paradigm shift—from a purely psychological model of literacy to one that includes sociological aspects as well. Such a shift requires that our emphasis moves from cognitive skill sets and instructional methods to the purposes to which literacy is aimed and the historical and cultural settings of literacy learners. Thus, knowing is increasingly understood not so much as an individual cognitive matter but as a social, relational process. Chapter 8 ends with a call to question existing perceptions of literacy, reflect on practices, and see literacy and learning within the larger context of a changing society.

Contributors to this middle section of the volume amplify the calls for societal involvement issued in Part I. They elaborate on the role of social contexts in literacy development across the life span and highlight the many purposes for which literacy is needed and aimed. Taken together, they expand our view of literacy development toward a broader, global perspective.

CHANGING LITERACY PRACTICES

Having explored literacy learners' development (Part I) and the social contexts of literacy development (Part II), in this final section attention is turned to an often-overlooked component: teacher development. Although the three contributors to Part III span diverse cultural contexts, they are uniform in their call for reforms in teacher development practices and revisit the cost of failing to attend to factors shown through research to be critical to literacy development. Seok Moi Ng examines teacher professional development from a systemic perspective, Ileana Seda-Santana describes problems associated with changing entrenched conceptions of literacy; and Michael W. Kibby and Debra Dechert discuss particular requirements of individual teacher change. Together, these three chapters offer a road map to effective teaching.

Ng's chapter 9 centers on answering the following question: How can we put what we know of literacy development into practice? Her extensive review of literacy research positions her to extend her work meaningfully into the domain of practice. Ng asserts that teacher development is critical to educational change and that such work must consider the interplay among teacher beliefs, instructional practice, and students' literacy achievement. She cites research from North America, Australia, New Zealand, and Singapore to support her call for adequate and appropriate teacher development programs and infrastructure that supports innovative practice. Beyond this, Ng maintains that underlying beliefs and attitudes of students, parents, and others in the community can impede or support change and that their involvement is critical in building support for educational change.

In chapter 10, Seda-Santana affirms the importance of attitudes and beliefs in teaching, looking at the specific conceptions of literacy students and teachers hold. Her position is that the approaches students and teachers take toward literacy tasks at school grow out of their conceptions and beliefs. On the basis of her review of North American and Mexican research on student and teacher conceptions, Seda-Santana urges that preservice and in-service teacher education focus on helping teachers to understand prior conceptions and develop new ones that are more closely aligned with current research-based knowledge of literacy development.

Kibby and Dechert, in the final chapter of this final section, take up the specifics of skilled literacy teaching, laying out a set of abilities that teachers need to support diverse learners' literacy development (e.g., reestablishing children's confidence in their reading ability, becoming a systematic observer of children, and balancing the difficulty level of text). Foundational to skilled teaching, they argue, is teachers' use of a problem-solving model for instructional decisions. They call for a shift in teacher focus from covering curriculum to *adaptive flexibility*, whereby teachers sculpt instruction to build from what children know to what they most need to learn. Such a reflective approach leads to instruction that is child centered rather than activity centered. Finally, they posit that the benefits of diagnostic teaching processes extend beyond positive student literacy outcomes to gains in teacher knowledge and confidence.

CONCLUSION

Although the chapters in this book are written by scholars from different parts of the globe who have diverse research interests, three clear, common themes emerge. First among these is *diversity*. Literacy learners come in all shapes and sizes, and thus the need for customizing instructional support is critical. One program, one innovation, one curriculum, one venue, or one approach to literacy simply does not fit all learners. Neither does it fit for all teachers. Learners and teachers differ in many ways, including in their cultural backgrounds, their material resources, their experiences with language, and their conceptual understanding (Neuman & Dickinson, 2001). Thus, the delivery of services to meet diverse needs and profiles must be specifically tailored. It doesn't matter which of the aspects of literacy development are considered, this point remains true. Customizing for specific needs is necessary in order to achieve success.

The second theme that emerges across the chapters is *research-based practice*. In the first section of the book, "Improving School-Based Literacy Development," this theme manifests in a focus on analyses of literacy learners. In Part II, "Literacy Development Beyond the School Walls," analysis of the social context of literacy development, including the beliefs and views of literacy learners and teachers, becomes the research lens. In the book's third section, "Changing Literacy Practices," the research lens is turned on teacher development. Each of our contributing researchers looks closely at the practices of front-line educators as they attempt to bring about positive change, recognizing in them a key component to improvement in literacy development.

The third theme involves the necessity for *integration*—integration of multiple reading skills (e.g., phonemic and morphological awareness, phonics and vocabulary knowledge, and comprehension strategies and skills), of multiple literacy contexts (school, home, and media environments), and of multiple aspects professional development (e.g., teacher knowledge and beliefs, collaborative mentorship, and reflective practice). This last theme is perhaps less completely articulated than the others; the challenge that now lies before us is to integrate our research-based analyses across literacy learners and literacy contexts.

Taken together, these three themes provide a launch, of sorts, from which educators and researchers are positioned to ask: Where are we now? Where do we go next?

REFERENCES

Allington, R. L. (2002). *What really matters for struggling readers: Designing research-based programs*. New York: Longman.

Bruner, J. (1990). *Acts of meaning*. Cambridge, MA: Harvard University Press.

DuFour, R., & Eaker, R. (1998). *Professional learning communities at work.* Bloomington, IN: National Educational Service.

Dunst, C. J. (2002). Family-centered practices: Birth through high school. *Journal of Special Education, 36*, 139–147.

Ingram Willis, A., Garcia, G. E., Barrera, R. B., & Harris, V. J. (2003). *Multicultural issues in literacy research and practice.* Mahwah, NJ: Lawrence Erlbaum Associates.

Kamil, M. L., Manning, J. B., & Walberg, H. J. (Eds.). (2002). *Successful reading instruction.* Greenwich, CT: Information Age.

Kamil, M. L., Mosenthal, P. B., Pearson, P. D., & Barr, R. (Eds.). (2000). *Handbook of reading research* (Vol. III). Mahwah, NJ: Lawrence Erlbaum Associates.

Neuman, S. B., & Dickinson, D. K. (Eds.). (2001). *Handbook of early literacy research.* New York: Guilford.

Olson, D. R. (2002). *Psychological theory and educational reform: How school remakes mind and society.* Cambridge, England: Cambridge University Press.

Olson, D. R., & Torrance, N. (2001). *The making of literate societies.* Oxford, England: Blackwell.

Slavin, R. E. (2002). Evidence-based educational policies: Transforming educational practice and research. *Educational Researcher, 31*, 15–21.

Storey, J. (1996). *Cultural studies and the study of popular culture: Theories and methods.* Athens: University of Georgia Press.

Taylor, B., & Pearson, P. D. (2002). *Teaching reading: Effective schools, accomplished teachers.* Mahwah, NJ: Lawrence Erlbaum Associates.

I

Improving School-Based
Literacy Development

2

The Child's Route Into Literacy: A Double-Track Journey

Ingvar Lundberg
Göteborg University

It can be claimed that the evolution of mankind from barbarism to civilization was the result of literacy. Thus, a major step in the development of human culture and society was the invention of a system for external representation of the sounds of human language giving us a cognitive tool, the art of reading and writing, with the most profound impact on society and human cognitive functioning. However, the acquisition of reading and writing does not come naturally in childhood in the same way as skills such as talking and walking. Reading and writing are, in fact, rather unnatural acts, and some children have great difficulties learning these important skills. Poor mastery of literacy skills in society has serious future consequences and puts the child in a risky future situation. Therefore, in order to take proper preventive and remedial measures, it is of critical importance to understand the conditions and prerequisites for learning to read and write and identify the major obstacles for children at risk.

A skilled reader recognizes printed words rapidly and without effort. In fact, the words are as transparent as spoken words are to a listener. However, automatic word recognition is only one aspect of skilled reading. Comprehension of texts involves higher order linguistic and cognitive skills such as sentence parsing, making inferences, dealing with text structure, and applying relevant background knowledge. Literacy activities in current society involve more than just reading a piece of conventional text;

they are also involved in the complex use of the enormously expanded memory bank provided by the media, the Internet, and printed documents and forms. Getting access to these sources is not only a question of decoding the printed words and using the normal listening comprehension skills developed in oral communication. Navigating in the sea of textual information also requires complex procedural memories and advanced cognitive strategies for locating items, for finding the right entries; using the right keywords; knowing the conventions of tabular packing of information; searching manuals, recipes, and diagrams; following directions; and remembering passwords, PIN codes, and efficient search procedures. These skills, certainly vulnerable to poor initial acquisition and loss due to disuse, accidents, or aging, deserve closer examination as the demands on literacy competence increase dramatically in postmodern society.

In this chapter, I examine the ontogenetic roots of literacy skills in the individual and try to understand why reading and writing acquisition is a particularly hard task for some children. Because reading and writing are primarily language-based skills, the focus is on aspects of linguistic development. My departure is the distinction between word recognition or decoding and comprehension in reading (Gough & Tunmer, 1986), and I argue that these two aspects have partly different ontogenetic roots.

An outline of the structure of this chapter is given in Fig. 2.1. The left part of the figure describes one track and includes the various developmental components related to decoding of printed words. Accurate representations of the sound structure of the native language start to develop very early in infancy and constitute prerequisites for the development of a vocabulary as well as phonological awareness. The child eventually comes to realize how the alphabetic script is mapped to the phonemic units of language.

The track to the right in Fig. 2.1 concerns the development of communicative and linguistic abilities projecting onto the comprehension aspect of reading. This track includes very basic prerequisites for social and cognitive development, such as secure attachment and the development of a theory of mind. Syntactic ability, vocabulary, and world knowledge are necessary dimensions in the development of comprehension.

EARLY STEPS IN LANGUAGE DEVELOPMENT

Long before children utter their first word, considerable activity related to language acquisition takes place. During the first year, infants come to recognize the perceptual properties of their native language, and mental maps are developed for the speech sounds of their mother tongue (Jusczyk, Friederici, Wessels, Svenkerud, & Jusczyk, 1993; Kuhl, 1998).

During the first weeks of life, an infant usually is asleep. However, an enormous development project is ahead: the acquisition of thousands of

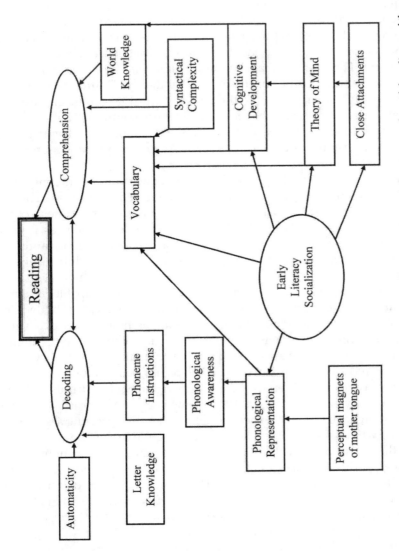

FIG. 2.1. The two developmental tracks of reading: The left half of the diagram indicates the route toward word decoding, and the right half indicates steps toward comprehension.

words in a short period of time, words that are constructed from a limited set of speech sounds. In view of this task, sleeping might not be the optimal way of spending useful learning time. In a fascinating study, Cheour et al. (2002) showed that newborns actually can learn to discriminate between similar vowel sounds—for example, /y/ and /y/i/—when they are asleep. In contrast, older children or adults are not expected to be able to learn while they are sleeping. Cheour et al. recorded a certain kind of electrophysiological brain response from electrodes attached to the skull of the newborns. This response, called *mismatch negativity,* indicates that a change in auditory stimulus has been detected by the child. After a full night of training (repeated exposure to the vowel contrast) a significant mismatch negativity response could be recorded, whereas nontrained babies did not show this response to the vowel contrasts. It is obvious that sleeping babies are able to use the surrounding speech sounds in a learning process of important future potential.

Infants, awake or asleep, thus learn a great deal about different aspects of the sound organization of their native language in a short span of time. They learn to categorize the sound units of their mother tongue, and they can extract words, and even the clauses and phrases of utterances, from the continuous speech stream (Jusczyk, 1997). The sound categorization process is well illustrated by a study in Japan (Kuhl, 1998). Adult speakers of Japanese have notorious difficulties in making the /r-l/ distinction (Strange, 1995). A newborn Japanese child, however, is capable of hearing the difference between /r/ and /l/. Eleven months later, this ability is lost, not because of impaired hearing but as a result of the extensive exposure to the native language, where relevant linguistic contrasts are highlighted and nonused contrasts are de-emphasized. Similarly, the vowel system of Swedish has an early impact on Swedish babies, who tend to perceive and categorize vowels differently from American babies (Kuhl, Williams, Lacerda, Stevens, & Lindblom, 1992). Thus, the phoneme categories of the native language function as perceptual magnets by attracting and patterning the world of speech sounds surrounding the infant. One can suspect that this early and delicate phase of phonological development might easily be disturbed by unfavorable influences, such as repeated and untreated middle ear infections (otitis media). This condition may impair hearing up to 20 dB, which may be enough to seriously affect the child's ability to make relevant phonological distinctions (Klein & Rapin, 1988; Nittrouer, 1996; for a research review, see also Roberts & Burchinal, 2001). Although some children may be genetically more vulnerable than others to develop otitis media, environmental factors do play a role. Passive smoking has been identified as a risk factor. Neglect, poor caring, and poor medical treatment are often socially determined factors that increase the risk for untreated otitis and delayed language development. Breastfeeding, however, is considered to be a powerful protective factor that strengthens the infant's immune defense and reduces the seriousness of an ear infection. One could also speculate on the role of breastfeeding in the development of attachment; at the least, it might be a good indicator of emotional bonds of beneficial value for the further development of communicative skills. In any case, infant caring conditions involve physical as well as psychological and social dimensions.

The early establishment of precise phonological representations of words is critical for the development of vocabulary (Locke, Hodgson, Macaruso, Roberts, Lambrecht-Smith, & Guttentag, 1997) and speaking skills. It also is a necessary achievement for the development of phonological awareness, which in turn is a critical prerequisite for understanding the alphabetic principle when children face the task of learning to read.

PHONOLOGICAL AWARENESS

When children begin to learn to read and write, they have to be able to deal with phonology more consciously than when they learned to speak. They need to understand the *alphabetical principle,* that is, to understand that the phonemes of a word can be represented by letters, and that the difference between words heard in the phonological structures is encoded by the letters of written words.

Why is it so difficult for some children to understand this principle and to gain conscious access to the phonology they already master so well in their spoken language? Let us see how speakers produce phonemes and how listeners hear them. Phonemes, when we produce them, are movements in the organs of speech. For example, a /b/ is a closing and opening of the lips, accompanied by an explosion of breath and voicing. But before we are finished with one phoneme, our speech organs have usually begun preparing for the next phoneme. If you are going to say *book,* you close your lips with a slight rounding, because you know your next phoneme is a vowel sound that needs rounded lips. If you are going to say *beetle,* you don't close your lips rounded, but laterally spread, in anticipation of the bright *ee*-sound. And so it goes all through the utterance, with sounds blurring, overlapping, and interfering with each other. This is the principle of *co-articulation* of speech (Liberman, Cooper, Shankweiler, & Studdert-Kennedy, 1967).

Why is spoken language so complex and yet so simple to process and produce? Surely it would have been easier for listeners if all the speakers pronounced their utterances as strings of discrete, tidy, unblurred phonemes. Here we should remember that speech has been around much longer than print and that speech is obviously the result of a long biological evolution. The good thing about co-articulation is that it lets us speak much faster than if we carefully articulated words one phoneme at a time, and this speed seems to have given us a biological advantage. We usually speak at the rate of 10 to 20 phonemes per second—much, much faster than if we delivered phonemes one at a time, like pearls on a string.

Another advantage of co-articulation is that it provides a higher degree of redundancy. The vowel sound in *book* is incorporated into both of the surrounding consonant sounds, so if the listener misses the middle part of the word—for example, because of some extraneous noise—then nothing is lost; the listener still hears the word *book*. So the redundancy that is created by co-articulation helps guard against what communication engineers call *noise*: the inevitable background buzz that accompanies any signal.

Just like other specialized processes that have evolved over great spans of time (another example is depth perception), co-articulation is fully automatic. Neither speakers nor listeners have to know anything at all about it; they just do it. Speakers need only to think of what they are saying and listeners to what is being said. Phonemes get chosen, blended, and spoken, then heard, unblended, and understood automatically. Our *specialized phonological module* takes care of these tasks for us.

In order to learn to talk, the only thing a child has to do is be around people who talk, but in order to learn to read, the child almost always has to submit to some kind of instruction—in school, or less formally by a parent or an older sibling. We see, then, that writing and speech are not truly analogous functions. Learning to talk is as natural as learning to walk or learning to experience depth perception. Learning to read is more like learning to play chess or program a computer. Once the child has grasped the alphabetical principle through explicit teaching, a powerful self-teaching device is available for further explorations of the print environment, where the reading skill is developed, refined, and automatized (Share & Stanovich, 1995).

If it is the case learning to read makes specific demands in the child's phonological system, is it then possible to predict, early on, which children will have trouble learning to read and write when they start school?

THE RELATION BETWEEN PHONOLOGICAL AWARENESS AND LEARNING TO READ

The association between lack of phonological awareness and failure in learning to read and write is in fact one of the most robust findings in developmental cognitive psychology and has been replicated over and over again across several languages, ages, and tasks used to assess phonological awareness (for a review, see, e.g. Höien & Lundberg, 2000).

One of the earliest demonstrations was presented by Lundberg, Olofsson, and Wall (1980). It provided an intensive examination of the linguistic abilities of kindergartners and addressed the question of whether the children's deficiency in phonological awareness is, in fact, linguistic in nature or whether it might be attributable to a deficiency in general cognitive analytical ability. The battery of 11 tests given to 200 children included both linguistic and nonlinguistic tasks. The linguistic category included word synthesis tasks that varied in two dimensions of two levels each: with or without memory load and using either phoneme or syllable units. Word analysis tasks analogous to those for synthesis were also used, as were tasks demanding the analysis of phoneme position in words, reversal of phoneme segments in words, and rhyming. The linguistic tasks required the child to shift attention from content or meaning to abstract form, thus possibly reflecting a general cognitive function not exclusively limited to language material. For this reason, nonlinguistic control tasks that simulated those cognitive demands were also included, making it possible to demonstrate a critical dissociation as support for a modular view of the phonological function.

The most powerful predictors of later reading and writing skills in the entire battery turned out to be those requiring phonological awareness, specifically the ability to manipulate phonemes in words. In contrast, the poor readers showed no particular deficiency in the nonlinguistic task. The causal model tested in the study was thus supported by the data. The longitudinal design implies a causal direction: Abilities developed at a later point in time cannot possibly be the cause of earlier achievement. Thus, phonological awareness seems to be an important prerequisite for learning to read, and nonreaders with a low level of phonological awareness at the preschool level have an elevated risk of a developing reading disability in school.

A commonly held view is that reading instruction is necessary for the development of phonemic awareness. I (Lundberg, 1991) studied more than 200 nonreading preschoolers aged 6 to 7 years and found that only about 10 children were able to deal with language segments at the phoneme level. Although these cases are exceptional, they demonstrate that it is possible, at least in principle, to develop phonemic awareness among nonreaders outside the context of formal reading instruction in school. The real stimulating force, however, seems to be involved in the acquisition of reading and spelling.

It has been demonstrated that phonemic awareness can be developed among preschoolers without the use of letters or other elements of early reading instruction. Lundberg, Frost, and Petersen (1988) designed a program that required daily games and exercises in group settings over a full preschool year. The program included listening games, rhymes and ditties, playing with sentences and words, and discovering the initial sounds of words and finally with full segmentation of words into phonemes. An American version of this program is now available (Adams, Foorman, Lundberg, & Beeler, 1998).

The effects of this program were very specific, being modest or even absent on general cognitive functions and on language comprehension, vocabulary, rhyming, and syllable segmentation, but rather dramatic on phonemic skills. Thus, Lundberg et al. (1988) concluded that phonemic awareness could be developed among preschoolers by training, without introducing letters or written text. A more crucial element seems to be the *explicit* guidance of children when they are trying to access, attend to, and extract the elusive, abstract, and implicit segments of language.

The crucial question now is whether explicit training in preschool also facilitates later reading and spelling acquisition in school. The preschool children studied by Lundberg et al. (1988) were followed up through 4 school years, and reading and spelling achievement was assessed on several occasions. The trained group outperformed the control group on each of 12 points of measurement, indicating the beneficial effect of the preschool program.

I (Lundberg, 1994) presented data from children in preschool with a high risk of developing reading disability as revealed on a pretest on phonological awareness and general language development. Children at risk who were involved in the training program had fairly normal reading and spelling development, whereas children at risk in the untrained control group showed the expected poor literacy development. Thus, it seems to be possible to prevent the development of reading and spelling disabilities in school by a carefully designed preschool program that brings the children to a level of phonological awareness that is sufficiently high to meet the demands involved in the alphabetic system. The at-risk children who did not enjoy the benefit of such training seemed to face serious obstacles on their way to literacy.

Studies of phonological awareness have also focused on more theoretical issues, such as, for example, the dimensionality of phonological awareness, the neurological substrate of phonological awareness, or phonological awareness as a core problem in dyslexia (Lundberg, 1999). I (Lundberg, 1978) argued that phonological awareness might be viewed as a continuum or hierarchy ranging from *shallow* to *deep* sensitivity, where the deeper levels require more explicit analysis of smaller sized phonological units. The task of deciding which words rhyme, for example, seems to require a small amount of conscious awareness of phonemic segments. The attention is more directed to global similarity between words. One should then not be surprised to find rhyming ability among nonreading children. Syllables are also accessible units of the speech signal, more easy to isolate, more salient, and less abstract than the phoneme units. To attend to and become aware of syllables, the child does not have to ignore the natural unity of the articulatory act, as is the case with attending to phonemes.

A study by Höien, Lundberg, Bjaalid, and Stanovich (1995) supported the view that there are different components of phonological awareness corresponding to the different levels of language analysis required by the task. More than 1,500 children in preschool and Grade 1 were tested with a battery of tasks, including rhyme recognition, syllable counting, initial phoneme identification, phoneme deletion, phoneme synthesis, and phoneme counting. Three basic factors were extracted in a principal-component analysis: a Phoneme factor, a Syllable factor, and a Rhyme factor. It was demonstrated that the three components of phonological awareness were separate predictors of early word reading ability, with the Syllable factor the weakest predictor. Not unexpectedly, the Phoneme factor proved to be the most powerful predictor of early reading acquisition. Among the various phonemic tasks, the phoneme identification tasks explained the highest proportion of unique variance.

I have outlined the first track in the child's route to reading leading to the skill of decoding written words. It started with the sleeping baby learning the phonetic contrasts of the mother tongue and ending up with the school beginner becoming aware of the phonemic segments of spoken words hitherto only implicitly embedded in the speech module of a talkative child. The other track leads to the art of comprehending and appreciating written texts. Because it involves general cognitive and linguistic functions outside the phonological module, it is a far more complex track, and only a few characteristics can be highlighted in this chapter.

VOCABULARY DEVELOPMENT

Children acquire new words with a miraculous speed. By the age of 16 to 17 years, they know the meaning of some 60,000 words. A simple calculation indicates that they must learn about 10 new words every day, or one new word each 90th minute, during their waking hours. How is it possible? There is yet no definite answer. Bloom (2000) conducted an interesting historic review of attempts to explain the remarkable learning process. Since St. Augustine (398/1961), several theories have been proposed. The church father pointed out the critical importance of the communicative intention of adults who mark their intentions by gestures and eye movements toward the object to be named. John Locke (1690/1964), on the other hand, suggested that children acquire a new word by associating it with objects that are pointed out or events occurring when the word is uttered. Bloom thinks that Augustine's view is more correct, although the acquisition process seems to be more complex and we know surprisingly little about it. In fact, there are several different ways to acquire new words, whereby various cues from the linguistic and extralinguistic contexts are used.

Bloom (2000) emphasized the importance of joint attention between the child and adult in language learning. A prerequisite for learning, according to Bloom, is that the child has a conception of the other's consciousness, or what is called a *theory of mind*. When a child learns the meaning of word, he or she also learns something about the thoughts of other human beings. *Joint attention* means that I understand that you see the same thing as I do. This is a first step toward the ability to take the other's role, to know what the other knows or does not know, that there is something important in the speech act that the other wants to express.

As already mentioned, children learn new words with a remarkable speed. However, there are wide individual differences. Hart and Risley (1995) observed pronounced differences in vocabulary among 3-year-olds in Kansas. They decided to take a closer look at the linguistic environment of children. During regular home visits to 42 families of various socioeconomic and educational backgrounds they carefully recorded parent–child communication from the age of 8 months to the age of 36 months. The observations were coded and analyzed for the type of verbal interactions that occurred. On the basis of the samples of observations, the researchers estimated the total number of words to which the children had been exposed to by the parents during the first 3 years of life. There were large differences in the quantity of language interactions as a function of social class.

Children of parents with higher education (professionals) had been exposed to an average of more than 30 million words during the first 3 years of living, whereas children of parents on social welfare had an average of about 10 million words. Children of working-class parents had an estimate somewhere in between (approximately 20 million words). These differences are certainly dramatic and probably explain much of the differences in vocabulary growth between children from these social strata. It seems as if a possible contribution from genetic factors in explaining interindividual variation is effectively masked by social factors. Not only does the sheer number or quantity of words exposed differ between the groups, but also the quality of speech directed to the children is different. The children of professionals were to a far higher extent exposed to encouragement, praise, warm suggestions and the like, whereas children of parents on welfare primarily listened to utterances intended to restrict their actions, disciplinary orders, blame, and so on. There is no doubt that the quality of speech input should have an impact on the development of the child's self-concept and future courage and willingness to learn in school.

The higher the socioeconomic level, the more the parents listened to their children, prompted children to elaborate their utterances, told their children what was worth remembering, and taught them how to cope with problems. The correlational nature of this fascinating study certainly requires care in the interpretation of causality. We cannot know with certainty that the linguistic development of the children is determined by the quantity and quality of the verbal interactions. However, in combination with evidence from other studies there is a great deal of support for an interpretation in the suggested direction.

ATTACHMENT AND LITERACY DEVELOPMENT DURING THE PRESCHOOL YEARS

Infants form strong emotional ties to their caregivers. Since Bowlby (1969) formulated a comprehensive theory on the biological and social mechanisms of attachment, the issue has been extensively studied, and Bowlby's original ideas have enjoyed substantial empirical support (Sroufe, 1996; Sroufe, Carlson, Levy, & Egeland, 1999). The establishment of a secure attachment during the first year of a child's life seems to be closely related to the sensitivity of the parents. The more secure the attachment, the more effective is the parent in helping the child to explore the world (Ainsworth, 1967). There is a correlation between secure attachment during infancy and subsequent cognitive interactions with parents (Borkowski & Dukewich, 1996; Frankel & Bates, 1990). The early attachment pattern has also an indirect effect: It plays an ongoing role during development in the child's selection of environments, in what type of activity the child will be engaged, the intensity of the engagement, and how the child interprets the experiences (Sroufe et al., 1999). The initial attachment pattern sets in motion particular styles of thinking, feeling, and interacting throughout development.

Attachment security is also related to the early informal literacy socialization (emergent literacy) during the preschool years (Bus & van Ijzendoorn, 1988). Securely attached children were more attentive and less easily distracted during literacy interactions. The more securely attached children spent more time reading together with their mothers than did less securely attached children (Bus, & van Ijzendoorn, 1995). The insecure children were inattentive during storybook reading and had greater difficulty in understanding the text.

Early Informal Literacy Socialization

Before reading instruction is given in the first school year, most children enjoy the benefit of a great deal of informal literacy socialization at home and in preschool settings. Without yet being able to read, many children come to know the conventions of print, its directionality and its layout principles (Hiebert, 1981; Mason, 1984). Certain basic ideas of literacy are learned in picture-book reading episodes where decontextualized language and overarticulated language is used. Children learn that books concern fictional worlds, and they discover the symbolic power of language, a magic vehicle taking them beyond the immediate present to new worlds of fiction and adventure.

Family functioning that positively influences later reading acquisition and provides a rich array of literacy experiences includes the following factors (Snow, Burns, & Griffin, 1998): (a) high value placed on literacy with positive regard by parents and others for literacy and its development in children (Morrow, 1997); (b) a certain press for achievement—children are expected to learn letters and words; (c) availability and instrumental use of reading materials from plastic refrigerator letters, writing materials, storybooks, magazines, and so on; (d) exposure to print—parents read to their children and they help children as they attempt to read; and (e) rich opportunities for verbal interactions with parents, siblings, and others.

Storybook Reading

According to Sulzby and Teale (1991), there are strong and positive correlations between amount of storybook reading during the preschool years and subsequent vocabulary and language development, children's interest in reading, and early success in reading. The interactions taking place during storybook reading have been studied in some detail, including questioning, scaffolding, the adult's eliciting of verbal interactions, expansion of the child's utterances, encouragements, and so on. (Lonigan, 1994; Snow, 1983).

The evidence of the value of early storybook reading for later language development and reading is basically correlational. It does not exclude the possibility that the child's interest in books and joint reading is rooted in a genetically determined trait for exploration of uncharted territories and enjoyment of verbal stimulation. Thus, book reading can be regarded as a by-product of a biological disposition favorable for verbal development. Other interpretations are also possible. Bus & van Ijzendoorn (1995) showed that storybook reading is not a happy and engaging event when children interact with parents with whom they are not securely attached. According to Scarborough and Dobrich (1994), parental storybook reading does not show a strong correlation with reading achievement in school. They reviewed a number of studies and estimated the median correlation to be 0.27, which means that less than 8% of the variance in reading achievement can be accounted for by early parental reading.

However, this sad conclusion has to be balanced against the fact that the reading achievement measure that has been most widely used is related to the word decoding aspect of reading. More relevant dimensions, such as reading interest, comprehension, and vocabulary, have not been as much in focus. Furthermore, assessing the amount and quality of book reading and the assessment of aspects of language development are difficult tasks. Lack of reliability and validity is a notorious problem in studies of young children. In addition, I have to mention successful intervention programs that give a more balanced and positive view of the impact of storybook reading. Thus, children's reading interest is as much a consequence of book reading as a prerequisite. Children with early experience of storybook reading display more interest in reading books than do comparable children who lack this early experience (Arnold, Lonigan, Whitehurst, & Epstein, 1994). Whitehurst et al. (1994) demonstrated that during storybook interactions it is possible to improve parental skills that thus positively affect the development of literacy in children.

To appreciate some of the power of storybook reading apart from its social benefits, a closer look at the basic differences between oral and written language may be enlightening.

Oral and Written Language.   The remarkable characteristic of human language is its offline capacity. The rich vocabulary and syntax make it possible to transcend the immediate present and to create a common history and culture, including purposeful, collective planning for the future. This is certainly a sharp distinction between animals and people and evolutionarily a giant step (Bickerton, 1990). The offline capacity of human language is particularly evident in written discourse. To really appreciate the power of text, we should compare typical oral speech—that is, dyadic communication—with typical connected prose found in books, newspapers, or magazines.

Besides modality, written language is different from oral language in many other important respects, and some of these differences may help to account for the great difficulties many individuals have in learning to read.

Speech Perception and Speech Production.   A given spoken utterance may be located on a continuum of articulatory precision, from extreme hypo-articulation to a very unnatural hyperarticulation. The actual location on the continuum is the result of a tug of war between two demands: (a) the need to facilitate the listener's comprehension and (b) the tendency to simplify articulation in order to minimize and smoothen the movements of the tongue and other parts of the articulatory apparatus. The latter reflects a general economic principle of minimizing the expenditure of physical energy in muscle activity, which also holds for all other motor systems. A dialogical situation offers conditions for rapidly reaching a point of acceptable equilibrium for the level of articulation through the listener's explicit demands for increased clarity ("What did you say?").

How, then, is it possible to understand spoken utterances, acoustically realized as mere hints rather than a fully articulated sequence of sounds? Apparently, we listen actively with departure from our knowledge of the language and the situational context of the speech communication. This knowledge helps us to reveal the speech signal and correctly interpret what the speaker intended to say despite ambiguous information in the acoustic event. In other words, the element of top-down processing is usually substantial in speech perception because of the reduced physical quality of the signal.

The closer the participants involved in spoken communication are, physically as well as psychologically, the stronger is the tendency to move toward the hypo-articulated region. Successful speech communication can take place with safety margins created by the listener's active perceptual strategies and the redundancy of language, which protect against disturbances and noise. The speech perception mechanism must be able to function, even with a highly degraded stimulus.

Written Words.   Whereas reductions, assimilations, and co-articulation are inevitable features of spoken language, printed words are fully articulated, especially in an alphabetic writing system, where the complete morphophonemic architecture of words is represented. Basically, of course, the hyperarticulated written representation reflects the different functions of written language. In its prototypical form, such as an expository text, the written message is essentially transmitted by linguistic means with little or no support from extralinguistic cues. This forces an explicitness and articulated precision from syntactic structure all the way down to the word-form level. Written language is normally also intended for a larger, often unknown, and variable audience with different oral conventions (e.g., dialects).

Chafe (1985) examined differences in structure between conversational speech and written texts. In writing, people use devices such as nominalization, subordination, and modification to pack many idea units within a single sentence. Chafe specified as many as 14 different linguistic devices that serve this function. Dependent clauses, appositives, and participial clauses are typical devices used to create a more elaborate and complex linguistic product. In typical written language, cohesion is achieved by lexicalization, anaphoric references, and various other cohesive ties, whereas in spoken discourse cohesion is often accomplished through the situational context or through paralinguistic or prosodic cues. Deictic terms, such as *here, he,* and *now,* are clarified by reference to the shared situation and by pointing, nodding, or other gestures. In the absence of nonverbal or paralinguistic channels, the author's attitude toward ideas must be lexicalized in writing.

CONCLUSION

Written language is in many respects a different kind of communication system compared with oral conversation. Early literacy socialization helps the child get used to the conventions of print, its functions, its decontextualized nature, and its specific syntax.

In most cases, however, early informal literacy socialization does not lead to the breaking of the alphabetic code. One probable outcome is rather an increased awareness of print (Lundberg & Höien, 1991). Although an understanding of the purposes and functions of print may be important, it is probably not related to reading skill in a very straightforward way. The correlations between tests of understanding literacy functions in kindergarten and reading achievement (decoding) in school typically are low (Ayers & Downing, 1982). Tomkins and McGee (1986) studied visually impaired and sighted children's emerging concepts about print. At the end of kindergarten, quite naturally, visually impaired children had very poorly developed concepts of written language. In the first grade, however, they quickly acquired many central concepts about Braille. By third grade, they had almost caught up with the sighted children. The initial absence of print awareness did not prevent the visually impaired children from acquiring reading skill. Thus, print awareness may not be a necessary prerequisite for reading acquisition. However, as I have said, by being exposed to written language through story reading, the child also gains familiarity with the particular syntactic organization and the more explicit, elaborated, and decontextualized character of written discourse that may be an important step in the acquisition of reading skill.

There are enormous differences among children in regard to the amount and quality of their early involvement in text and print. Some of this variation is certainly related to differences in opportunity due to cultural traditions or socioeconomic conditions. However, another, much-neglected source of individual variation in literacy stimulation, at which I already have hinted, might be related to genetic dispositions.

In Western societies, a vast majority of people grow up in environments where there is at least a potential of rich literacy stimulation (environmental print, preschool settings, literate adults, newspapers, books, libraries, etc.). Children, almost regardless of social background, have thus a rich potential, an abundant source for "niche picking" (Scarr & McCartney, 1983). Provided they have a favorable genetic disposition, they can construct their realities by influencing adults and by selecting stimulation and experiences that optimally fit their talents. In a sense, one can say that genes drive experience (Hayes, 1962), which is true for literacy as well as for a large number of other skill domains. The genes do not determine what we will become but how we react on the affordances offered by the environment. Children with a natural facility with language may encourage adults to read more to them, take them to libraries and bookstores, provide them with writing tools, send them postcards, and so on. Thus, the primary source of early literacy socialization is not only the benevolent adult; the child too plays an active and crucial role.

On the other hand, children with a less favorable genetic disposition, maybe with genes implying high risk for developing reading difficulties in school, even in a potentially rich environment, tend to avoid situations involving the cognitive demands typically associated with written language. Even ambitious parents will eventually give up their effort to stimulate their child, to expose him or her to print. Thus, my basic assumption is that I ascribe to the children an active and constructive role in selecting and shaping their course of mental development. The dynamic interaction between genetic dispositions and environment is a continuous process that warrants study.

REFERENCES

Adams, M. J., Foorman, B. R., Lundberg, I., & Beeler, T. (1998). *Phonemic awareness in young children*. Baltimore: Brookes.

Ainsworth, M. D. S. (1967). *Infancy in Uganda: Infant care and the growth of love*. Baltimore: Johns Hopkins University Press.

Arnold, D. H., Lonigan, C. J., Whitehurst, G. J., & Epstein, J. N. (1994). Accelerating language development through picture book reading: Replication and extension to a videotape training format. *Journal of Educational Psychology, 86,* 235–243.

Augustine, St. (1961). *The confessions of Saint Augustine*. New York: Random House. (Original work published 398)

Ayers, D., & Downing, J. (1982). Testing children's concept of reading. *Educational Research, 24,* 277–283.

Bickerton, D. (1990). *Language and species*. Chicago: University of Chicago Press.

Bloom, P. (2000). *How children learn the meaning of words*. Cambridge, MA: MIT Press.

Borkowski, J. G., & Dukewich, T. L. (1996). Environmental covariations and intelligence: How attachment influences self-regulations. In D. K. Detterman (Ed.), *Current topics in human intelligence: Vol 5. The environment* (pp. 3–15). Norwood, NJ: Ablex.

Bowlby, J. (1969). *Attachment and loss: Vol 1. Attachment*. New York: Basic Books.

Bus, A. G., & van Ijzendoorn, M. H. (1988). Mother–child interactions, attachment, and emergent literacy: A cross-sectional study. *Child Development, 59,* 1262–1272.

Bus, A. G., & van Ijzendoorn, M. H. (1995). Mothers reading to their 3-year-olds: The role of mother–child attachment security in becoming literate. *Reading Research Quarterly, 30,* 998–1015.

Chafe, W. L. (1985). Linguistic differences produced by differences between speaking and writing. In D. R. Olson, N. Torrance, & A. Hildyard (Eds.), *Literacy, language, and learning. The nature and consequences of reading and writing* (pp. 105–123). Cambridge, England: Cambridge University Press.

Cheour, M., Martynova, O., Näätänen, R., Erkkola, R., Sillanpää, M., Kero, _., et al. (2002). Speech sounds learned by sleeping newborns. *Nature, 415,* 599–600.

Frankel, K. A., & Bates, J. E. (1990). Mother–toddler problem solving: Antecedents in attachment, home behaviour, and temperament. *Child Development, 61,* 810–819.

Gough, P. B., & Tunmer, W. E. (1986). Decoding, reading, and reading disability. *Remedial and Special Education, 7,* 6–10.

Hart, B., & Risley, T. R. (1995). *Meaningful differences in the everyday experience of young American children.* Baltimore: Brookes.

Hayes, K. J. (1962). Genes, drives and intellect. *Psychological Reports, 10,* 299–342.

Hiebert, E. (1981). Developmental patterns and interrelationships of preschool children's print awareness. *Reading Research Quarterly, 16,* 236–260.

Höien, T., & Lundberg, I. (2000). *Dyslexia: From theory to intervention.* Dordrecht, The Netherlands: Kluwer Academic.

Höien, T., Lundberg, I., Bjaalid, I. K., & Stanovich, K. E. (1995). Components of phonological awareness. *Reading and Writing: An Interdisciplinary Journal, 7,* 1–18.

Jusczyk, P. W. (1997). *The discovery of spoken language.* Cambridge, MA: MIT Press.

Jusczyk, P. W., Friederici, A. D., Wessels, J. M., Svenkerud, V. Y., & Jusczyk, A. M. (1993). Infants' sensitivity to the sound patterns of native language words. *Journal of Memory and Language, 32,* 402–420.

Klein, S. K., & Rapin, I. (1988). Intermittent conductive hearing loss and language development. In D. Bishop & K. Mogford (Eds.), *Language development in exceptional circumstances* (pp. 96–97). Edinburgh, Scotland: Churchill Livingstone.

Kuhl, P. K. (1998). The development of language. In C. von Euler, I. Lundberg, & R. Llinàs (Eds.), *Basic mechanisms in cognition and language* (pp. 175–195). Oxford, England: Pergamon.

Kuhl, P. K., Williams, K. A., Lacerda, F., Stevens, K. N., & Lindblom, B. (1992). Linguistic experience alters phonetic perception in infants by 6 months of age. *Science, 255,* 606–608.

Liberman, A. M., Cooper, F. S., Shankweiler, D., & Studdert-Kennedy, M. (1967). Perception and the speech code. *Psychological Review, 74,* 431–461.

Locke, J. (1964). *An essay concerning human understanding.* Cleveland, OH: Meridian. (Original work published 1690)

Locke, J., Hodgson, J., Macaruso, P., Roberts, J., Lambrecht-Smith, S., & Guttentag, C. (1997). The development of developmental dyslexia. In C. Hulme & M. Snowling (Eds.), *Dyslexia: Biology, cognition and intervention* (pp. 97–107). London: Whurr.

Lonigan, C. J. (1994). Reading to preschoolers exposed: Is the emperor really naked? *Developmental Review, 14,* 303–323.

Lundberg, I. (1978). Linguistic awareness as related to reading. In A. Sinclair, R. J. Jarvella, & W. J. M. Levelt (Eds.), *The child's conception of language* (pp. 83–96). New York: Springer-Verlag.

Lundberg, I. (1991). Phonemic awareness can be developed without reading instruction. In S. A. Brady & D. P. Shankweiler (Eds.), *Phonological processes in literacy: A tribute to Isabelle Y. Liberman* (pp. 47–53). Hillsdale, NJ: Lawrence Erlbaum Associates.

Lundberg, I. (1994). Reading difficulties can be predicted and prevented: A Scandinavian perspective on phonological awareness and reading. In C. Hulme & M. Snowling (Eds.), *Reading development and dyslexia* (pp. 180–199). London: Whurr.

Lundberg, I. (1999). Towards a sharper definition of dyslexia. In I. Lundberg, F. E. Tonnessen, & I. Austad (Eds.), *Dyslexia: Advances in theory and practice* (pp. 9–29). Dordrecht, The Netherlands: Kluwer Academic.

Lundberg, I., Frost, J., & Petersen, O. P. (1988). Effects of an extensive program for stimulating phonological awareness in pre-school children. *Reading Research Quarterly, 33,* 263–284.

Lundberg, I., & Höien, T. (1991). Initial enabling knowledge and skills in reading acquisition: Print awareness and phonological segmentation. In D. J. Sawyer & B. J. Fox (Eds.), *Phonological awareness and reading: The evolution of current perspectives* (pp. 73–95). New York: Springer-Verlag.

Lundberg, I., Olofsson, A., & Wall, S. (1980). Reading and spelling skills in the first school years predicted from phonemic awareness skills in kindergarten. *Scandinavian Journal of Psychology, 21,* 159–173.

Mason, J. M. (1984). Early reading from a developmental perspective. In D. E. Pearson (Ed.), *Handbook of reading research* (pp. 505–543). New York: Longman.

Morrow, L. M. (1997). *Literacy development in the early years: Helping children read and write* (3rd ed.). Englewood Cliffs, NJ: Prentice Hall.

Nittrouer, S. (1996). The relation between speech perception and phoneme awareness: Evidence from low-SES children with chronic OM. *Journal of Speech and Hearing Research, 39,* 1059–1070.

Roberts, J. E., & Burchinal, M. R. (2001). The complex interplay between biology and environment: Otitis media and mediating effects on early literacy development. In S. B. Neuman & D. K. Dickinson (Eds.), *Handbook of early literacy research* (pp. 232–241). New York: Guildford.

Scarborough, H., & Dobrich, W. (1994). On the efficacy of reading to preschoolers. *Developmental Review, 14,* 245–302.

Scarr, S., & McCartney, K. (1983). How people make their own environments: A theory of genotype–environment effects. *Child Development, 54,* 424–453.

Share, D., & Stanovich, K. E. (1995). Has the phonological recoding model of reading acquisition led us astray? *Issues in Education, 1,* 1–57.

Snow, C. (1983). Literacy and language: Relationships during the preschool years. *Harvard Educational Review, 53,* 165–189.

Snow, C., Burns, M. S., & Griffin, P. (1998). *Preventing reading difficulties in young children.* Washington, DC: National Academy Press.

Sroufe, L. A. (1996). *Emotional development.* New York: Cambridge University Press.

Sroufe, L. A., Carlson, E. A., Levy, A., & Egeland, B. (1999). Implications of attachment theory for developmental psychopathology. *Development and Psychopathology, 11,* 1–13.

Strange, W. (Ed.). (1995). *Speech perception and linguistic experience: Issues in cross-language research.* Timonium, MD: York.

Sulzby, E., & Teale, W. (1991). Emergent literacy. In R. Barr, M. L. Kamil, P. B. Mosenthal, & P. D. Pearson (Eds.), *Handbook of reading research* (Vol. 2, pp. 727–758). New York: Longman.

Tomkins, G. E., & McGee, L. M. (1986). Visually impaired and sighted children's emerging concepts about written language. In D. B. Yaden, Jr. & S. Templeton (Eds.), *Metalinguistic awareness and beginning literacy* (pp. 259–275). Portsmouth, NH: Heineman.

Whitehurst, G. J., Epstein, J. N., Angell, A. L., Payne, A. C., Crone, D. A., & Fishel, J. E. (1994). Outcomes of an emergent literacy intervention in Head Start. *Journal of Educational Psychology, 86,* 542–555.

3

How to Avoid Reading Failure: Teach Phonemic Awareness

Tom Nicholson
University of Auckland

> *My twin 7 year olds have been falling behind in reading and writing, possibly every-*
> *thing. There report card was all c's and beginning of reading and writing. Is there*
> *any help out there for us. If so please let me know if there is some funding for there*
> *school or something.*

I received this e-mail from a parent in Canada at the time I was writing this chapter. I sent it to one of the editors of this book, and she arranged for a family literacy center to contact the distressed parent. It was a message that I have received many times before. A letter I remember most was sent to me when I carried out a parent survey that asked questions about reading (Nicholson, 1999). The parent wrote to me: "*I have two children how [sic] need books bad. They are very backwood in their readying at school. How do I get the right books for them? I am give you my name and address would you let me know about the books for my children I hope so.*" I wrote to the parent and gave her a list of book titles, but I felt bad, because at the time there were no specialist services that I could recommend to her. There are more services available nowadays, but there are still many parents who desperately need help for their children, yet schools struggle to find resources to help them.

In New Zealand, statistics indicate that up to 1 in 4 children have difficulties with reading. Ministry of Education figures show that 19% of 6-year-old children receive Reading Recovery tuition, although it is accessible only to 68% of schools. If all pupils had the service available to them, an estimated 25% would be receiving this extra tuition (Anand & Bennie, 2005). The situation is similar in other places as well, such as England, Australia, Canada, and the United States (Nicholson, 2000). The current New Zealand statistics may be an underestimate, because in the most disadvantaged schools, located in low-income parts of the country, there are far more 6-year-old children with reading difficulties than there are Reading Recovery teachers. The situation for older children is worse, even though the New Zealand government recently doubled the number of specialist teachers to 120. These teachers are called *Resource Teachers of Literacy*, and they have now been given formal training in the form of four courses on reading. At present, however, for every specialist teacher there are many children who need help. The official figure is 12 students on a waiting list for every reading specialist, but this may be an underestimate. According to an International Association for the Evaluation of Educational Achievement (IEA) international survey conducted in 1990 (Elley, 1992), the mean number of New Zealand Grade 3 students in need of reading help but not receiving it was 1.40 per class. Given that there are about 2,000 primary schools in New Zealand, this suggests a long waiting list at Grade 3, let alone across the 12 school grades. The report mentioned that the mean number of students in need of reading help per Grade 3 class for all countries in the survey, including Canada and the United States, was 1.60 (Wagemaker, 1993).

When governments become aware of poor literacy rates, the first response is to spend more money on interventions. Yet there are several reasons to be cautious about relying only on this approach. First, many interventions do not deliver on their promises. An example is Reading Recovery in New Zealand, where results have not matched expectations (Elbaum, Vaughn, Hughes, & Moody, 2000; Glynn, Crooks, Bethune, Ballard, & Smith, 1989; Hiebert, 1994; Nicholson, 1989; Shanahan & Barr, 1995; Tunmer, 1990; Tunmer, Chapman, Ryan, & Prochnow, 1998). For a long time it was believed that children who fell behind in the first year of school could easily catch up again through Reading Recovery. Although large numbers of children went into Reading Recovery, the common belief was that almost all of them would catch up to their classmates at the end of the intervention. A steady accumulation of research now indicates that Reading Recovery does not provide enough help to give these children the long-term catch-up skills they need. A possible reason for this is that Reading Recovery does not provide sufficient attention to the teaching of phonological decoding skills. Children at entry into Reading Recovery programs tend to be very low in phonological awareness skills, and these skills do not seem to improve sufficiently during the program (Fletcher-Flinn, White, & Nicholson, 1999).

Second, young children should not have to get to the point where intervention is needed. Once children start to fail, they lose confidence in themselves. It is better to get as many children as possible off to good start at once rather than put them into a catch-up program when they are older. When the whole-language approach to teaching reading was first introduced in New Zealand, there was an expectation that all children could learn to read by reading, without having to have a strong classroom focus on the teaching of phonological recoding skills. However, research over the last several decades has shown that the whole-language approach is more effective for children who start school with good alphabet recognition and phonemic awareness than it is for children to start school lacking such skills (Ehri et al., 2001; Tunmer, Chapman, & Prochnow, 2002). In the last several years, the Ministry of Education has commissioned task force reports to address this issue, especially the disparities in reading between rich and poor schools, and among European, Maori, and Pacific Island children. Each report has recommended increased attention to the teaching of phonological recoding skills (Ministry of Education, 1999a, b). The need for a more phonological approach to the teaching of reading has been even strongly stated in a recent Education and Science Select Committee Report, *Let's All Read* (Education and Science Select Committee Report on Reading, 2001). There have been similar recommendations made in the United States (National Reading Panel, 2000). Children with poor phonological skills at entry to school benefit from instruction that targets these skills. We need better initial teaching that benefits the maximum number of children. At the present time in New Zealand, and in many other places as well, too many children are not learning to read.

Third, we need to think outside the school day, to external services such as family literacy centers, summer schools that focus on reading skills, and after-school reading centers to provide parents with additional options for their children. These services should be especially available to parents who lack the financial resources to pay for private tuition. In the Faculty of Education at The University of Auckland, we have introduced an after-school reading program with specially trained tutors who work with struggling readers using research methods that focus on phonological recoding, and the results have been very encouraging (Nicholson, 2003, 2005). Research is continuing to determine whether this tuition has lasting effects, because long-term success is the litmus test of every intervention.

THE PHONOLOGICAL APPROACH
TO TEACHING READING

There is an increasing consensus among researchers around the world that schools must include, from the first days of schooling, a strong phonological approach in the teaching of reading. There is converging evidence from many studies that children who experience difficulties in learning to read do not understand how to recode words phonologically; that is, they do not know how to blend the sounds of letters together to realize the spoken forms of written words. A major challenge for the beginner reader of English or any language that uses an alphabetic writing system is to become consciously aware that words are composed of phonemes and that these phonemes are encoded in the letters of written words. Phonological awareness has a strange role in learning to read because it is an unnatural awareness to acquire. However, it plays an important role and must be taught.

WHAT IS PHONOLOGICAL AWARENESS?

Phonological awareness is part of a more general metalinguistic awareness that appears in middle childhood. During this period, from about 5 to 12 years of age, children become more conscious that the language they speak has a structure; that sentences are made of words; that sentences have grammatical rules about what is acceptable or not; that words are composed of syllables; and that syllables can be broken into smaller units, down to the phoneme level. Phonological awareness is broader than the phoneme; it includes syllable awareness as well as awareness that the syllable itself can be broken into its onset and rime.[1]

A child has the beginnings of phonological awareness when he or she can break a spoken word into syllables (e.g., *cow-bell*). The next level of awareness is the ability to break syllables into onsets and rimes (e.g., /c/-/ow/, /b/-/ell/). If the child can tell you the first sound in a one syllable word such as /fish/, then the child is showing awareness that /fish/ has an onset that can be separated from the rest of the syllable. The child has some awareness of the phonological structure of a word but does not have full phonemic awareness (Share, 1995). A child who has phonemic awareness has the ability to segment a spoken word completely into all of its phonemes (e.g., the sounds in /fish/ are /f/-/i/-/sh/).

WHAT IS PHONEMIC AWARENESS?

Phonemes are the smallest distinctive sound units in a language. In English, for example, there are 40 phonemes. Other languages have more or fewer phonemes than in English. Phonemes are abstract concepts in the mind because each phoneme can vary in terms of its phonetic quality in speech. This is why phonemic awareness is not a naturally acquired skill.

---

[1]The *onset* is the beginning consonant(s), and the *rime* is the remainder of the syllable, including the vowel and optional consonants. Thus, the onset of *cat* is "c," and the rime is "-at." The rime (e.g., *at*) can be broken into the *peak* (a) and the *coda* (t).

Is Phonemic Awareness Like Phonics?

Some publishers say their programmes teach phonemic awareness when they really mean *phonics*, a way of teaching how to associate letters to sounds so as to sound out words in reading. It assumes phonemic awareness but does not necessarily teach it. In contrast, phonemic awareness instruction involves teaching how to analyze sounds within spoken words, not written ones. The easiest way to distinguish phonemic awareness from phonics is to ask yourself: Is this activity just focusing on spoken language, or am I teaching alphabet letters as well? If you are teaching about how letters correspond to phonemes, then you aren't teaching phonemic awareness; you are teaching phonics. When teaching phonemic awareness, the teacher will use spoken words, or illustrations, but will not use letters of the alphabet. In practice, though, it is hard to resist combining phonemic awareness instruction and phonics. It is not only hard to resist, but it also is more effective than teaching phonemic awareness on its own (Bradley & Bryant, 1983; Coles, 2000; Krashen, 1999; Mann, 1991; Nicholson, 2000; Share, 1995).

Is Phonemic Awareness Like Phonetics?

Phonetic analysis is a way of describing how speech sounds are made. It is not phonemic awareness, and it is not phonics. What is the difference? In phonetics, the interest is in the *phone*, that is, the way the phoneme is expressed. For example, the same phoneme can sound slightly different in different words because of the sounds that precede or follow it. The /p/ in *pin* is different phonetically to the /p/ in *spin* or *nip*. You can easily tell this by holding your hand to your mouth when saying these words. There is a puff of air when you say *pin*, less so when you say *spin*, and none at all when you say *nip*. Another example is the sound of /b/ when you say *bunny* or *big* or *beautiful*. In these words, the /b/ is slightly different phonetically, though we hear it as the same phoneme. A phonetician is interested in such small variation (called *allophonic variation*). But phonemic awareness is not concerned with that. In teaching phonemic awareness, we want the child to break free of phonetic sensitivity and realize that sounds like the /b/ in *bunny* and *bounce* are phonemically the same. Thus, phonemic awareness is the abstract ability to think about the sounds of words separately from their spellings and separately from the slight phonetic variations that occur within the structure of phonemes.

TESTING FOR PHONOLOGICAL AWARENESS

Tests of phonological awareness usually involve looking at pictures of objects, or else listening to spoken words. The assessment of phonological awareness includes awareness of syllables in words (e.g., "Can you say *bunny* without the *ny*?") and awareness of the onset-rime structure of syllables (e.g., "I'll say the sounds in *Mike*. M-ike. Now, can you say the sounds in *shop*?"). A phonological awareness test will assess children's developmental knowledge of syllables, onset rime, and phonemes, but a phonemic awareness test will assess only awareness of the phonemes in words.

Phonemic awareness does not just happen overnight; instead, it dawns gradually across the word. The stages, according to Gough, Larson, and Yopp (1993), appear to be (a) blending phonemes (e.g., m-a-t), (b) isolating the last phoneme (e.g., /m/ in *thumb*), (c) isolating the first phoneme (e.g., /f/ in *fish*), and (d) deleting a phoneme (e.g., *spot* = *pot*).

Some tests of phonemic awareness are easier than others. It is easier for a child to say what is left if we take the last sound (/t/) off *meat* (the answer is *me*) than it is to say what is left if we take the off first sound (/m/) of *meat* (the answer is *eat*). This is because it is mentally harder to take off a beginning phoneme than an ending one. Also, it is easier for a child to verify to you that *cat* and *hat* rhyme than it is for the same child to think of a word that rhymes with *cat*. Why? The reason is that the *cat–hat* task gives the child a 50% chance of being right. To think of another word is much harder. The key skill of phonemic awareness is that the child has to ignore the meaning of a word and focus on its form. The child has to think about sounds in words, not meanings of words. This can be difficult. For example, a 5-year-old who can think only of the meaning in a word is likely to say that the sounds in *cat* are meow.

WHAT PHONEMIC AWARENESS TEST SHOULD I USE?

A test of phonemic awareness that I strongly recommend is the Gough–Kastler–Roper Test of Phonemic Awareness, which was developed at the University of Texas at Austin and has reliabilities greater than $r = .70$ (see Nicholson, 2005; Roper, 1984). My own longitudinal research shows that phonemic awareness, along with alphabet recognition, are very good predictors of children's reading progress through the first 5 years of school. Children with poor alphabet recognition and low phonemic awareness at school entry are likely to have difficulties in learning to read. Alphabet recognition at school entry is a very good predictor of reading success in the first year of school, but phonemic awareness is a better predictor of success after that (Nicholson, 2003).

A SHORT HISTORY OF PHONEMIC AWARENESS RESEARCH

Research on phonological awareness and reading is quite recent (Leong, 1991). Researchers in Moscow in the 1960s (e.g., D. B. Elkonin) were aware that preschool children lacked phonological awareness. This was called *glass theory* (Elkonin, 1971, 1973). For beginner readers, it was as if spoken words were a glass through which the child looked at the world. If children could be taught that the glass was there, then they would have phonemic awareness. The Russian researchers wanted to put a smudge on that window in the mind, so that the child became aware that words could be analyzed in terms of their sounds.

In the 1960s, at the same time, U.S. researchers were also tackling the phonological awareness problem. Alvin Liberman (1968, cited in Bertelson & de Gelder 1993) wrote that if phonemes "are real they are not necessarily real at a high level of awareness. That is to say, it does not follow from anything I have said that the man in the street can tell you about phonemes, or that he can even tell you how many phonemes there are in particular utterances" (p. 394). In 1970, Isabelle Liberman presented a paper in which she also linked phonological awareness with the task of learning to read (cited in Bertelson & de Gelder, 1993). Looking back, it seems clear that the Russian researchers had an intuitive understanding that phonemic awareness was a problem for school beginners. However, the American researchers had a better understanding of why it was a problem. They had done the speech research that showed how phonemes were *not* like beads on a string (A. M. Liberman, 1996, 1997, 1999). They had found that phonemes do not exist separately in the speech stream; instead, information about particular phonemes is also found in phonemes that precede and follow them. This process of phonemic overlap is called *parallel transmission*. This is why it is difficult mentally to split phonemes off from spoken words. We can learn to do it, but it doesn't come naturally. Some phonemes can be said in isolation (e.g., /m/ and /s/), but others are not like this. For example, it is impossible to pronounce the phoneme /b/ in *bag* separately from the /a/ that follows it. If we try to say /b/ on its own, we say /beh/, which is two phonemes. Thus, children have a difficult task in learning about phonemes.

The following studies are examples of the large number of studies that have been carried out since the 1960s.

A 1960s study from England found that many children had difficulty with deletion of phonemes (Bruce, 1964). For example, when asked to say what word would be left if the *s* were taken from the middle of *nest*, one child said, "I can't actually do it. You see, I can't say the last letter without the middle" (Bruce, 1964, p. 169).

A 1970s study in the United States found that only 20% of 5-year-olds could tap the number of phonemes in words like *ice* (2) and *spy* (3) (I. Liberman, Shankweiler, Fischer, & Carter, 1974). Oxford University researchers in England in the early 1980s found that older, poor readers were significantly worse than younger, average readers in picking one word out of four that did not follow the same phonological pattern (e.g., *weed, peel, need, deed,* where *peel* is the odd one out); (Bradley & Bryant, 1978).

A longitudinal study in the 1980s in the United States found that children who became poor readers entered first grade with little or no phonemic awareness. In contrast, children who became good readers entered first grade with much higher levels of phonemic awareness (Juel, 1988).

RECENT DEBATES ON PHONEMIC AWARENESS

Some whole-language writers have questioned the research on phonemic awareness instruction. They say that training studies have improved phonemic awareness and the reading of made-up words, but not real words in real text (see Coles, 2000; Krashen, 1999; McQuillan, 1998). They argue that training studies have short-term effects that disappear when children are assessed 1 and 2 years later. Their solution is that the problems lie in the home and that parents must do more to build literate environments. The problem with their solution, however, is that many families do not have the financial or emotional resources to do this. In many poor homes, day-to-day living is a struggle. It is difficult for these parents to provide for their children's education as well. Some children come from violent homes, others from homes where they are neglected, and some from homes where they have to complete many hours of chores and help care for siblings. As Horin (1995) put it, asking parents to read to their children "may not work for kids whose lives already lack structure and whose parents, coping with unemployment, desertion, violence, or illness, may not feel like a cosy read at night" (p. 2). Of course, it will be possible to help some families to provide more literate environments for their children, but this will never be the whole solution. The school, or some additional after-school service, will always be needed to help children who start school without the home environment advantages of other children. Children who lack alphabet and phonemic awareness skills on entry to school will have to be taught these skills outside of the home.

Other criticisms of the effects of phonemic awareness studies have highlighted design flaws in the research (Troia, 1999). Scientific design flaws include lack of random assignment to treatment conditions, failure to control for Hawthorne effects, poor measurement sensitivity, insufficient attention to fidelity of treatment, and inadequately described research samples.

A way to answer these criticisms is to look at the weight of evidence from a large number of studies rather than getting bogged down in particular studies. This is called *meta-analysis*. What happens is that the effects of all the training studies are averaged out to assess their general significance. A recent meta-analysis that looked at effect sizes in a number of studies concluded that the case for training effects from phonological awareness instruction was so strong that "About 500 studies with null results in the file drawers of disappointed researchers would be needed to turn the current results into non-significance" (Bus & van Ijzendoorn, 1999, p. 411). The National Reading Panel, a U.S.-government appointed body of reading experts, also conducted a meta-analysis of more than 40 peer-reviewed and published articles that were relatively free of design flaws. A summary of part of the findings of the panel was recently published in *Reading Research Quarterly* (Ehri et al., 2001). The researchers concluded that children's reading progress was more likely to benefit if it was accompanied by phonological awareness instruction.

TEACHING PHONEMIC AWARENESS

Elkonin (1973), a researcher in Moscow, was one of the first writers to discuss the teaching of phonemic awareness. He taught preschoolers to segment spoken words. The child would name a picture (e.g., *gusi* is Russian for *goose*), and then say the word sound by sound (e.g., g-u-s-i), at the same time putting down a cardboard chip (a different color for consonants and vowels) for each sound. Children in kindergarten and first grade were able to learn how to analyze sounds in words in 10 to 12 lessons.

Bradley and Bryant (1983) reported that 5-year-old children who received phonological awareness training, along with the use of letters of the alphabet, for 2 years of instruction, made significant gains in reading and spelling. In a similar vein, a 1-year Scandinavian training study produced significant gains in the phonological awareness skills of preschool children before they began formal schooling. Follow-up assessments of the progress of these children indicated that the training contributed to reading progress 2 years after the training had ended (Lundberg, Frost, & Petersen, 1988).

Oxford University researchers in England found that children's knowledge of traditional English nursery rhymes at 3 years of age strongly predicted their reading ability at 6 years of age (Bryant, Bradley, Maclean, & Crossland, 1989). Another study in England reported that prereading children in nursery school (i.e., 4-year-olds) responded better to rhyme activities (e.g., What is wrong with this: "Jack and Jill / Went up the road?") than to training involving word onsets (Layton, Deeny, Tall, & Upton, 1996). A difficulty with training of onsets is the concept of beginning sound. Phil Gough (personal communication, March 1, 1997) has suggested using I Spy games to teach preschoolers about beginning sounds (e.g., "I spy with my little eye, something beginning with /f/," where the first phoneme is said, not the letter name of the thing that is spied).

A New Zealand study found that phonemic awareness training, when added to a whole-language program, had a positive effect on 5-year-old children's reading and spelling progress (Castle, Riach, & Nicholson, 1994).

Children received phonological awareness training that focused specifically on phonemes. Researchers taught slowed pronunciation of words (e.g., What word is mmmm-ou-sss?), segmenting of the initial phoneme (e.g., What is the first sound in bbbbb-bear?), rhyme (e.g., Which pictures rhyme?—the child looks at pictures of *log*, *dog*, and *sun*), phoneme deletion and substitution (e.g., Say *cat*. Now, instead of *cuh*, let's start it off with *m*), and complete phonemic segmentation (e.g., using the Elkonin method, where the child places counters in square boxes below the picture of an object, one counter for each sound in the word). The odd-one-out game focuses on onsets (e.g., Which of these pictures does not start with the same sound as the others? [Show pictures of apple, ball, and ambulance.]) (Castle, 1999). Note that in these studies teaching phonemic awareness is usually done verbally, without using letters of the alphabet. The focus is on teaching children to hear sounds in words, not to relate sounds to letters.

A design difficulty with some of the research on phonological awareness is that phonological training has been accompanied by reading instruction, which makes it difficult to know whether it is the phonological awareness training or the reading instruction that makes the difference. So there is a possibility that phonemic awareness is a result of learning to read rather than a result of phonological awareness instruction by itself. It can be argued that the process of learning to read teaches children phonological awareness. The invisible nature of phonemes is made visible in print. As children learn to read, they are exposed to the sounds of letters. The names of letters enable some children intuitively to analyze letter–phoneme correspondences (Treiman, 1993). Children who use invented spelling use letter names to write words phonemically (e.g., *kat* for *cat*). Read (1978), who was the one of the first researchers to study the phenomenon of invented spelling among preschoolers—that is, children who used letter names as clues for spelling words—argued that the emergence of phonemic awareness while learning to read was "highly suspicious" (p. 73) in that teaching reading probably facilitates phonemic awareness. However, the weight of studies nowadays indicates that phonological awareness is an important prerequisite in learning to read. It helps children get off to a better start in reading and spelling (Ehri et al., 2001).

Which Phonemes Should Be Taught?

For what level of phonological awareness does the teacher aim? Do you have to aim for complete segmentation ability (e.g., where the child can explicitly segment all of the sounds in *cat*)? Some researchers argue that children need full segmentation skill, because this will make it easier for the child to infer letter–sound correspondences (Gough et al., 1993). Training activities such as blending can facilitate segmentation skills. For example, a blending activity is where the teacher says each phoneme separately, as in *t-r-u-ck*, and asks the child to tell her the word she has said (i.e., *truck*). Where do you start? One simple approach is to start with the 26 typical phonemes that go with the letters of the alphabet. Teach the common sound for each consonant (e.g., *geh* for *goat*, *c* for *cat*) and the short vowel sound for each vowel (e.g. *a* as in *at*). Start with the phoneme *a*, then *b*, then *k*, then *d*, and so on. Later, you can teach other phonemes, such as *sh*, *ch*, and so on. An alternative is to start with a limited set of phonemes and then add others later. In one study, researchers used large posters with many illustrations of same-sounding objects (Byrne & Fielding-Barnsley, 1991). The program they used, which they developed themselves, was called *Sound Foundations*. They focused on commonly occurring phonemes: *s, m, p, g, l, t, sh,* as well as the two vowels *a* and *e*. They taught children to recognize the consonant phonemes at the beginning of words (e.g., *g* in *goat*) and at the end of words (e.g., *g* in *dog*). They taught only the beginning vowel phonemes. They used posters with lots of pictures starting with a particular phoneme (e.g., *a* in *ant, axe, anchor, astronaut, apple*) or ending with a phoneme (*s* in *mouse, house, nurse, moose*). They taught beginning phonemes first, and then moved to final-position phonemes.

How to Pronounce Phonemes

There are approximately 40 phonemes in English. These phonemes are each represented by a special phonetic code (Treiman, 1993). When teaching phonemes, you will sometimes have to distort them. For example, sometimes you need to use the iteration technique *beh, beh, beh, bottle* to get the concept of /b/ across, even though the actual phoneme *b* does not have an *eh* attached to it. Children will usually figure out that the *eh* is extra, because quite a few consonants have the same *eh* sound attached to them.

To reduce phoneme distortion, it is useful to introduce continuant phonemes at first, to make the segmenting task easier (e.g., *f, m, n, s, v, z,* and *r, l*). These phonemes can be stretched but still have the same sound (e.g., *fffff*). The stop sounds, with *eh* attached, can follow later (e.g., *b, d, g, k, j, p, t*). Start with the initial phonemes (e.g., *s* in *sun*), then teach final phonemes (e.g., *n* in *sun*), and then teach middle phonemes (e.g. *u* in *sun*).

POSSIBLE TEACHING STRATEGIES

In this section, I describe some possible teaching strategies (Calfee & Patrick, 1995; Nicholson, 1999, 2005).

One strategy is the *lip-popper technique*. Children are taught to attend to their articulation, so as to understand how a phoneme is made. For example, rather than ask the class to listen carefully to the *p* in *pig*, demonstrate how to articulate the *p* (e.g., *pan, pop, top*). Children close together and pop their lips as they say the phoneme /p/. Some teachers ask children to look into a hand mirror to see what they tongue and lips do when they form each phoneme. Other sounds are tongue-tipper (e.g., *t* and *d*) and tongue-back (e.g., *k* and *g*) sounds. Nosey sounds (hold your nose) are *m*, *n*, and *ng*.

Gamelike onset-rime activities, described next, include I Spy, Turtle Talk, bingo, the Elkonin technique, and Making and Breaking. In the I Spy game, it is possible to segment the onset (i.e., initial phoneme) of spoken words. Use toys and objects, such as a toy mouse, a toy dog, a rubber fish, a rubber duck, a clothes peg, sunglasses, a toy sheep, and so on, and lay then out on the floor.

Teacher:	I spy with my little eye, something that starts with the "sound _____." (Then you say a particular sound, like *M*.)
Children:	"Is it a dog?"
Teacher:	"No. It starts with the sound of *mmmm*."
Children:	"Is it a mouse?"
Teacher:	"Yes, that's right. Can you all say the sound that's at the beginning of *mouse*? That's great. Yes, the sound is *mmmm*.

Another version of I Spy involves asking children to listen for the sound that is at the end of the word. This is harder because children have to segment the final phoneme, whereas the more natural break is the initial phoneme. Thus, make sure objects are easy to spy and use no more than three objects.

Teacher:	"I spy with my little eye something that ends with the sound *sh*."
Children:	"Is it a fish?"
Teacher:	"Wow. Excellent. Well done. Can you all say the sound at the end of *fish*?"

The game Turtle Talk can be used to reduce distortion of phonemes by saying the word slowly (e.g., b-o-tt-le). Use a turtle puppet to talk turtle talk. The teacher says to the children, "Is a turtle faster than a rabbit, or slower?" The children all agree that the turtle is very slow, compared to a rabbit. The teacher then asks, "Do you think a turtle will also talk slowly?" The children may not be too sure about this but will probably agree. Then the teacher shows the puppet and explains to the children that this turtle talks very slowly, but that they should try to understand what the turtle says. "m-ou-se," says the turtle. The teacher asks "What did he say?" The children then say the word *mouse*. As children understand what is involved, they can take turns talking back to the turtle very slowly. This activity is a good way of teaching children to blend the phonemes in words.

In the bingo game, each child has a bingo card. The teacher has a pack of picture cards, which he or she places face down on the floor. The child picks up a picture card. Does the initial phoneme match one of a series of pictures on her bingo card? If child can make a match, the child puts a counter on the matching picture on his or her card, and then puts the picture back on the floor. The first child to fill up his or her bingo card wins the game.

The Elkonin technique requires the child to do full segmentation of phonemes in the word. The teacher draws a table. The child selects a picture card and has to place counters in each cell of the table, according to the number of phonemes in the picture name. The child says the name of picture slowly (e.g., t-r-ai-n), while placing a counter in each cell as each phoneme is said. Later, letters are introduced to replace counters

In the Making and Breaking activity (Clay, 1993), the whole class can delete and add phonemes. This activity can be done verbally at first, without using letters. For example, "Everybody say *and*. Now put *s* at start of *and*. That's right, *sand*. Now take off the *s* and put *b* in front of *and*. Now take off *b* and replace it with *st*." Once the children can do this activity, introduce alphabet cards or magnetic letters to show how to add and delete phonemes to make new words.

AFTER PHONEMIC AWARENESS, WHAT?

Phonemic awareness by itself is not enough to learn to read. A child who can read has learned to *decode*. This means teaching the child phonics, which enables the child to apply letter–sound knowledge to the decoding of written words. Phonics, however, will make little sense to the child unless he or she has a foundation of phonemic awareness. Once the child has at least some phonemic awareness, instruction in phonics can begin. Teaching phonics requires considerable instruction and should be done systematically. The approach my colleagues and I have found most successful is that devised by Robert Calfee and his associates at Stanford University, called *Project Read* (Calfee & Patrick, 1995). We have adapted it for struggling readers who attend our after-school reading program and have found that it is an effective approach (Nicholson, 2003). It starts by teaching the letter–sound rules of the everyday words of English of Anglo-Saxon derivation. When these rules are learned, the focus moves to teaching how to read the large number of borrowed words that have come into English from Latin, French, and Greek (Nicholson, 2005). First, however, the child has to acquire the letter–sound rules that apply to the most common words in English. These are the words that beginners must first learn to decode. This means learning Anglo-Saxon letter–sound associations as shown in the Appendix (Nicholson, 1997, 2005).

CONCLUSION

Children get off to a better start in learning to read if they are introduced to phonemic awareness instruction as early as possible, even before they learn the alphabet. Phonemic awareness can be taught without using the letters of the alphabet, although teaching phonemes together with letters is more effective. Research suggests it is better to teach phonemic awareness than to wait for phonemic awareness to dawn on the child, because many beginners have no idea that spoken words are made of sounds, or that letters in words represent phonemes. The sooner children realize that words are made up of phonemes, the sooner they will be able to crack the alphabetic code and begin the process of learning the letter–sound rules of English. The child who can use letter–sound rules is able to read words on his or her own, which means that the door to the world of books has begun to open. The key to that door, however, is phonemic awareness.

REFERENCES

Anand, V., & Bennie, N. (2005, February). *Annual monitoring of Reading Recovery: The data for 2003.* Wellington: Research Division, Ministry of Education. www.minedu.govt.nz

Bertelson, P., & de Gelder, B. (1993). The emergence of phonological awareness: Comparative approaches. In I. G. Mattingly & M. Studdert-Kennedy (Eds.), *Modularity and the motor theory of speech perception* (pp. 393–412). Hillsdale, NJ: Lawrence Erlbaum Associates.

Bradley, L., & Bryant, P. E. (1978). Difficulties in auditory organisation as a possible cause of reading backwardness. *Nature, 271,* 746–747.

Bradley, L., & Bryant, P. E. (1983). Categorizing sounds and learning to read—A causal connection, *Nature, 301,* 419–421.

Bruce, D. J. (1964). The analysis of word sounds by young children. *British Journal of Educational Psychology, 34,* 158–170.

Bryant, P. E., Bradley, L., Maclean, M., & Crossland, J. (1989). Nursery rhymes, phonological skills and reading. *Journal of Child Language, 16,* 407–428.

Bus, A. G., & van Ijzendoorn, M. H. (1999). Phonological awareness and early reading: A meta-analysis of experimental training studies. *Journal of Educational Psychology, 91,* 403–414.

Byrne, B., & Fielding-Barnsley, R. (1991). Evaluation of a program to teach phonemic awareness to young children. *Journal of Educational Psychology, 83,* 451–455.

Calfee, R. C., & Patrick, C. P. (1995). *Teach our children well.* Stanford, CA: Stanford University Press.

Castle, J. M. (1999). Teaching phonological awareness. In G. B. Thompson & T. Nicholson (Eds.), *Learning to read: Beyond phonics and whole language* (pp. 55–73). New York: Teachers College Press.

Castle, J. M., Riach, J., & Nicholson, T. (1994). Getting off to a better start in reading and spelling: The effects of phonemic awareness instruction within a whole language program. *Journal of Educational Psychology, 86,* 350–359.

Clay, M. M. (1993). *Reading Recovery: A guidebook for teachers in training.* Portsmouth, NH: Heinemann.

Coles, G. (2000). *Misreading reading: The bad science that hurts children.* Portsmouth, NH: Heinemann.

Education and Science Select Committee Report on Reading. (2001). *Me panui tatou katoa—Let's all read. Report of the Education and Science Committee on the Inquiry Into the Teaching of Reading in New Zealand.* Wellington: New Zealand Parliament.

Ehri, L., Nunes, S. R., Willows, D. M., Schuster, B. V., Yaghoub-Zadeh, Z., & Shanahan, T. (2001). Phonemic awareness instruction helps children to learn to read: Evidence from the National Reading Panel's meta-analysis. *Reading Research Quarterly, 36,* 250–287.

Elbaum, B., Vaughn, S., Hughes, M. T., & Moody, S. W. (2000). How effective are one-to-one tutoring programs in reading for elementary students at risk of reading failure. A meta-analysis of the intervention research. *Journal of Educational Psychology, 92,* 605–619.

Elkonin, D. B. (1971). Development of speech. In A. V. Zaporozhets & D. B. Elkonin (Eds.), *The psychology of preschool children* (pp. 111–185). Cambridge, MA: MIT Press.

Elkonin, D. B. (1973). USSR. In J. Downing (Ed.), *Comparative reading: Cross-national studies of behavior and processes in reading and writing* (pp. 551–580). New York: Macmillan.

Elley, W. B. (1992). *How in the world do students read?* Hamburg, Germany: International Association for the Evaluation of Educational Achievement.

Fletcher-Flinn, C. M., White, C. Y., & Nicholson, T. (1998). Does Reading Recovery improve phonological skills? *Queensland Journal of Educational Research, 14,* 4–28.

Glynn, T., Crooks, T., Bethune, N., Ballard, K., & Smith, J. (1989). *Reading Recovery in context.* Wellington: Ministry of Education, New Zealand.

Gough, P. B., Larson, K., & Yopp, H. (1993, July). *The structure of phonemic awareness.* Paper presented to the International Society for the Study of Behavioral Development, Recife, Brazil. Available at www.psy.utexas.edu/psy/klarson/recife.html

Hiebert, E. H. (1994). Reading Recovery in the United States: What difference does it make to an age cohort? *Educational Researcher, 23,* 15–25.

Horin, A. (1995, February 4). Poverty marks its victims in kindergarten. *Sydney Morning Herald,* p. 2.

Juel, C. (1988). Learning to read and write. A longitudinal study of 54 children from first through fourth grades. *Journal of Educational Psychology, 80,* 437–447.

Krashen, S. (1999). Training in phonemic awareness: Greater on tests of phonemic awareness. *Perceptual & Motor Skills, 89,* 412–416.

Layton, L., Deeny, K., Tall, G., & Upton, G. (1996). Researching and promoting phonological awareness in the nursery class. *Journal of Research in Reading, 19,* 1–13.

Leong, C. K. (1991). From phonemic awareness to phonological processing to language access in children developing reading proficiency. In D. J. Sawyer & B. J. Fox (Eds.), *Phonological awareness in reading* (pp. 217–254). New York: Springer-Verlag.

Liberman, A. M. (1996). *Speech: A special code.* Cambridge, MA: MIT Press.

Liberman, A. M. (1997). When theories of speech meet the real world. *Applied Psycholinguistics, 27,* 111–122.

Liberman, A. M. (1999). The reading researcher and the reading teacher need the right theory of speech. *Scientific Studies of Reading, 3,* 95–112.

Liberman, I., Shankweiler, D., Fischer, W. F., & Carter, B. (1974). Explicit syllable and phoneme segmentation in the young child. *Journal of Experimental Child Psychology, 18,* 201–212.

Lundberg, I., Frost, J., & Petersen, O. P. (1988). Effects of an extensive program for stimulating phonological awareness in preschool children. *Reading Research Quarterly, 23,* 267–284.

Mann, V. A. (1991). Phonological awareness and early reading ability: One perspective. In D. J. Sawyer & B. J. Fox (Eds.), *Phonological awareness in reading* (pp. 191–216). New York: Springer-Verlag.

McQuillan, J. (1998). *The literacy crisis: False claims, real solutions.* Portsmouth, NH: Heinemann.

Ministry of Education. (1999a). *Report of Literacy Taskforce.* Wellington, New Zealand: Author.

Ministry of Education. (1999b). *Literacy Experts Group Report to the Secretary of Education.* Wellington, New Zealand: Author.

National Reading Panel. (2000). *Teaching children to read: An evidence based assessment of the scientific literature on reading and its implications for reading instruction.* Washington, DC: National Institute of Child Health and Human Development.

Nicholson, T. (1989). A comment on Reading Recovery. *New Zealand Journal of Educational Studies, 24,* 95–97.

Nicholson, T. (1997). *Solving reading problems across the curriculum.* Wellington: New Zealand and Australian Councils for Educational Research.

Nicholson, T. (1999). Literacy in the family and society. In G. B. Thompson & T. Nicholson (Eds.), *Learning to read: Beyond phonics and whole language* (pp. 1–22). New York: Teachers College Press and International Reading Association.

Nicholson, T. (2000). *Reading the writing on the wall: Debates, challenges and opportunities in the teaching of reading.* Melbourne, Australia: Thompson.

Nicholson, T. (2003). Risk factors in learning to read. In B. R. Foorman (Ed.), *Preventing and remediating reading difficulties: Bringing science to scale* (pp. 165–196). Timonium, MD: York.

Nicholson, T. (2005). *Phonics Handbook.* Chichester, England: Wiley and Son.

Read, C. (1978). Children's awareness of language with emphasis on sound systems. In A. Sinclair, R. J. Jarvella, & W. J. Levelt (Eds.), *The child's conception of language* (pp. 65–82). Berlin, Germany: Springer-Verlag.

Roper, H. D. (1984). *Spelling, word recognition and phonemic awareness among first grade children.* Unpublished doctoral dissertation, University of Texas at Austin.

Shanahan, T., & Barr, R. (1995). Reading Recovery: An independent evaluation of the effects of an early instructional intervention for at-risk learners. *Reading Research Quarterly, 30,* 958–996.

Share, D. L. (1995). Phonological recoding and self-teaching: Sine qua non of reading acquisition. *Cognition, 55,* 151–218.

Treiman, R. (1993). *Beginning to spell.* New York: Oxford University Press.

Troia, G. A. (1999). Phonological awareness intervention research: A critical review of the experimental methodology. *Reading Research Quarterly, 34,* 28–52.

Tunmer, W. E. (1990). The role of language prediction skills in beginning reading. *New Zealand Journal of Educational Studies, 25,* 95–114.

Tunmer, W. E., Chapman, J. W., & Prochnow, J. E. (2003). *Preventing negative Matthew effects in at-risk readers: A retrospective study.* In B. R. Foorman (Ed.), *Preventing and remediating reading difficulties: Bringing science to scale* (pp. 121–164). Timonium, MD: York.

Tunmer, W. E., Chapman, J. W., Ryan, H. A., & Prochnow, J. E. (1998). The importance of providing beginning readers with explicit training in phonological processing skills. *Australian Journal of Learning Disabilities, 3,* 4–14.

Wagemaker, H. (1993). *Achievement in reading literacy. New Zealand's performance in a national and international context.* Wellington, New Zealand: Ministry of Education.

APPENDIX

Anglo-Saxon words are the words of the Angles and Saxons, who inhabited England before the Romans arrived. They are the common words of English. Later additions to English came from Latin words (Roman invasion), French words (French invasion), and Greek words (scientific terms). English has words from more than 100 different languages.

Letter–sound correspondences in Anglo-Saxon words.

- Consonants are all letters except *a, e, i, o,* and *u.* In English, there are 21 consonants. In Anglo-Saxon words, each consonant has one sound except *c* (*cup, cent*), and *g* (*go, gel*).
- *Consonant blends* are two or three adjacent consonants in same syllable (e.g., *cl, gr, str*), but each consonant keeps its own sound.
- *Consonant digraphs* are two adjacent consonants in one syllable (e.g., *ch, sh, th, wh*) that have single sounds different from their own.
- Vowels are *a, e, i, o,* and *u.* They each have two sounds (short and long). The short and long sounds are marked. There is a silent e marker for the long sound (as in *made* and *like;* exceptions are *have, give, live,* etc). There is a doubling marker for the short sound (e.g., *scrubbing, rapping*).
- *R-* and *l-* affected vowels have unique sounds (*ar, er, ir, or, ur, all*) that are different from their short and long sounds.
- *Vowel digraphs* are two adjacent vowels that have one sound (as in *oat*) or two sounds (as in *cow, tow*). Vowel digraphs that end in *i* (*rain*) or *u* (*sauce*) change to *y* (*say*) or *w* (*law*) at the end of word.

Decoding Anglo–Saxon words.

- Children learning to read English usually start to learn to read with books that contain Anglo-Saxon words.
- Unfortunately, some common words have weird spellings (e.g., *the, to, was, come, do, break, who, could, rough*). They have to be learned as *sight words* through lots of practice.
- Most Anglo-Saxon words have one or two syllables. If the word has two syllables, it is easier to read if the child knows how to break the word into syllables (see next section).
- Compound words (e.g., *rain-coat*) are common in Anglo-Saxon.
- There are some prefixes (e.g., *dis*like).
- There are some suffixes (e.g., like*ly*).

Dividing words into syllables.

- Every syllable has a vowel sound.
- Sometimes a vowel digraph is used to represent one vowel sound (e.g., b*ee*-per).
- Sometimes a word will have a vowel that does not have a sound, for example, the silent *e* (e.g., lik*e*) signals that the preceding vowel is pronounced by its name, not its sound.
- There are some helpful rules for dividing syllables. One rule is divide two syllable words after the first vowel (e.g., *shi-ny*). Another rule is if the vowel is followed by two consonants, divide between the consonants (e.g., *ten-nis*).

4

Teaching Reading Comprehension

Michael Pressley
Katie Hilden
Michigan State University

When Pressley first began studying comprehension in the middle 1970s, few others were interested in the topic. There was slightly greater interest in memory for text, reflecting that researchers, trained in basic memory using traditional paradigms (paired-associate learning, serial list learning), had found connections between their previous work and a form of learning that more realistically connected to the demands on students. Even so, educational practitioners offered advisement to high school and college students to use study skills, such as SQ3R, which entailed skimming a text, asking questions based on the title or headers or pictures, reading the text, attempting to recite it, and then reviewing it. Sometimes a fourth "R" was added: rereading of the text. The study skills techniques, however, had not been subjected to empirical research, and when they were examined, they were not convincingly validated as causing large improvements in reading achievement. In short, in the 1970s, there was not much science for those who wished to improve the comprehension of students.

Given that state of affairs, it is not surprising Dolores Durkin (1978) found little teaching of comprehension when she looked in the elementary classrooms of the 1970s. Instead, she found a lot of testing of comprehension, often in the form of questions posed by the teacher following student reading of a text. In fact, teacher question-and-answer exchanges were the most typical type of discourse in classrooms during that era (Mehan, 1979), with IRE sequences dominating classroom discussions (i.e., the teacher initiated questions, students attempted responses, and the teacher evaluated their responses). Questions ranged from factual and literal to higher order and inferential (Redfield & Rousseau, 1981). Higher order questions often produced more learning, although there was evidence that lower order questions helped weaker students more, whereas more inferential questions promoted the learning of stronger students more certainly (Brophy & Evertson, 1976).

Given the popularity of questioning in the classroom in the 1960s and 1970s, perhaps it should not be surprising that placing questions in text was undoubtedly the most popular approach to increasing student learning from text in the era, following the lead of Ernst Rothkopf (1966). Both questions before and after a text tended to promote learning from text, although questions before text seemed especially to do so by focusing attention on the ideas tapped by the prequestions, resulting in inattention to other ideas in the text (e.g., R. C. Anderson & Biddle, 1975). Also, such adjunct question effects were never very large, especially with child readers (Pressley & Forrest-Pressley, 1985).

In summary, in the 1970s, the relevant research literature on comprehension was small. The effects that were reported for approaches intended to increase learning from text often were not very impressive. Questioning as a process was at the center of many of the most prominent interventions, from SQ3R, to teacher-led IREs, to questions printed either before or after a text. Researchers who would come to define the field of comprehension instruction in the decades ahead (e.g., Pearson & Johnson, 1978) did so largely in response to their recognition that little was known in the 1970s about how to improve comprehension, despite the recognition that many students could read the words but failed to get the meaning of texts read (e.g., Wiener & Cromer, 1967).

THE FINAL QUARTER OF THE 20TH CENTURY: MUCH RESEARCH ON COMPREHENSION STRATEGIES

A great deal happened in the concluding quarter of the 20th century that increased dramatically the options available to educators who wanted to increase student learning from text, with this being an arena where theoretical advances certainly stimulated applied research that could be translated into realistic classroom instruction. In particular, cognitive psychologists proposed and studied many ways that humans can represent texts (Adams, Treiman, & Pressley, 1998): The mature mind processes the many small ideas in text but manages to condense across these ideas to retain the gist (e.g., van Dijk & Kintsch, 1983). When reading narratives, good readers especially seem to understand and remember parts of the story that are consistent with the typical structure of stories; that is, setting and character information is encoded as are problems encountered by the protagonists in the story and the means for solving those problems (e.g., Mandler, 1984; Stein & Glenn, 1979). Skilled readers often translate the verbal ideas in text into mental images representing the ideas expressed in words by the author (Clark & Paivio, 1991). In short, a number of ways for representing the ideas in text were considered by cognitive psychologists in the 1970s, 1980s, and 1990s.

Educational psychologists, in particular, were inspired by the theoretical work on representation to devise interventions intended to encourage readers to create text representations as they read; that is, educational psychologists devised comprehension strategies, including summarization, attention to story grammar elements, and construction of mental images. In addition, educational psychologists had the insight that good readers understand and remember text by relating it to knowledge they already possess, knowledge encoded in holistic schemas that have been acquired through real experiences and prior reading (e.g., R. C. Anderson & Pearson, 1984). Thus, a story about a cruise is more understandable to people who have taken a cruise previously, for previous cruisers have a cruise schema that noncruisers have had no opportunity to acquire. The cruise schema is a huge package of knowledge, from understanding the characteristics of a stateroom, to knowledge of the events of a cruise (embarking, days at sea, port-of-call, disembarkation), to awareness of the various staff roles on a cruise ship, to detailed understanding of etiquette requirements for meals and entertainment events on a ship. That schematic knowledge could be used by readers to understand text inspired teaching readers to predict what might be in text based on prior knowledge (i.e., prediction strategies) and to relate ideas encountered in text to readers' prior knowledge (i.e., associating to text).

How did cognitive psychologists become so certain that skilled readers use representational strategies? They conducted many studies during which they asked skilled readers to think aloud as they read (see Pressley & Afflerbach, 1995, for a summary). Such readers were very active, using their prior knowledge to relate to text and constructing representations to understand and remember text. Thus, good readers made predictions about what might be in the text based on prior knowledge of the topic of the text. They constructed images and explicitly looked for main points that were essential to the gist of the text. The big events in stories were explicitly noted. Ideas and events often reminded good readers about something they already knew. In short, the good readers were extremely active as they read. The verbal protocols of reading reviewed by Pressley and Afflerbach (1995) did much to fuel interest in teaching children to construct text representations—that is, to teach them strategies for encoding the meaning of text the way good readers encode the meaning of text.

The verbal protocols also did much to make obvious that good readers monitor extensively when they read; that is, they are very aware of what they want to learn from text and whether they are learning it. When good readers are failing to comprehend, they take that as a signal to change strategies or reprocess text (e.g., go back and reread). That the monitoring done by good readers is important in text comprehension was validated in analytical experiments demonstrating the value of teaching readers to monitor their understanding as they proceeded through text (Elliott-Faust & Pressley, 1986).

Thus, there were many, many studies of comprehension strategies inspired by the representational theories. Elementary school students were taught to summarize text as they read, for example, by looking for main ideas. They were instructed about the value of setting, character, problem, and problem-resolution information in stories, and they were encouraged to notice that information in particular as they processed stories. They also were encouraged to construct images depicting the ideas portrayed in text and how the ideas related to one another. Young readers were taught to relate ideas being encountered in text to what they already knew. In general, instruction in any one of these cognitive strategies improved understanding and memory of text (e.g., Pressley, Johnson, Symons, McGoldrick, & Kurita, 1989).

Why did children's comprehension and memory of text improve when they were taught to use comprehension strategies? It was because they were not using such strategies on their own: They were production deficient (e.g., Flavell, 1970) with respect to the strategies used by really skilled readers. Like many strategy production deficiencies, however, children can learn to use strategies they do not naturally discover through instruction. A great challenge for strategies instructors of all sorts, however, is students' continued use of strategies that are taught, especially transfer to situations slightly different than the situations in which the strategies were taught. Good information processing is self-regulated information processing, with learners using the strategies they have learned appropriately (see Schneider & Pressley, 1997, chap. 7). It was very clear from the work on instruction of single comprehension strategies that their continued use was anything but guaranteed. What was also clear was that the information-processing single-strategy instruction encouraged was not anything like the information processing observed in very good readers: As Pressley and Afflerbach (1995) clearly documented, good readers use a variety of comprehension strategies as they go through texts, not just one—that is, good readers broadly transfer the strategies they know!

Thus, it was sensible that there was research focusing on continued use of strategies following instruction, including appropriate transfer of strategies, typically a small repertoire of strategies taught to students. Palincsar and Brown (1984) dubbed their approach to the development of self-regulated use of reading strategies *reciprocal teaching*. Their study included Grade 7 readers who could read the words of text but who had problems comprehending what they read. The participants in the treatment condition were taught four comprehension strategies: (a) prediction based on prior knowledge, (b) generating questions about ideas encountered in text, (c) seeking clarification when confused, and (d) summarizing. In the initial lessons, the teacher extensively explained and modeled the strategies, but very quickly the students were practicing use of the strategies in small groups, with the students taking turns leading the group through the application of the four strategies to short texts. There were 20 instruction and practice sessions.

The strategies-instructed students in Palincsar and Brown's (1984) study were taught the value of the strategies they were learning. In particular, the students were explicitly informed that questioning, summarization, prediction, and seeking clarification were strategies that improved comprehension. They also were encouraged to use the strategies when they read on their own. For example, teachers emphasized that being able to summarize passages and predict the questions on upcoming tests were good ways to assess whether what was read was understood.

Reciprocal teaching affected several different measures of comprehension, from the answering of short-answer questions to passage retellings. Palincsar and Brown's (1984) study inspired many replications, which were reviewed by Rosenshine and Meister (1994). Across investigations, there was clear evidence that children can learn to carry out the cognitive processes that are part of the reciprocal-teaching package. There was also clear evidence of improvement on measures such as standardized tests of comprehension, although sometimes the effects were not particularly large. More positively, the more direct was the teaching of the four strategies by the teacher, the greater the effects on standardized comprehension were. Improved performance on measures such as standardized tests is important for, at a minimum, such gains as a function of reciprocal teaching are evidence of strategy transfer (i.e., students were not trained with standardized tests).

Reciprocal teaching was an important starting point for many educators who decided to teach packages of comprehension strategies to their students. Even so, many educators who were inspired by Palincsar and Brown (1984) ended up teaching multiple comprehension strategies very differently than as operationalized in the original experiment on the approach (Marks & Pressley, 1993). In particular, the use of strategies was not quite as rigid. In the original formulation, the strategies were always executed in the order of prediction, questioning, clarification, and summarization. Marks and Pressley (1993) observed teachers encouraging students to use the strategies as demanded by the text (e.g., summaries whenever they made sense, questions whenever they made sense). In addition, Marks and Pressley (1993) observed multiple-strategies instruction that was occurring over many more lessons than occurred in Palincsar and Brown's study—in many cases, over the entire school year or several years.

Marks and Pressley's (1993) observations were complemented by other observations of multiple comprehension strategies instruction in elementary schools (Pressley, El-Dinary et al., 1992). Pressley, El-Dinary, et al. (1992), consistently observed that when multiple comprehension strategies instruction seemed to be producing greater achievement, students were encouraged to use a small repertoire of comprehension strategies, with such instruction occurring over semesters and years rather than days and weeks. Although the four strategies favored by Palincsar and Brown (1984) often were observed by Pressley, El-Dinary, et al., they also observed other strategies in the mix, including construction of mental images representing the meanings expressed in text and relating the ideas encountered in text to prior knowledge. Pressley, El-Dinary, et al. often observed comprehension strategies instruction occurring most intensely in small reading groups but with students encouraged to use the comprehension strategies across the school day and text tasks. What was apparent in the small groups was that when students were using strategies, they were interpreting text: Their predictions reflected their interpretations of what might happen. Their images and summaries reflected ideas that they found significant and interesting. Their questions were their own, reflecting an intermixing of the readers' prior knowledge and the literal messages in texts. In short, Pressley, El-Dinary, et al. observed that during comprehension strategies instruction, readers transacted with text (Rosenblatt, 1978)—mixing their own thinking and ideas in the text as they transacted with one another—conversing, with the conversations filled with predictions, questions, comments about images formed during reading, and interpretive summaries of text. Hence, Pressley, El-Dinary, et al. named the teaching they observed *transactional strategies instruction*.

Brown, Pressley, Van Meter, and Schuder (1996) conducted a year-long quasi-experimental investigation of the effects of transactional strategies instruction on Grade 2 children's reading. Five Grade 2 classrooms receiving transactional strategies instruction were matched with Grade 2 classrooms taught by teachers who were well regarded as language arts teachers but who were not using a strategies-instruction approach. In each classroom, a group of readers who were low achieving at the beginning of Grade 2 were identified.

In the fall of the year, the strategies-instruction condition and control participants in the study did not differ on standardized measures of reading comprehension and word attack skills. By the spring, there were clear differences on these measures favoring the transactional strategies instruction classrooms. In addition, there were differences favoring the strategies-instructed students on strategies use measures as well as interpretive measures (i.e., strategies-instructed students made more diverse and richer interpretations of what they read than did control students).

There have been two other well-controlled evaluations of transactional strategies instruction. Collins (1991) provided a semester of such instruction to Grade 5 and 6 students, with clear improvements on a variety of measures, including standardized tests. V. Anderson (1992) targeted middle-school students (i.e., Grades 6–9) who could read the words in texts but experienced comprehension problems. Again, there were clearly greater improvements after a semester of transactional comprehension strategies instruction relative to the improvements of comparable middle school students who did not learn to use comprehension strategies.

In summary, there was a great deal of research in the concluding quarter of the 20th century establishing that good readers use comprehension strategies as they read and that such strategies can be taught to child readers, who do not discover such strategies on their own. Successful instruction involves teaching a small repertoire of strategies over a relatively long period of time—a semester to a year in the validating studies conducted to date. So much attention was given to comprehension strategies here because so much attention was given to it during the past 30 years. That said, there are other elements of reading instruction that can and do affect reading comprehension positively, and those are taken up in the next section.

WHAT SHOULD BE INCLUDED IN COMPREHENSION INSTRUCTION?

Although the most work on comprehension instruction has involved study of comprehension strategies instruction, other elements of instruction also enjoy some empirical validation. The empirical bases for these other factors have been provided in several documents in recent years, including the report of the National Reading Panel (2000; henceforth NRP), Pressley (2002), and the RAND Reading Study Group (2002; henceforth RRSG). For exhaustive reviews of the literature, readers should refer to those sources. The point of this section is simply to establish the variety of activities that should be included in comprehension strategies instruction in the elementary grades.

As we discuss each of the components, we include some commentary and questions. These reflect issues that audiences across the United States have reflected back to me as we have talked about comprehension instruction. We do this because we have been impressed by the consistency of the points made by audience members and the questions asked. Although reports such as those of the NRP and RRSG include many, many questions that could be studied by researchers, the questions included in this section are the ones that seem most critical, at least to the audiences with whom we have interacted. There are far fewer questions that come up again and again in audience responses than are contained in the published reports. There are so many questions in the published reports that only some will get studied; in our view, the ones included here should be considered for priority in funding, given that they reflect the issues that real teachers and education professionals think are critical, and this is an audience we want to influence with research on comprehension instruction. Specifically, we should be in the business of doing research that informs the educators who are willing enough to consider doing comprehension instruction to come to a talk on the topic!

Before beginning this review of elements of instruction, an interesting question is "Why there is so much contemporary interest in comprehension instruction?" Several years ago, we received many invitations to talk about balanced literacy instruction but never an invitation to talk about comprehension. Perhaps our positions on balance now are so well accepted or understood (Pressley, 2002) that there is no need for us to talk about it additionally in public! More realistically, we think a number of factors have combined to increase interest in comprehension instruction.

The RRSG (2002) concluded that contemporary interest in comprehension instruction reflects a number of factors, including increasing demands for comprehension, with job places, in particular, demanding more and better literacy all the time. The flood of standardized test data that are now available continually reminds us that students' comprehension often is not good. Even so, we are convinced by audience reactions that two factors are more prominent than others. Teachers do not think about the test data when they reflect on poor comprehension by students; they reflect on the poor comprehension they observe day after day, week after week, in their students. If you walk into a middle-school classroom that is doing some reading, it is easy to observe multiple examples of obvious miscomprehension during the course of an hour of teaching. Wharton-McDonald, Pressley, and Hampston (1998) determined there was still little comprehension instruction, but that research is not how teachers know that little comprehension instruction is occurring: They know there is little such instruction because they themselves are not doing it. When this realization is combined with the understanding, based on daily student miscomprehensions, that students need to be taught how to comprehend better, there is great motivation for teachers to find out how they can develop comprehension competencies in their students. In the following sections, we describe what we tell educators to do, in addition to teaching of comprehension strategies, to encourage comprehension in their students.

Decoding Instruction

Except for picture-books with little or no text, comprehension of text is logically impossible when the reader cannot read the words. Thus, it is critical that readers learn how to decode. The NRP (2000), in particular, made the case that, before reading instruction begins (e.g., during kindergarten), instruction that develops phonemic awareness is helpful. That is, it makes sense to provide 10 minutes or so of daily activity intended to make children aware that words are composed of sounds blended together. This type of instruction helps prepare children for phonics instruction, which involves blending the sounds made by letters to sound out words. Learning letters and their sounds and learning to blend them is not logically sensible for a child who lacks phonemic awareness. Once a child knows that words are blends of sounds and understands that the blended sounds are mapped by letters, then phonics instruction makes sense as something to do as part of reading.

In fact, young readers benefit from systematic phonics instruction when they are first learning to read words, which was one of the NRP's (2000) most visible conclusions. There is a great deal of accumulated evidence that learning to sound out words is a good start on reading. That said, sounding out of words is just a start on word recognition, a waystation that needs to be moved through as certainly as possible. When young readers must sound out words, they have to devote a lot of mental effort to the activity. Having done that, there is little mental capacity left over for comprehending either the individual word that is being sounded out or other words in the text (LaBerge & Samuels, 1974). Fortunately, what begins as sounding out and blending often becomes more automatic recognition of word chunks (e.g., *log* is at first sounded out as three sounds and then sounded out as two, the *l* sound and the sound of the chunk *-og*, which has been encountered previously in *dog, log,* and *pog*; Goswami, 2000). Recognition of chunks is easier than blending one sound at a time.

The ultimate goal of word recognition instruction, however, is fluent recognition of whole words, recognition of words as sight words. The correlation between fluent reading and comprehension is well established (e.g., NRP, 2000). Even more important, when fluency is developed through instruction and practice, comprehension improves (e.g., Tan & Nicholson, 1997; see also Breznitz, 1997a, 1997b).

When I discuss word recognition instruction as critical to developing comprehension abilities, there are a few frequent questions: Is some form of phonics training more effective than others in promoting comprehension? Many reading programs include decodable texts as an approach to improving fluency: Is there an optimal proportion of decodables that makes sense? Every so often, someone asks about *Dolch words*: high-frequency function words; Dolch (1941) advanced the idea that these words should be taught as sight words during the primary years. Does the teaching of such words make sense in contemporary classrooms? For the most part, these questions are not answerable on the basis of existing data. That said, I am struck that at least trends in summary analyses of phonics instruction (including the NRP's [2000]) favor synthetic phonics over alternatives. I also recall vividly many decodables being read in the classrooms of provably effective primary teachers that I have studied (e.g., Pressley, Allington, Wharton-Mc-Donald, Block, & Morrow, 2001). Finally, the hypothesis that it should help comprehension to acquire high frequency (e.g., Dolch) words to the point of fluency is so logically compelling that I cannot believe their presence in classrooms would be anything but a good thing. The Dolch words just seem like words that kids ought to be learning because they will encounter them so often. We provide more details about the words kids ought to be learning in the next section.

Vocabulary Instruction

The correlation between good reading and extensive vocabulary is common knowledge among reading researchers. What is more impressive is that teaching students vocabulary increases their comprehension skills (NRP, 2000; RRSG, 2002).

The questions that always come up when I present this result are the following: Is there a list of vocabulary words that children need to know? Should the words encountered in basal stories or trade books drive vocabulary instruction? The answer to the first question is "no"; the answer to the second is "in part." Students should be taught words that they are likely to encounter again, ones that literate people know. Teachers do not need a word list to make this determination. Rather, when unfamiliar words are encountered, the degree of attention given to the word should be driven, at least in part, by how likely the reader is to encounter the word in the future. Everyone knows whether a word falls in that category. Thus, if a third-grade story includes the word *spitfire*, it might make sense to mention to the reading group in passing that a *spitfire* is someone who is very emotional. I wouldn't go much further. If the story also included the word *entrepreneur*, it would also make sense to give this word more attention, perhaps looking it up in the dictionary to determine that it means someone who "owns, launches, and undertakes the risks of a business." I'd then ask for examples of entrepreneurs from the students and explanations from them about why the character in the story is an entrepreneur. *Entrepreneur* is an important enough word to include on the formal vocabulary list for the story, a list of words reviewed several times and ones students are encouraged to think about and use. Why? Because I am certain that most third graders will encounter the word again at some time. The stories children read contain some words that are essential for them to learn and some that are not so essential: Fortunately, by living in the world, the adults who are teachers have had ample opportunity to learn which words are which! Common sense should guide their selection of vocabulary words for explicit teaching and emphasis.

Develop Students' World Knowledge

One great contribution of the 35 years of the Center for the Study of Reading at the University of Illinois was that Richard Anderson and his colleagues established very well that world knowledge matters: The more one knows, the better and more certain comprehension will be (R. C. Anderson & Pearson, 1984). A recent demonstration of the power of worthwhile world knowledge comes from work inspired by E. D. Hirsch's (1988) conception of cultural literacy: Hirsch believes that schools should explicitly teach worthwhile scientific and social scientific knowledge as well as the best of literature and mathematics. Some schools are doing this, attempting to emphasize the knowledge he identified as appropriate in each of the elementary grades (Core Knowledge Foundation, 1998). These Core Knowledge Schools—about 800 of them—have now been operating long enough that some preliminary data have been gathered. So far, reading achievement does seem to be at least slightly improved by the Core Knowledge approach (Datnow, Borman, & Stringfield, 2000).

The obvious question is how to build excellent world knowledge. Most students are not enrolled in Core Knowledge programs. What every student can do, however, is read and, in particular, to choose to read worthwhile books, ones that are informative about important social scientific, scientific, literary, and mathematical contents. This is a controversial stance, however, for it means favoring such worthwhile books over some books that many kids prefer, including the *Goosebumps* series and the *Baby Sitters Club* series. Although a case can be made that reading of such books positively affects fluency, no reasonable case can be made that reading these volumes will result in important shifts in world knowledge.

Something else that students can do is to watch worthwhile television. Informative television in general, such as the fare on the Discovery Channel, influences literacy positively (Koolstra, van der Voort, & van der Kamp, 1997; Wright et al., 2001). Moreover, the effects of watching such child-informative programming during the preschool years carry over at least into adolescence, with heavier preschool viewers of child-informative programming doing better in school than other children, even controlling for alternative variables that might produce boosts in literacy achievement (D. R. Anderson, Huston, Schmitt, Linebarger, & Wright, 2001). Informative television also provides opportunity for the literacy rich to get richer: For example, 5-year-olds who are more advanced with respect to literacy are more likely to watch informative television than less literacy advanced 5-year-olds (Wright et al., 2001). In doing so, they gain more opportunities to learn information and skills that can affect literacy development positively. Getting children to turn on something other than The Cartoon Network or reruns of situation comedies should be a high priority for all teachers.

In addition to building knowledge, it is also essential to encourage students to make use of the prior knowledge they have. My students and I provided many demonstrations of the underuse of prior knowledge (Pressley, Wood, et al., 1992; see especially Martin & Pressley, 1991). For example, when we asked Canadian students to read about events that had occurred in each of the Canadian provinces, they often failed to use their prior knowledge to situate the events sensibly in the provinces where the events had occurred (Martin & Pressley, 1991; Woloshyn, Pressley, & Schneider, 1992). More positively, when students were prompted to ask themselves why it made sense for the events to occur where they did, they did use their prior knowledge, with huge increases in memory of what they read. When it comes to factual text, it is often very helpful for students to ask themselves why the facts are sensible, for it is often the case that readers will be able to explain the facts by relating the new information to their prior knowledge. Unfortunately, however, students often do not use what they know to understand new material.

When I make the recommendation to encourage students to ask themselves "why" questions when they read, or to use strategies of any sort, I often encounter the following challenges: Wouldn't students rather just read the text straight through? Isn't such reflection really interfering with reading? The answer is "absolutely not"! Remember the verbal protocols of reading summarized by Pressley and Afflerbach (1995): Skilled readers do not read straight through from the first word to the last; instead, they are reflective when they read, including asking themselves "why" questions and relating ideas encountered in text to what they already know. Those who advocate simply encouraging students to read the text straight through from first word to last are, in fact, encouraging students to read the way that weak readers read!

Monitoring

One of the most dramatic discoveries in my work was that even good college students can read texts, completely miss the point of the reading, and still believe they got it (Pressley, Ghatala, Woloshyn, & Pirie, 1990)! Monitoring is not perfect, even at the college level. That said, readers can be taught to be sensitive to whether they understand what they are reading and to react to feelings of miscomprehension proactively, for example, by rereading parts of text that are confusing. Comprehension strategies instruction that results in continued and effective use of strategies invariably includes teaching students to monitor as they read (e.g., Klingner & Vaughn, 1999; Palincsar & Brown, 1984; Pressley, El-Dinary, et al., 1992). Monitoring instruction always begins with the teacher modeling monitoring and providing explanations of monitoring, with students then encouraged to monitor on their own. Such reminders must continue for some time, for effective monitoring clearly develops slowly. Such monitoring is essential to teach, for high comprehension depends on it (e.g., Baker, 2002).

Read, Read, Read

One of the most common signs posted in elementary classrooms is "Read, Read, Read." During the early 1990s, however, when whole-language approaches dominated reading instruction, there was a belief that skilled comprehension would be a natural by-product of large doses of reading alone. Educators now know that it makes a great deal of sense to teach word recognition skills, vocabulary, and comprehension strategies and monitoring as well as to encourage habits of life that develop worthwhile world knowledge (e.g., encourage broad reading, viewing of worthwhile television, habitual reflection on why facts as stated in text make sense on the basis of prior knowledge). More is needed for skilled comprehension to develop than just massive reading.

Massive reading does do much good for the developing reader, however, and in ways that affect comprehension positively. It promotes fluency at the word level; increases vocabulary; and permits opportunities to apply the comprehension strategies being learned, including monitoring and relating new information encountered in text to prior knowledge. Massive reading is an essential part of elementary comprehension development, even though it is not sufficient to develop skilled comprehension.

CONCLUSION

No single component is sufficient, however, for, the summary point of this final section is that skilled comprehension involves the addition and interaction of word recognition, vocabulary, comprehension strategy, and world knowledge components. That is why skilled comprehension requires years to develop, why really skilled comprehension is seen only in very mature readers, typically individuals who are past the K–12 years (Pressley &

Afflerbach, 1995). We are confident that much better comprehenders can be developed by instruction that saturates elementary children with excellent word recognition instruction, vocabulary building, comprehension strategies instruction, teaching of monitoring, and experiences that develop worthwhile world knowledge that students learn to use habitually to interpret the world, including worlds in texts.

REFERENCES

Adams, M. J., Treiman, R., & Pressley, M. (1998). Reading, writing, and literacy. In I. Sigel & A. Renninger (Eds.), *Handbook of child psychology: Vol. 4. Child psychology in practice* (pp. 275–355). New York: Wiley.

Anderson, D. R., Huston, A. C., Schmitt, K. L., Linebarger, D. L., & Wright, J. C. (2001). Early childhood television viewing and adolescent behavior. *Monographs of the Society for Research in Child Development, 66,* (Serial No. 264).

Anderson, R. C., & Biddle, W. B. (1975). On asking people questions about what they are reading. In G. Bower (Ed.), *The psychology of learning and motivation* (Vol. 9, pp. 89–132). New York: Academic.

Anderson, R. C., & Pearson, P. D. (1984). A schema-theoretic view of basic processes in reading. In P. D. Pearson (Ed.), *Handbook of reading research* (pp. 255–291). New York: Longman.

Anderson, V. (1992). A teacher development project in transactional strategy instruction for teachers of severely reading-disabled adolescents. *Teaching & Teacher Education, 8,* 391–403.

Baker, L. (2002). Metacognition in comprehension instruction. In C. C. Block & M. Pressley (Eds.), *Comprehension instruction: Research-based best practices* (pp. 77–95). New York: Guilford.

Breznitz, Z. (1997a). Effects of accelerated reading rate on memory for text among dyslexic readers. *Journal of Educational Psychology, 89,* 289–297.

Breznitz, Z. (1997b). Enhancing the reading of dyslexic children by reading acceleration and auditory masking. *Journal of Educational Psychology, 89,* 103–113.

Brophy, J., & Evertson, C. (1976). *Learning from teaching: A developmental perspective.* Boston: Allyn & Bacon.

Brown, R., Pressley, M., Van Meter, P., & Schuder, T. (1996). A quasi-experimental validation of transactional strategies instruction with low-achieving second grade readers. *Journal of Educational Psychology, 88,* 18–37.

Clark, J. M., & Paivio, A. (1991). Dual coding theory and education. *Educational Psychology Review, 3,* 149–210.

Collins, C. (1991). Reading instruction that increases thinking abilities. *Journal of Reading, 34,* 510–516.

Core Knowledge Foundation. (1998). *Core knowledge sequence: Content guidelines for grades K–8.* Charlottesville VA: Author.

Datnow, A., Borman, G., & Stringfield, S. (2000). School reform through a highly specified curriculum: Implementation and effects of the core knowledge sequence. *Elementary School Journal, 101,* 167–191.

Dolch, E. W. (1941). *Teaching primary reading.* Champaign, IL: Gerrard Press.

Durkin, D. (1978). What classroom observations reveal about reading comprehension instruction. *Reading Research Quarterly, 15,* 481–533.

Elliott-Faust, D. J., & Pressley, M. (1986). Self-controlled training of comparison strategies increase children's comprehension monitoring. *Journal of Educational Psychology, 78,* 27–32.

Flavell, J. H. (1970). Developmental studies of mediated memory. In H. W. Reese & L. P. Lipsett (Ed.), *Advances in child development and behavior* (Vol. 5, pp. 181–211). New York: Academic.

Goswami, U. (2000). Phonological and lexical processes. In M. Kamil, P. B. Mosenthal, P. D. Pearson, & R. Barr (Eds.), *Handbook of reading research* (Vol. 3, pp. 251–267). Mahwah, NJ: Lawrence Erlbaum Associates.

Klingner, J. K., & Vaughn, S. (1999). Promoting reading comprehension, content learning, and English acquisition through collaborative strategic reading (CSR). *Reading Teacher, 52,* 738–747.

Koolstra, C. M., van der Voort, T. H. A., & van der Kamp, L. J. T. (1997). Television's impact on children's reading comprehension and decoding skills: A 3-year panel study. *Reading Research Quarterly, 32,* 128–152.

LaBerge, D., & Samuels, S. J. (1974). Toward a theory of automatic information processing in reading. *Cognitive Psychology, 6,* 293–323.

Mandler, J. M. (1984). *Stories, scripts, and scenes: Aspects of schema theory.* Hillsdale, NJ: Lawrence Erlbaum Associates.

Marks, M., & Pressley, M. (with Coley, J. D., Craig, S., Gardner, R., Rose, W., & DePinto, T.). (1993). Teachers' adaptations of reciprocal teaching: Progress toward a classroom-compatible version of reciprocal teaching. *Elementary School Journal, 94,* 267–283.

Martin, V. L., & Pressley, M. (1991). Elaborative interrogation effects depend on the nature of the question. *Journal of Educational Psychology, 83,* 113–119.

Mehan, H. (1979). *Social organization in the classroom.* Cambridge, MA: Harvard University Press.

National Reading Panel. (2000). *Teaching children to read: An evidence-based assessment of the scientific research literature on reading and its implications for reading instruction: Reports of the subgroups.* Washington, DC: National Institute of Child Health and Development.

Palincsar, A. S., & Brown, A. L. (1984). Reciprocal teaching of comprehension-fostering and monitoring activities. *Cognition and Instruction, 1,* 117–175.

Pearson, P. D., & Johnson, D. D. (1978). *Teaching reading comprehension.* New York: Holt, Rinehart and Winston.

Pressley, M. (2002). *Reading instruction that works: The case for balanced teaching* (2nd ed.). New York: Guilford.

Pressley, M., & Afflerbach, P. (1995). *Verbal protocols of reading: The nature of constructively responsive reading.* Mahwah, NJ: Lawrence Erlbaum Associates.

Pressley, M., Allington, R., Wharton-McDonald, R., Block, C. C., & Morrow, L. M. (2001). *Learning to read: Lessons from exemplary first grades.* New York: Guilford.

Pressley, M., El-Dinary, P. B., Gaskins, I., Schuder, T., Bergman, J. L., Almasi, J., & Brown, R. (1992). Beyond direct explanation: Transactional instruction of reading comprehension strategies. *Elementary School Journal, 92,* 511–554.

Pressley, M., & Forrest-Pressley, D. L. (1985). Questions and children's cognitive processing. In A. Graesser & J. Black (Ed.), *Psychology of questions* (pp. 277–296). Hillsdale, NJ: Lawrence Erlbaum Associates.

Pressley, M., Ghatala, E. S., Woloshyn, V., & Pirie, J. (1990). Sometimes adults miss the main ideas in text and do not realize it: Confidence in responses to short-answer and multiple-choice comprehension items. *Reading Research Quarterly, 25,* 232–249.

Pressley, M., Johnson, C. J., Symons, S., McGoldrick, J. A., & Kurita, J. A. (1989). Strategies that improve memory and comprehension of what is read. *Elementary School Journal, 90,* 3–32.

Pressley, M., Wood, E., Woloshyn, V. E., Martin, V., King, A., & Menke, D. (1992). Encouraging mindful use of prior knowledge: Attempting to construct explanatory answers facilitates learning. *Educational Psychologist, 27,* 91–110.

RAND Reading Study Group. (2002). *Reading for understanding: Toward an R & D program in reading comprehension.* Santa Monica, CA: RAND.

Redfield, D. L., & Rousseau, E. W. (1981). A meta-analysis of experimental research on teacher questioning behavior. *Review of Educational Research, 51,* 237–246.

Rosenblatt, L. M. (1978). *The reader, the text, the poem: The transactional theory of the literary work.* Carbondale: Southern Illinois University Press.

Rosenshine, B., & Meister, C. (1994). Reciprocal teaching: A review of nineteen experimental studies. *Review of Educational Research, 64,* 479–530.

Rothkopf, E. Z. (1966). Learning from written materials: An exploration of the control of inspection of test-like events. *American Educational Research Journal, 3,* 241–249.

Schneider, W., & Pressley, M. (1997). *Memory development between two and twenty* (2nd ed.). Mahwah, NJ: Lawrence Erlbaum Associates.

Stein, N. L., & Glenn, C. G. (1979). An analysis of story comprehension in elementary school children. In R. O. Freedle (Ed.), *New directions in discourse processing* (Vol. 2, pp. 53–120). Norwood, NJ: Ablex.

Tan, A., & Nicholson, T. (1997). Flashcards revisited: Training poor readers to read words faster improves their comprehension of text. *Journal of Educational Psychology, 89,* 276–288.

van Dijk, T. A., & Kintsch, W. (1983). *Strategies of discourse comprehension.* New York: Academic.

Wharton-McDonald, R., Pressley, M., & Hampston, J. M. (1998). Outstanding literacy instruction in first grade: Teacher practices and student achievement. *Elementary School Journal, 99,* 101–128.

Wiener, M., & Cromer, W. (1967). Reading and reading difficulty: A conceptual analysis. *Harvard Educational Review, 37,* 620–643.

Woloshyn, V. E., Pressley, M., & Schneider, W. (1992). Elaborative interrogation and prior knowledge effects on learning of facts. *Journal of Educational Psychology, 84,* 115–124.

Wright, J. C., Huston, A. C., Murphy, K. C., St. Peters, M., Piñon, M., Scantlin, R., & Kotler, J. (2001). Oral discussion, group-to-individual transfer, and achievement in cooperative learning groups. *Journal of Educational Psychology, 77,* 60–66.

5

A Cross-Language Perspective on Learning to Read

Richard C. Anderson
Wenling Li
Center for the Study of Reading
University of Illinois at Urbana–Champaign

Across the world there are many varieties of written language. Various orthographies are constructed on distinct principles and present linguistic information in diverse forms. European languages, such as English, employ an alphabetic writing system in which the elements represent minimal units of sound. There are, however, other writing systems, notably Chinese, in which the symbols most directly encode meaning. Because of these differences, it is useful to carry out reading research across languages. Such research can reveal both universal and orthography-specific processes important for learning to read, which in turn can help to build a genuinely comprehensive theory of how people learn to read and comprehend written information. At a personal level, in addition to satisfying curiosity about other languages and the challenges faced by children learning other languages, a cross-language perspective can help to make the familiar strange, calling to our attention features of our own language that we otherwise take for granted, presenting them in a new light so that we more fully appreciate their significance.

"To the extent that a spoken language and associated writing system are connected in a logical way, it is only reasonable to suppose that children who understand the logic will more easily acquire and use the written language" (Nagy & Anderson, 1998, p. 155). On the other hand, when the pronunciation and meaning of new words cannot be reliably predicted from principles relating speech and print, or children don't understand the principles, then they must memorize words one by one in order to correctly pronounce them and identify their meanings.

Metalinguistic awareness is the ability to identify, reflect on, and manipulate language forms. Learning to read is fundamentally metalinguistic (Nagy & Anderson, 1998; Shu & Anderson, 1998). According to Nagy and Anderson (1998):

> A child must first realize that print represents speech, and then work out the details of how print represents speech. Understanding the mapping between print and speech requires figuring out which units of language are represented by the elements of the writing system. A child cannot make progress in learning to read without understanding whether the marks on a page represent phonemes, syllables, morphemes, words, or something else. (p. 155)

The nature of the metalinguistic insights that are important for reading depends on the language and its associated writing system. Languages may differ in terms of the units of language to which a reader must attend and the principles that govern the mapping between units of speech and elements of written language. Metalinguistic awareness may be considered to consist of phonological awareness, morphological awareness, syntactic awareness, pragmatic awareness, and awareness of genre function and structure. In this chapter, we compare and contrast two very different languages—English and Chinese—with respect to the two most basic classes of metalinguistic awareness: (a) *phonological awareness* and (b) *morphological awareness.*

PHONOLOGICAL AWARENESS IN ENGLISH AND CHINESE

Phonological awareness is the ability to identify, reflect on, and manipulate sound units of language. It subsumes syllable awareness, onset/rime awareness, and phoneme awareness. Several ways of assessing each level of phonological awareness have been developed by psycholinguists. Here are illustrations: Syllable awareness can be assessed by asking a child to reverse the order of syllables in words and phrases; for instance, when she hears *river,* the child is supposed to say *er riv.* Rime awareness can be assessed by asking a child to select from among sets of three words the one that has a different ending; on hearing *beach, bright,* and *reach,* the child should pick *bright.* Phoneme awareness can be assessed by asking a child to delete phonemes in words; asked to say *fit* without the /f/ sound, the child should say *it.*

Learning to read entails understanding the principles that govern the relationships between speech and writing. In English, the overarching principle is that letters represent segmental phonemes. The alphabetic principle motivates and rationalizes the assimilation of specific letter–sound associations for the young reader. However, to become skilled readers of English, children have to acquire a more sophisticated understanding of orthography–phonology relationships as they learn to cope with variability in the pronunciation of letters and letter clusters.

Syllables, onsets, rimes, and phonemes are descriptive sound units of every language; however, the level or levels most important in learning to read depends on the language and how it maps onto the writing system. In English, the phonemic level is critical because letters represent phonemes. There are a lot of studies showing that phoneme awareness correlates highly with success in learning to read English (e.g., Blachman, 2000; Cunningham, 1990). Furthermore, training children in phoneme awareness has been shown to benefit their later progress in reading, demonstrating a causal link from phoneme awareness to reading (e.g., Byrne & Fielding-Barnsley, 1995; Lundberg, Frost, & Petersen, 1988). Phoneme awareness is by definition a metalinguistic skill and hence depends on the learner's cognitive and metacognitive development (Tunmer, Herriman, & Nesdale, 1988). It is often assumed that children have tacit linguistic knowledge that words are represented in terms of phonemes and that developing phoneme awareness is a primarily matter of bringing this tacit knowledge to the level of consciousness (Gombert & Fayol, 1992).

Phoneme awareness can be acquired, to some extent, prior to learning how to read and apart from any knowledge of letters (Bradley & Bryant, 1983; Mann & Liberman, 1984). Importantly, though, there is a reciprocal relationship among phoneme awareness, learning letters, and learning to read an alphabetic script. Some level of phoneme awareness is necessary to get started in learning to read a language with an alphabetic writing system. Once started, learning to read an alphabetic script promotes further advances in phoneme awareness. This was shown in a study by Huang and Hanley (1995; see also, Mann, 1986), who found that Taiwanese children learning to read Chinese characters with the aid of a script for representing speech sounds, called *zhu yin fu hao*, had greater phoneme awareness than Hong Kong children learning to read Chinese characters without the aid of a script, and both groups of Chinese children lagged behind British children learning to read English. Many English-speaking parents and teachers have noticed a young child who makes a "breakthrough" in learning to read and shows an accompanying surge in the distinctness of his or her speech; this is an indication of heightened phoneme awareness.

What about syllable awareness and onset/rime awareness in learning to read English? Conceptually, syllable awareness is important. Any child trying to learn to read English who did not have it would be in trouble. However, for most children, even troubled readers, distinguishing syllables is not difficult; so, practically speaking, syllable awareness is of lesser importance in reading English. Syllable awareness is not difficult for most Japanese children, either. But syllable awareness is the critical phonological insight for Japanese children because in the *hiragana*, the first script that Japanese children learn to read, each symbol represents one syllable in spoken Japanese. Thus, Mann (1986) found that whereas most Japanese children in her study displayed perfect or near-perfect performance on a syllable awareness task, there was a fairly high correlation between syllable awareness and reading proficiency, suggesting that the few children who did not possess good syllable awareness were poor readers.

Onset/rime awareness is fairly important in learning to read English (Goswami, 2000). A probable reason for this is that much of the irregularity at the letter-sound level disappears when one considers the rime level (Treiman, Mullennix, Bijeljac-Babic, & Richmond-Welty, 1995). An example is the varying pronunciation of *ea* in such words as *ready, meat, break,* and *ocean.* In contrast, *eam* has the same pronunciation in every word in which this rime appears, for instance, *team, cream, beam, seam.* Another example is the blatantly irregular word *could.* It doesn't seem so exceptional when one considers the other members of its rime "family" or "neighborhood," *should* and *would.* Thus, it can be an advantage to read English words in chunks corresponding to onsets and rimes. Often, words that are irregular at the letter-sound level are easy to pronounce by analogy with other words sharing the same rime. An instructional program that teaches analysis of words into onsets and rimes has been developed for children having problems learning to read English and, although the program has not been subjected to rigorous evaluation, the indications are that it is successful (Gaskins, 1998).

We turn now to the Chinese language, the Chinese writing system, and the mapping between the two. Compared with the thousands of syllables in English, a notable feature of Chinese is that it contains only about 400 syllables. A Chinese syllable consists of an onset (also called an *initial*) and a rime (or *final*). Table 5.1 displays all of the valid syllables in modern standard Chinese, which in the West we call *Mandarin* and which in China is called *putonghua,* meaning "common language." As can be seen, Mandarin syllables are combinations of a limited number of onsets and rimes. The pronunciations in Table 5.1 are represented in *pinyin*—literally, "spell sound"—an alphabetic script that mainland Chinese children learn in the first 10 weeks of first grade as an aid to learning character pronunciations. Be forewarned that the sound values of letters in pinyin are not identical to their sound values in English.

Each Mandarin syllable is further differentiated according to one of four *tones,* or voice inflections, making in all about 1,200 distinct *tone syllables.*

TABLE 5.1
Combinations of Onsets and Rimes That Form Valid Syllables in Mandarin

	a	o	e	i	er	ai	ei	ao	ou	an	en	ang	eng	ong	ia	iao	ie	iu
	a	o	e	yi	er	ai	ei	ao	ou	an	en	ang	eng		ya		ye	you
b	ba	bo		bi		bai	bei	bao		ban	ben	bang	beng			biao	bie	
p	pa	po		pi		pai	pei	pao	pou	pan	pen	pang	peng			piao	pie	
m	ma	mo	me	mi		mai	mei	mao	mou	man	men	mang	meng			miao	mie	miu
f	fa	fo					fei		fou	fan	fen	fang	feng					
d	da		de	di		dai	dei	dao	dou	dan	den	dang	deng	dong		diao	die	diu
t	ta		te	ti		tai		tao	tou	tan		tang	teng	tong		tiao	tie	
n	na		ne	ni		nai	nei	nao	nou	nan	nen	nang	neng	nong		niao	nie	niu
l	la		le	li		lai	lei	lao	lou	lan		lang	leng	long	lia	liao	lie	liu
z	za		ze	zi		zai	zei	zao	zou	zan	zen	zang	zeng	zong				
c	ca		ce	ci		cai		cao	cou	can	cen	cang	ceng	cong				
s	sa		se	si		sai		sao	sou	san	sen	sang	seng	song				
zh	zha		zhe	zhi		zhai	zhei	zhao	zhou	zhan	zhen	zhang	zheng	zhong				
ch	cha		che	chi		chai		chao	chou	chan	chen	chang	cheng	chong				
sh	sha		she	shi		shai	shei	shao	shou	shan	shen	shang	sheng					
r			re	ri				rao	rou	ran	ren	rang	reng	rong				
j				ji											jia	jiao	jie	jiu
q				qi											qia	qiao	qie	qiu
x				xi											xia	xiao	xie	xiu
g	ga		ge			gai	gei	gao	gou	gan	gen	gang	geng	gong				
k	ka		ke			kai	kei	kao	kou	kan	ken	kang	keng	kong				
h	ha		he			hai	hei	hao	hou	han	hen	hang	heng	hong				

(continued)

TABLE 5.1 (*continued*)

	ian	in	iang	ing	iong	u	ua	uo	uai	ui	uan	un	uang	ueng	Ü	ue	uan	un
	yan	yin	yang	ying	yong	wu	wa	wo	wai	wei	wan	wen	wang	weng	yu	yue		
b	bian	bin		bing		bu												
p	pian	pin		ping		pu												
m	mian	min		ming		mu												
f						fu												
d	dian			ding		du		duo		dui	duan	dun						
t	tian			ting		tu		tuo		tui	tuan	tun						
n	nian	nin	niang	ning		nu		nuo			nuan				nu	nue		
l	lian	lin	liang	ling		lu		luo			luan	lun			lu	lue		
z						zu		zuo		zui	zuan	zun						
c						cu		cuo		cui	cuan	cun						
s						su		suo		sui	suan	sun						
zh						zhu	zhua	zhuo	zhuai	zhui	zhuan	zhun	zhuang					
ch						chu	chua	chuo	chuai	chui	chuan	chun	chuang					
sh						shu	shua	shuo	shuai	shui	shuan	shun	shuang					
r						ru	rua	ruo		rui	ruan	run						
j	jian	jin	jiang	jing	jiong										ju	jue	juan	jun
q	qian	qin	qiang	qing	qiong										qu	que	quan	qun
x	xian	xin	xiang	xing	xiong										xu	xue	xuan	xun
g						gu	gua	guo	guai	gui	guan	gun	guang					
k						ku	kua	kuo	kuai	kui	kuan	kun	kuang					
h						hu	hua	huo	huai	hui	huan	hun	huang					

The same syllable with a different tone has a completely different meaning. For instance, mā means *mother*, and mǎ means *horse*. The diacritical mark in mā, which in English would mean a long vowel, in pinyin means the first tone (high, even voicing). The diacritical mark in mǎ, which in English is used to represent a short vowel sound, in pinyin stands for the third tone (low falling then rising voice inflection).

Which levels of phonological awareness are implicated in learning to read Chinese? Theoretically, syllable awareness is important because Chinese characters are pronounced with a single syllable but, as we have seen, syllable awareness is not difficult for most children around the world. Tone awareness is a phonological insight, not needed for English or other Western languages, that is implicated in learning to read Chinese. Because every syllable in Mandarin is differentiated with a tone, it is to be expected that a child who cannot or does not pay attention to tone will often be confused. Finally, most scholars investigating Chinese reading agree that onset/rime awareness is important. Looking at Table 5.1 reveals an obvious reason why: Chinese syllables are constructed from a restricted set of onsets and rimes. The valid syllables are formed using just 21 onsets and 36 rimes. There is another, more subtle reason why onset/rime awareness may be important that we explain after we describe the Chinese writing system.

How about phoneme awareness? Is it implicated in Chinese reading? The answer is probably not. As a rule of thumb, young readers do not make finer distinctions than required to use their language. In fact, research we have already mentioned suggests that Chinese children who learn characters without a script, such as *zhu yin fu hao* or *pinyin*, have relatively poor phoneme awareness (Huang & Hanley, 1995). Phoneme awareness does not correlate highly with Chinese reading proficiency.

In the 6 years of elementary school, mainland Chinese children are expected to learn about 2,500 visually complex Chinese characters. Chinese characters are usefully divided into two categories: (a) simple characters and (b) compound characters. Simple characters are not further divisible into pronounceable, meaningful parts. Simple characters include pictographs and ideographs, so called because 5,000 years ago when characters were invented they were constructed so that the visual form conveyed something about the meaning. For instance, the characters for up 上 and down 下 may be considered to give a clue to their meanings from the directions in which they point. However, characters have been simplified and stylized over centuries of use, and only a few remain in which there is an obvious connection between form and meaning.

The largest class of Chinese characters are semantic–phonetic compounds or, more simply, phonetic compounds. This type of character contains a part that gives a clue to meaning and a part that gives a clue to pronunciation. An example of a phonetic compound character is 妈 which means *mother* and, as we said before, is pronounced mā. On the left is 女, which is the part (called the *semantic radical*) that gives a clue to the meaning. On the right is 马, which is the part (called the *phonetic*) that gives a clue to pronunciation. When 女 appears alone as a simple character, it means *female* and is pronounced nǚ, but as the semantic radical in the compound character 妈 mother, 女 contributes aspects of its meaning but not its pronunciation. When 马 appears alone as a simple character, it means *horse* and is pronounced mǎ, but as the phonetic component in the compound character 妈 mother, it contributes an approximate pronunciation but not its meaning.

In Chinese, the principle for mapping between speech and print, which corresponds to the alphabetic principle in English, might be called the *phonetic principle*. Anderson, Li, Ku, Shu, and Wu (2003), who coined the phrase, explain, "The phonetic principle is simply that the phonetic components of compound characters represent syllables in spoken Chinese." Young readers—and older, poor readers—are not necessarily aware of, or functionally able to use, this principle (Ho & Bryant, 1997; Shu, Anderson, Wu, 2000). One kind of evidence that mastery of the alphabetic principle is critical for learning to read English and other alphabetic languages is the high correlation of pseudoword reading with word recognition and reading comprehension (e.g. Siegel, 1993), where the pseudowords represent monosyllables without obscure or tricky letter–sound relationships. Comparable evidence has been found in support of the importance of the phonetic principle in learning to read Chinese. Ho and Bryant (1997) asked Hong Kong first and second graders to pronounce compound characters, two-character words, and pseudocharacters. The pseudocharacters were novel combinations of familiar semantic radicals and familiar phonetic components in their legal positions. Pseudocharacter pronunciation was found to correlate highly with the pronunciation of both compound characters and two-character words. The only way to pronounce a pseudocharacter is to use information in the phonetic component; therefore, this finding implies that children who are aware of and attempting to use the information in the phonetic component are making better progress in learning to read. Similarly, C. K. Chan and Siegel (2001) had Hong Kong children in the first through the sixth grades read aloud a list of characters about 80% of which were semantic phonetic compounds. Among the younger children, normal readers had significantly higher scores on a pseudocharacter pronunciation task than poor readers. This finding again implies that children making good progress in reading are trying to use the information in the phonetic component.

Now comes the bad news. Like written English, written Chinese is not very regular. Shu, Chen, Anderson, Wu, and Xuan (2003) completed a comprehensive analysis of all of the characters listed to be taught in the six grades of elementary school by the Chinese Ministry of Education. They found that only 23% of the compound characters in elementary school Chinese are entirely regular in the sense that the compound has exactly the same pronunciation as its phonetic component—same onset, same rime, and same tone. It is apparent, therefore, that a Chinese child cannot reliably predict the pronunciations of unfamiliar compound characters.

Now, some more encouraging news: Shu and her colleagues (2003) estimated that an additional 42% of the compound characters in school Chinese are semiregular and contain partial information about pronunciation. These include tone-different characters, in which the compound is pronounced with the same onset and same rime as its phonetic, but in a different tone. Earlier we introduced an example of a tone-different character, *mother* 妈, which is pronounced mā, while its phonetic, 马, is pronounced mǎ. Semiregular characters also include onset-different characters, which, as the name suggests, are pronounced with the same rime but a different onset than their phonetics. An example of an onset-different character is 精 /jīng/, which contains the phonetic 青 /qīng/. Finally, semiregular characters include rime-different characters that have the same onset but a different rime than their phonetics, such as the character 结 /jié/ and its phonetic, 吉 /jí/. Shu et al. (2003) estimated that 16% of the phonetic compound characters in school Chinese are tone different, 20% are onset different, and 6% are rime different.

The partial information about pronunciation available in less-than-fully-regular characters would not enable a child to accurately *predict* the pronunciations of unfamiliar characters, but it might be helpful for *assimilating* the characters, once the pronunciation has been provided by the teacher, looked up in the dictionary, or figured out from context while reading. Ehri (1991, p. 402) illustrated the use of partial information in English using the example *sword*. Although the word is irregular, and an English-speaking child who did not know the word would not be able to predict its pronunciation or spelling, the letters *s, o, r,* and *d* have their normal sound values. Ehri's research shows that a phonemically aware child can use this partial information to readily encode and remember *sword* and other English words containing partial information.

Can Chinese children use the partial information about pronunciation in semiregular characters? Anderson, Li, Ku, Shu, and Wu (2003) tried to answer this question in an investigation that included more than 300 second graders and fourth graders from working class schools in Beijing in the north of China and Guangzhou in the south of China. The children had two brief opportunities to learn the pronunciation of 28 unfamiliar compound characters. After each opportunity to learn, the children received a test in which they indicated the pronunciations of the characters. The children were taught and tested on the pronunciation of four types of unfamiliar characters: (a) fully regular, (b) tone different, (c) onset different, and (d) phonetic unknown (unknown to children of a specific age). The results are displayed in Fig. 5.1. Compared with phonetic-unknown characters, which provide a baseline because they convey no information about pronunciation, children learned and remembered the pronunciation of not only more regular characters but also significantly more tone-different and onset-different characters. Performance on regular characters was significantly better than performance on tone-different characters, which in turn was significantly better than performance on onset-different characters. The information in onset-different characters was less accessible to children, although the contrast of onset-different characters with phonetic-unknown characters was statistically significant.

So, the answer is yes, Chinese children can use the partial information in tone-different—and, to some extent, onset-different—characters to learn and remember the pronunciations of the characters. Whether they can use the information in rime-different characters has not been investigated, but a guess is that they cannot, because there are not many of these characters, and they contain negligible information. It is now possible to appreciate another, more subtle reason why tone awareness and onset/rime awareness are important for learning to read Chinese: Chinese children have to be sensitive to differences in tone, onset, and rime in order to use the partial information in tone-different; onset-different; and, perhaps, rime-different characters.

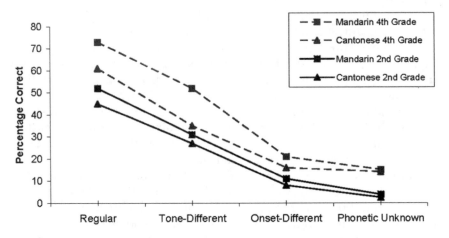

FIG. 5.1.   Percentage correct pronunciations as a function of character type, grade, and home language. From "Use of Partial Information in Learning to Read Chinese Characters," by R. C. Anderson, W. Li, Y. Ku, H. Shu, and N.-N. Wu, 2003, *Journal of Educational Psychology, 95.* Copyright 2003 by the American Psychological Association. Reprinted with permission.

Anderson et al. (2003) also found that children from Beijing, whose home language is Mandarin, learned more Mandarin pronunciations than children from Guangzhou, whose home language is Cantonese. Although called *dialects* of Chinese, Mandarin and Cantonese are actually mutually unintelligible languages. From the first grade on, Cantonese-speaking children experience immersion Mandarin. Mandarin is the language of instruction throughout the school day. Children are admonished to speak Mandarin in the hallways and on the playground. Probably Cantonese-speaking children learned to pronounce fewer characters because they suffered interference from Cantonese or lacked fluent access to Mandarin pronunciations. Another finding is that children rated by their teachers as making the best progress in learning to read were the ones who learned the most tone-different and onset-different characters. Fourth graders learned more pronunciations than second graders, which may indicate that they have learned how to learn new characters.

As Chinese children mature as readers, their grasp of the phonetic principle is not as rudimentary as it may appear to be among beginners. At the beginning stage, children's understanding of the principle might be something like "The part on the right tells the pronunciation" (Shu et al., 2000, p. 61). At this stage, children recognize the phonetic component of a semantic phonetic character and use it directly to name the character. As they become more experienced in reading, children who are making good progress learn how to cope with more complicated relationships between the phonetic component and the pronunciation of a character, especially characters in which the phonetic component conveys partial information. They may eventually learn to forecast the pronunciations of unfamiliar compound characters by analogy with familiar characters that contain the same phonetic component (see Chen, Shu, Wu, & Anderson, 2003).

To summarize, despite the obvious large differences in the English and Chinese languages and writing systems, not to mention huge differences in cultures and approaches to teaching reading (Wu, Li, & Anderson, 1999), there are common features in learning to pronounce English and Chinese words. In each language, aspects of phonological awareness are important. In each language, children who understand and use the principle for mapping speech to print make more rapid progress. In each language, there are large numbers of less-than-fully regular words from which the best young readers learn to extract useful partial information about pronunciation. In several specific respects, learning to pronounce words in the two languages is different. Phoneme awareness is important in English but probably unimportant in Chinese. Tone awareness is an aspect of phonological awareness peculiar to Chinese. The mapping principles in the two languages—the alphabetic principle in English, the phonetic principle in Chinese—are different.

MORPHOLOGICAL AWARENESS IN ENGLISH AND CHINESE

Morphological awareness is the ability to identify, reflect on, and manipulate word units that convey meaning. The basic word unit representing meaning is the *morpheme*. In English, a string of letters is required to represent a morpheme—for instance, *act*, which can appear in many words from *acts*, *acted*, and *actress* to *reaction* and *radioactivity*. *Act* is a free morpheme; that is, it can stand alone as a basic or root word. Other morphemes, such as *-ed* and *tele-*, are bound; that is, they cannot stand alone and must be combined with other morphemes to form words. The same general types of morphemes are found in English and Chinese (Packard, 2000), as is shown in Table 5.2, which is reproduced from Ku and Anderson (2003). English has more inflectional morphemes (*-s, -ed*) and derivational morphemes (*-tion, -ly*) than Chinese, whereas Chinese has more bound roots (*anti-, -logy*).

Morphological awareness can be assessed in several ways. For illustration, we will describe two of the four tasks used by Ku and Anderson (2003) in a recent study of the development of morphological awareness among Chinese and American children. In the Recognize Morpheme task, children judged whether the second word in pairs of words "comes from" the first one. For example, English-speaking children were asked to indicate whether the word *teacher* comes from the word *teach*. Chinese-speaking children were asked to indicate whether the meaning of the two-character word 书架 /shūjià/ (bookshelf) is related to meaning of the first character 书 /shū/ (book). The Discriminate Morphemes task was designed to determine whether children understand that words that share a certain part may

TABLE 5.2
Types of Morphemes and Examples in Chinese and English

Morpheme type	Chinese	English
Root word	山 /shān/ (mountain)	book
	狗 /gǒu/ (dog)	hand
Bound root	房 /fáng/ (house)	anti- (against, opposite)
	桌 /zhuō/ (desk)	-logy (study)
Inflectional affix	-了 /le/ verbal aspect	-ed (past tense)
	-们 /mén/ plural	-s (plural)
Derivational affix	无- /wú/ (not)	-er (agentive)
	-化 /huà/ verbalizing	-ly (adverb)

have different meanings. Children saw groups of three words that share a part. In two words, the common part had about the same meaning. They were supposed to circle the odd word, the one in which the common part had a different meaning. For an English example, among the words *classroom*, *bedroom*, and *mushroom*, the meaning of *room* in the first two words means a division of a building, with its own walls, floor, and ceiling, but the *room* in *mushroom* does not have this meaning. For a Chinese example, among the words 商品/shāngpǐn/ (merchandise), 商店/shāngdiàn/ (shop, store), and 商量/shāngliàng/ (to consult), the last one is odd because in this word the meaning of the character 商/shāng/ does not have to do with a business, at least in everyday usage.

Chinese morphology is more transparent than English morphology. In Chinese, each syllable in speech and each character in writing represents one morpheme. Morpheme boundaries are less certain in English and do not have a simple one-to-one correspondence with syllables, as is illustrated by *sign* and *signature*. Shifts in the spelling and pronunciation of words containing the same morpheme make it difficult for a child to identify the shared morpheme (Carlisle, 1995; Leong, 1989; Singson, Mahony, & Mann, 2000). Such shifts are common in English, as in *pronounce* and *pronunciation* or *deep* and *depth*, but rare in Chinese. One of the few cases of pronunciation shift in Chinese is that when two third-tone syllables are spoken one after the other the first one is pronounced with a second tone. An illustration is 你, which means *you* and is ordinarily pronounced with the third tone nǐ, but is pronounced with the second tone in the greeting, 你好, pronounced ní hǎo and literally translated, You good!

In English, often nothing in the surface forms of sets of words marks that the words have related meanings. For instance, there is no clue in the words themselves that *lake, pond, river, brook, creek, stream, sea,* and *ocean* are names for bodies of water. In contrast, the Chinese words for bodies of water all have a character that contains the water radical. A Chinese child who encounters one of these words for the first time will know right away that it has something to do with water and, with a little help from context, may be able to determine its meaning precisely. Shu et al. (2003) estimated that 58% of the compound characters in school Chinese contain a semantic radical that provides a direct and obvious cue to meaning, whereas another 30% contain an indirect or weak cue to meaning that might be useful under some circumstances.

In another way, the Chinese child may be at a disadvantage as compared to a Canadian, British, or American child. English has some homophones, for example *bear$_1$* (big animal), *bear$_2$* (to carry), and *bare* or *to, too,* and *two,* but because of the language's large stock of syllables and tendency toward long words (at least compared to Chinese), homophony probably is not a major stumbling block for young readers of English. Because of the small stock of syllables in Chinese, and the tendency toward short words of one or two syllables, there are numerous homophones in Chinese. Ku and Anderson (2003) stated that Chinese may average five morphemes per syllable. Thus, a Chinese child who is not morphologically aware, always alert to distinguishing meanings and habitually searching for information to discriminate meanings, is vulnerable to frequent misunderstandings. One major basis for discriminating homophones is the semantic radical in compound characters. The semantic radical is a *graphomorphological* feature, by which we mean a feature of written language that provides information about meaning that is not available in the spoken language.

Some morphological relationships are more obvious than others. Even literate English-speaking adults probably have not noticed that *business* comes from *busy* and *-ness* or the similarity in form and meaning of *frail* and *fragile*. English-speaking children from the United States may not even have noticed that *Thanksgiving* has anything to do with giving thanks while English-speaking adults may not have noticed that *breakfast* has anything to do with breaking a fast. These words are frozen—or lexicalized. Their use today has drifted away from original meanings and they do not invite decomposition into parts. For another example of a lexicalized word/phrase, the White House is a white house, but this is not the aspect of meaning that comes most readily to the minds of readers, rather it is something more like 'seat of executive authority in the U.S. government.'

Nonetheless, there is evidence from both Chinese and English studies that skilled adult readers habitually decompose most complex words into parts during the process of reading them and accessing their meanings (Andrews, 1986; Nagy, Anderson, Schommer, Scott, & Stallman, 1989; Taft, 1985; Zhou, Marslen-Wilson, Taft, & Shu, 1999). This is only reasonable for many complex words, notably regular inflections and derivatives involving *-ly, -able, -ize,* and *-ity,* among other common and productive suffixes. It would be clumsy to have separate entries in one's internal lexicon for *walk, walks, walked,* and *walking* and all the other regular verbs in one's vocabulary. Much more elegant would be a single entry for each root word plus rules of inflection; research suggests this is how peoples' lexicons are organized, which illuminates why decomposing words into parts seems to be a habitual process for skilled readers.

Morphological awareness is considered an important factor in children's rapid vocabulary growth during the elementary school years (Anglin, 1993; Nagy & Anderson, 1984; Shu, Anderson, & Zhang, 1995; Tyler & Nagy, 1990; White, Power, & White, 1989). Carlisle (1995) proposed that morphological awareness might be important for English-speaking children because "morphological decomposition and problem-solving provide one way to understand and learn the large number of derived words used in the books they read" (p. 205). The prevalent belief is that children who are knowledgeable about morphology decompose unfamiliar words into familiar meaningful units—prefixes, roots, and suffixes—and then derive the meanings of the words by combining the units. For example, the prefix *un-* means *not* or *"do the opposite,"* so when encountering the word *untidy* for the first time, children have an excellent chance of getting the right meaning—not tidy, or messy—using their morphological knowledge. Even unusual complex words, such as *teleprompter* or *breastplate*, may be understandable provided the context is helpful. The process of breaking an unfamiliar complex word into units, and then recombining the units into a meaningful whole, enables children to figure out the meanings of newly encountered words and probably enhances memory for these words.

Parenthetically, the other main factor considered to be important for vocabulary growth during the elementary school years is amount of experience with rich, interesting language (Anderson, 1996; Anderson, Wilson, & Fielding, 1988; Stanovich, 1993). This means good children's literature, not cartoons and shoot-'em-up TV shows.

There have been many studies of the morphological awareness of English-speaking children (Carlisle, 1995, 2000; Freyd & Baron, 1982; Singson et al., 2000). One of the most comprehensive was Tyler and Nagy's (1989) investigation of fourth-, sixth-, and eighth-grade American students' knowledge of different aspects of derivational suffixes. To test the relational aspect of suffix knowledge, children were given a multiple-choice test containing low-frequency derivatives of high-frequency base words and were asked to select the correct meanings of the derivatives. Most students were able to capitalize on the relationship between the derivatives and the base words. Failures were attributed to lack of vocabulary rather than deficient morphological knowledge.

To examine children's knowledge of the syntactic properties of suffixes, Tyler and Nagy (1989) asked children to select suffixed words to fit into blanks in sentences. The task required students to choose among sets of four derived words that differed only in their suffixes, for example:

You can _____ the effect by turning off the light.

intensify   intensification   intensity   intensive

To choose a suffixed word to complete each sentence appropriately, students have to understand the syntactic contribution of the suffixes. The results indicated that children's knowledge of the syntactic function of suffixes increases with grade level.

To investigate knowledge of distributional constraints on the use of suffixes, Tyler and Nagy (1989) asked children to distinguish between well-formed and ill-formed derivatives. Suffixes are constrained by the syntactic category of the base to which they attach. For example, *-ness* is restricted to nouns, so *butterness* is unusual but well formed, whereas *eatness* is ill formed. Overall, students were able to distinguish well-formed derivatives from ill-formed ones, and older students were better than younger students at judging whether the derivatives were well formed. Confirming Tyler and Nagy's prediction, knowledge of distributional constraints was acquired later than relational and syntactic knowledge.

Until recently, there have been few empirical studies of the morphological knowledge of Chinese children, although theorists have reasoned that the transparent morphology of Chinese might help children learn unfamiliar complex words (Hoosain, 1991; Nagy & Anderson, 1998). Some evidence for this conjecture comes from Shu et al.'s (1995) cross-cultural study of Chinese and American children learning unfamiliar words from context during normal reading. As compared to American children, Chinese children were more likely to learn the meanings of morphologically transparent words than of morphologically opaque words. This implies that Chinese children made more use of morphological analysis to assimilate word meanings.

Three recent studies have investigated Chinese children's awareness of the graphomorphological information in the semantic radicals of compound characters. In a creative writing task, L. Chan and Nunes (1998) gave 6- to 9-year-old Hong Kong children six semantic radicals and six phonetics and asked them to generate names for the novel objects in six pictures. Each radical was related in meaning to the object in one picture. For example, the plant radical 艹 was associated with grass or a flower. By the age of 6, the children were able to select the appropriate radical to represent a given meaning and put it in the correct position alongside a phonetic. The results suggest that from an early age Chinese children are sensitive to both the function and position of radicals.

Shu and Anderson (1997) investigated first-, third-, and fifth-grade Beijing children's use of semantic radicals in reading characters. Certain characters familiar to the children in oral language appeared in *pinyin* in two-character words. The children were asked to replace the *pinyin* with one of four characters. The choices shared the same phonetic component but had different semantic radicals. The target characters varied in morphological transparency. One third were morphologically transparent, with radicals that provide useful information about the meaning of the characters. One third were morphologically opaque, with radicals that provide no information that a child could use. The rest were simple characters that didn't have radicals. The results indicated that children performed better on morphologically transparent characters than opaque or simple characters. Transparency had a bigger effect on unfamiliar and recently learned characters than familiar characters; the effect was also bigger among third and fifth graders than among first graders. The results suggest that children can use the information in radicals to read characters and that radical awareness increases throughout the primary school period. In a second study, Shu and Anderson (1997) confirmed that children's performance was affected by familiarity of the radicals and demonstrated an influence from the conceptual difficulty of the words. Children were better able to use semantic components to derive meaning of characters when the semantic components were familiar and the words were conceptually easy.

Ho, Wong, and Chan (1999) examined whether children can use semantic analogy to understand the meanings of characters. Children learned "clue characters" and then read target characters with clue characters in sight. The task was to select from four pictures the one that represented the semantic category of the target character. There were three types of target characters: (a) an *analogous* character, which had the same semantic radical as the clue characters; (b) a *common-phonetic* character, which had the same phonetic component; and (c) a *control* character, which had nothing in common. Children made more improvement from pretest to posttest on semantically analogous characters than control characters or common-phonetic characters. The improvement was smallest in reading common-phonetic characters, because children sometimes mistakenly used the phonetic component as a semantic cue. It seems that children are able to use semantic analogy to read unfamiliar characters, but they sometimes confuse phonetic components with semantic radicals.

The foregoing studies indicate that children as young as 6 years old are aware of the position and function of semantic radicals (L. Chan & Nunes, 1998; see also Shu & Anderson, 1998), and their radical awareness increases throughout the primary school period (Shu & Anderson, 1997). Children are able to make semantic analogies when encountering unfamiliar characters in a supportive context (Ho et al., 1999). On the other hand, research also demonstrates that children's radical awareness is limited: There are many radicals young children do not know, and they sometimes confuse radicals with phonetic components.

Chinese children's development of morphological awareness through the elementary school years has not been studied until recently. The first comprehensive study was completed by Ku and Anderson (2003), who investigated the development of morphological awareness in both Chinese and English, giving tasks equated for difficulty in the two languages to about 700 Taiwanese and American students in second, fourth, and sixth grades. The study addressed children's understanding of compounds (*washcloth, microscope*), which had not been studied in previous research, as well as derivatives (*caution, likeable*), which have been much studied in the West but not in China. The results from both Chinese-speaking and English-speaking students indicate that morphological awareness develops with grade level and is strongly related to reading ability. More proficient

readers outperformed less proficient readers when asked to (a) recognize
morphological relationships between words, (b) discriminate word parts
having the same or different meanings, (c) select the best interpretations of
low-frequency derivatives and compounds composed of high-frequency
parts, and (d) judge the well-formedness of novel derivatives and compounds. The results indicate that the morphological awareness develops
significantly with grade level. More skilled readers outperformed less
skilled readers on every task at every grade in both countries. Correlations
between morphological awareness and reading proficiency ranged from
.60 to .73 and were somewhat higher among Taiwanese students than
American students.

Ku and Anderson's (2003) results suggest that the overall level of morphological awareness of Taiwanese and American children is similar. As
Fig. 5.2 shows, Taiwanese second graders lagged behind American second
graders; this was entirely due to their lack of understanding of derivational
morphology, probably because there are fewer derivatives in Chinese than
English and apparently no instruction in Taiwan about how derivatives are
formed, but the Taiwanese children had caught up and slightly surpassed
American children by sixth grade. Almost certainly, the Taiwanese children
would have outperformed the American children if the full range of compounds and derivatives in Chinese and English had been examined. As we
indicated before, English-speaking children have trouble when the pro-

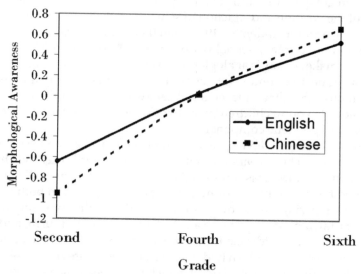

FIG. 5.2. Morphological awareness as a function of grade and language. From *Development of Morphological Awareness in Chinese and English* (p. 415), by Y. Ku and R. C. Anderson, 2003. Copyright 2002 by Reading and Writing—An Interdisciplinary Journal.
Reprinted with permission.

nunciation or spelling of morphemes shifts from word to word (e.g., Singson et al., 2000), but such words were excluded because in Chinese there are seldom shifts in spoken or written forms of morphemes, and Ku and Anderson were attempting to equate difficulty in the two languages.

Li, Anderson, Nagy, and Zhang (2002) reasoned that morphological awareness is more important than phonological awareness in learning to read Chinese for the following reasons: because the phonological insights required by Chinese are easy for most children, because the Chinese writing system provides more reliable information about meaning than about pronunciation, and because graphomorphological information in written characters and words provides the basis for distinguishing the numerous homophones in Chinese. To evaluate this theory, a battery of tests was developed and administered to about 400 first-grade and 400 fourth-grade students in 10 average-level primary schools in Beijing. The tests assessing phonological awareness consisted of syllable reversal, onset deletion, rime deletion, and tone judgment. The tests assessing morphological awareness included two measures assessing understanding of semantic radicals, plus measures assessing morpheme discrimination and morpheme recognition. The tests given in one or both grades to assess reading comprehension were vocabulary, syntactic knowledge, cloze completion, comprehension of sentences written in characters, comprehension of sentences written in *pinyin*, and paragraph comprehension. Tests were administered to one sample of first graders and fourth graders early in the school year and another sample of first graders and fourth graders late in the school year.

Figure 5.3 is a reproduction of Li et al.'s (2002) structural equation model of performance early in the first grade. The model relates reading proficiency to the two facets of metalinguistic awareness. The numbers in the figure are standardized path coefficients; rectangles represent observed variables, and ovals represent latent variables. Both morphological awareness and phonological awareness are significantly related to reading proficiency. The relationship of morphological awareness is stronger than that of phonological awareness. Li et al. found that similar models fit children's performance late in the first grade, early in the fourth grade, and late in the fourth grade. At each point in time, morphological awareness accounted for more unique variance in reading proficiency than phonological awareness. For instance, early in the first grade morphological awareness accounted for 22.6% of the variance in reading proficiency, after removing the variance due to phonological awareness, whereas phonological awareness accounted for a much smaller, although still significant, 4.4% of the variance in reading proficiency, after removing the variance due to morphological awareness. By early fourth grade, morphological awareness and phonological awareness accounted, respectively, for 37.5% and 1.2% of the unique variance in reading proficiency.

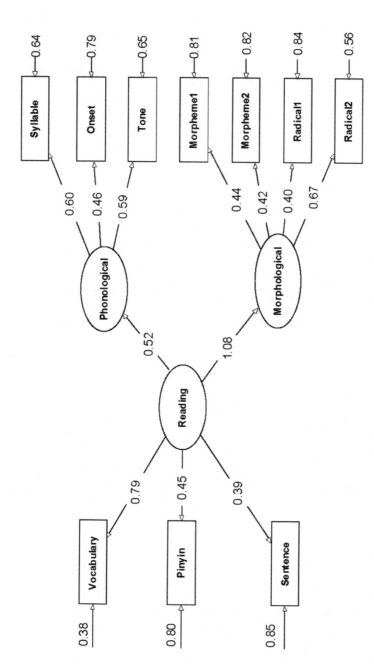

FIG. 5.3.   Early first-grade model predicting reading as a function of phonological and morphological awareness. Numbers are standardized path coefficients; rectangles represent observed variables; ovals represent latent variables. From "Facets of Metalinguistic Awareness That Contribute to Chinese Literacy" by W. Li, R. C. Anderson, W. E. Nagy, and H. Zhang, in W. Li, G. Gaffney, and J. L. Packard (Eds.), *Chinese Children's Reading Acquisition: Theoretical and Pedagogical Issues*, 2002, Norwell, MA: Kluwer Academic. Copyright 2002 by Kluwer Academic Publishers. Reprinted with permission.

Building on the idea that morphological awareness is especially important for learning to read Chinese, our research team has completed a year-long intervention study in Beijing elementary schools. The study had the theoretical goal of determining whether morphological awareness is a cause of reading proficiency and the practical goal of improving reading education in China. We revised every lesson in the first grade and the fourth grade Chinese language textbooks to more explicitly and systematically teach the morphology of Chinese (Wu, Anderson, Li, Chen, & Meng, 2002). We met every week throughout the year with the teachers to discuss how to teach Chinese in a way that heightens children's morphological awareness. Results with about 250 first graders and 250 fourth graders showed that, at both grade levels, morphological instruction significantly increased students' performance on reading and writing tasks that entail character-level knowledge (Nagy et al., 2002). This implies that morphological awareness is a *cause*—not just a correlate—of growth in character and word knowledge. Morphological instruction also had a significant influence on reading comprehension in the fourth grade, but not the first grade.

Here is the reflection of one of the first grade teachers about morphological instruction. Notice that she believes that the payoff was that children learned "how to teach themselves new characters":

> Morphological instruction was difficult at the beginning because we must teach so much more about the characters, but now the children understand the structure of characters. This was hard work for the teacher, because the children attending this school don't know much about characters. But, once they learned the structure of characters children were able to teach themselves new characters. So, later the method was easier than the traditional method.[1]

To summarize, the English and Chinese languages contain the same kinds of morphemes. The rules for forming complex words are similar in the two languages, although inflections and derivatives are more common in English, whereas compounds, especially compounds containing bound roots, are the most common form of complex word in Chinese. English morphology is less transparent than Chinese morphology. In English, groups of words with related meanings may be completely unrelated in surface form, whereas groups of Chinese words with related meanings usually contain characters with the same semantic radical. In English, the spoken or written representation of a morpheme may change in different words, which makes the morpheme more difficult to identify, whereas in Chinese the spoken and written representation of morphemes almost always remains the same from word to word. Morphological awareness develops with grade

---

[1]From an interview with De Xiuqi, first grade teacher in Fuxingmenwai Elementary School, Western District, Beijing, as told to Richard Anderson on November 5, 1998.

level and has strong relationships with vocabulary knowledge and reading proficiency at each grade among both English-speaking and Chinese-speaking children.

CONCLUSION

In this chapter, we have considered basic factors in learning to read two very different languages, English and Chinese. We have summarized research showing that, in both languages, reading requires phonological awareness and morphological awareness. Children who have the key phonological and morphological insights usually make good progress in learning to read; children who do not possess these insights usually do not. Because English and Chinese are so different, we may provisionally conclude that phonological and morphological awareness are universally important in learning to read (provisionally, of course; we haven't looked at children everywhere learning any language whatsoever).

That phonological awareness should be so important ought to be obvious. Children who can decode written words into spoken words have access to everything they know from oral language. This access is blocked when a child cannot decode or decodes inaccurately or too slowly. Furthermore, information in working memory is primarily in the form of abbreviated inner speech. Working memory is the holding place for incoming information while readers work out who did what to whom, how the current proposition relates to previous propositions, and where to modify the representation they are building of the situation described in the text. It stands to reason that if the acoustic–articulatory information in a reader's working memory is incomplete, indistinct, or garbled, comprehension will suffer.

Although morphological awareness has been less studied by researchers, and probably is less central in the thinking of reading teachers, it should be obvious why it, too, is important for learning to read. Reading is about getting meanings. Every language has a morphological system for representing meanings. It stands to reason that children who understand and use the system have a better chance of becoming good readers. Much of the research on morphological awareness reviewed in this chapter is recent and not widely known, and this fact increases its newsworthiness. The research makes a strong case for the importance of morphological awareness. In the words of Ku and Anderson (2003), "the following conclusion is warranted: Children who are good readers for their age are aware of the information in word parts, able to decompose complex words into informative parts, and able to use information in word parts to estimate the meanings of unfamiliar complex words" (p. 31).

Phonological and morphological awareness empower young readers in two ways. First, these facets of metalinguistic awareness enable young readers to anticipate the possible pronunciation and meaning of unfamiliar words. Although the English and Chinese writing systems are among the least regular in the world, and phonological and morphological analysis will seldom be sufficient, when combined with other information—from oral language, background knowledge, the situation, the context of other words—phonological and morphological analysis contribute to unlocking a word's pronunciation and meaning. Second, these two facets of meta-linguistic awareness enable rapid learning of new words, and maximally stable mental representations of them, even words that are less than per-fectly regular and transparent. Every reading teacher sees children who seem to know some words perfectly one day but who are completely un-able to recognize the words the next day. In all likelihood the problem is idiosyncratic, incomplete, or arbitrary mental representations of the words, representations not founded on the design principles of the writing system. For instance, an English-speaking child may seem to know how to read some animal names, but the child has encoded *elephant* as "the long one that starts with *e*," *monkey* as "the one with a tail on the end," and so on. Such representations are unstable; the words are easily confused with other words and likely to be forgotten.

There is a tension between the concept of metalinguistic awareness and another concept important for reading, the concept of *automaticity* (e.g., LaBerge & Samuels, 1974; Logan, 1997; Perfetti, 1988). Automaticity is a concept to explain reading fluency. The idea is that basic processes of word decoding must run quickly and smoothly without requiring much con-scious attention. If metalinguistic awareness implies *thoughtful* reading, then automaticity implies *thoughtless* reading, at least with respect to basic processes of word identification. The theory is that when basic processes are automatic then mental capacity is freed for higher level processes that necessarily involve thinking, such as resolving the reference of pronouns, making inferences to bridge propositions, constructing an understanding of the plot of a story, and critically evaluating an argument.

How are the concepts of metalinguistic awareness and automaticity to be reconciled? Our conjecture is that metalinguistic awareness is impor-tant at the frontiers of a child's reading competence. The first time a child encounters *plentiful*, she has a problem to solve. Here she needs to be thoughtful, strategic, reflective. But when she sees *plentiful* a second time—or if not the second time, the third time or the fifth time—we hope that it has become a sight word whose pronunciation and meaning she can access automatically.

One final thought: *Teaching is pointless without the concept of metalinguistic awareness.* The old-fashioned didactic teacher explains things about lan-guage and reading. Explanation presupposes a glimmer of awareness in children, that explanation can extend awareness, and that enhanced aware-

ness enables better reading. The fashionably modern teacher creates a literature rich classroom expecting children to make discoveries about
language and reading. Discovery presupposes insight and that greater
insight enables better reading.

REFERENCES

Anderson, R. C. (1996). Research foundations to support wide reading. In V.
Greaney (Ed.), *Promoting reading in the developing world* (pp. 55–77). Newark, DE:
International Reading Association.

Anderson, R. C., Li, W., Ku, Y., Shu, H., & Wu, N.-N. (2003). Use of partial information in learning to read Chinese characters. *Journal of Educational Psychology, 95,*
52–57.

Anderson, R. C., Wilson, P., & Fielding, L. (1988). Growth in reading and how children spend their time out of school. *Reading Research Quarterly, 23,* 285–303.

Andrews, S. (1986). Morphological influences on lexical access: Lexical or
nonlexical effects? *Journal of Memory and Language, 25,* 726–740.

Anglin, J. M. (1993). Vocabulary development: A morphological analysis. *Monographs of the Society for Research in Child Development, 58*(10), 1–166.

Blachman, B. A. (2000). Phonological awareness. In M. L. Kamil & P. B. Mosenthal
(Eds.), *Handbook of reading research* (Vol. III, pp. 483–502). Mahwah, NJ: Lawrence
Erlbaum Associates.

Bradley, L., & Bryant, P. E. (1983). Categorizing sounds and learning to read: A
causal connection. *Nature, 301,* 419–421.

Byrne, B., & Fielding-Barnsley, R. (1995). Evaluation of a program to teach phonemic
awareness to young children: A 2- and 3-year follow-up and a new preschool
trial. *Journal of Educational Psychology, 87,* 488–503.

Carlisle, J. F. (1995). Morphological awareness and early reading achievement. In L.
B. Feldman (Ed.), *Morphological aspects of language processing* (pp. 189–209).
Mahwah, NJ: Lawrence Erlbaum Associates.

Carlisle, J. F. (2000). Awareness of the structure and meaning of morphologically
complex words: Impact on reading. *Reading & Writing, 12,* 169–190.

Chan, C. K., & Siegel, L. S. (2001). Phonological processing in reading Chinese
among normally achieving and poor readers. *Journal of Experimental Child Psychology, 80,* 23–43.

Chan, L., & Nunes, T. (1998). Children's understanding of the formal and functional
characteristics of written Chinese. *Applied Psycholinguistics, 19,* 115–131.

Chen, X., Shu, H., Wu, N., & Anderson, R. C. (2003). Stages in learning to pronounce
Chinese characters. *Psychology in the Schools, 40,* 115–124.

Cunningham, A. (1990). Explicit vs. implicit instruction in phonemic awareness.
Journal of Experimental Child Psychology, 50, 429–444.

Ehri, L. C. (1991). Development of ability to read words. In R. Barr, M. Kamil, P.
Mosenthal, & D. Pearson (Eds.), *Handbook of reading research* (Vol. II, pp. 383–417).
New York: Longman.

Freyd, P., & Baron, J. (1982). Individual differences in acquisition of derivational
morphology. *Journal of Verbal Learning and Verbal Behavior, 21,* 282–295.

Gaskins, I. W. (1998). A beginning literacy program for at-risk and delayed readers. In J. Metsala & L. Ehri (Eds.), *Word recognition in beginning literacy* (pp. 209–232). Mahwah, NJ: Lawrence Erlbaum Associates.

Gombert, J., & Fayol, M. (1992). Writing in preliterate children. *Learning & Instruction, 2,* 23–41.

Goswami, U. (2000). Phonological and lexical processes. In M. Kamil, P. B. Mosenthal, P. D. Pearson, & R. Barr (Eds.), *Handbook of reading research* (Vol. 3, pp. 251–268). Lawrence Erlbaum Associates.

Ho, C. S.-H., & Bryant, P. (1997). Learning to read Chinese beyond the logographic phase. *Reading Research Quarterly, 32,* 276–289.

Ho, C. S.-H., Wong, W.-L., & Chan, W.-S. (1999). The use of orthographic analogies in learning to read Chinese. *Journal of Child Psychology, 40,* 393–403.

Hoosain, R. (1991). *Psycholinguistic implications for linguistic relativity: A case study of Chinese.* Hillsdale, NJ: Lawrence Erlbaum Associates.

Huang, H. S., & Hanley, J. R. (1995). Phonological awareness and visual skills in learning to read Chinese and English. *Cognition, 54,* 73–98.

Ku, Y.-M., & Anderson, R. C. (2003). Development of morphological awareness in Chinese and English. *Reading and Writing: An Interdisciplinary Journal, 16,* 399–422.

LaBerge, D., & Samuels, S. J. (1974). Toward a theory of automatic information processing in reading. *Cognitive Psychology, 6,* 293–323.

Leong, C. K. (1989). The effects of morphological structure on reading proficiency: A developmental study. *Reading and Writing: An Interdisciplinary Journal, 1,* 357–379.

Li, W., Anderson, R. C., Nagy, W. E., & Zhang, H. (2002). Facets of metalinguistic awareness that contribute to Chinese literacy. In W. Li, J. Gaffney, & J. L. Packard (Eds.), *Chinese children's reading acquisition: Theoretical and pedagogical issues* (pp. 87–106). Norwell, MA: Kluwer Academic.

Logan, G. D. (1997). Automaticity and reading: Perspectives from the instance theory of automatization. *Reading & Writing Quarterly: Overcoming Learning Difficulties, 13,* 123–146.

Lundberg, I., Frost, J., & Petersen, O. P. (1988). Effects of an extensive program for stimulating phonological awareness in preschool children. *Reading Research Quarterly, 23,* 263–284.

Mann, V. A. (1986). Phonological awareness: The role of reading experience. *Cognition, 24,* 65–92.

Mann, V. A., & Liberman, I. Y. (1984). Phonological awareness and verbal short-term memory. *Journal of Learning Disabilities, 17,* 592–598.

Nagy, W. E., & Anderson, R. C. (1984). How many words are there in printed school English? *Reading Research Quarterly, 19,* 304–330.

Nagy, W. E., & Anderson, R .C. (1998). Metalinguistic awareness and the acquisition of literacy in different languages. In D. Wagner, R. Venezky, & B. Street (Eds.), *Literacy: An international handbook* (pp. 155–160). Boulder, CO: Westview Press.

Nagy, W. E., Anderson, R. C., Schommer, M., Scott, J. A., & Stallman, A. (1989). Morphological families in the internal lexicon. *Reading Research Quarterly, 24,* 262–282.

Nagy, W. E., Kuo-Kealoha, A., Wu, X., Li, W., Anderson, R. C., & Chen, X. (2002). The role of morphological awareness in learning to read Chinese. In W. Li, J. Gaffney, & J. Packard (Eds.), *Chinese children's reading acquisition: Theoretical and pedagogical issues* (pp. 59–86). Norwell, MA: Kluwer Academic.

Packard, J. L. (2000). *The morphology of Chinese: A linguistic and cognitive approach.* Cambridge, England: Cambridge University Press.

Perfetti, C. A. (1988). Verbal efficiency in reading ability. In M. Daneman & G. E. Mackinnon (Eds.), *Reading research: Advances in theory and practice* (Vol. 6, pp. 109–143). San Diego, CA: Academic.

Shu, H., & Anderson, R. C. (1997). Role of radical awareness in the character and word acquisition of Chinese children. *Reading Research Quarterly, 32,* 78–89.

Shu, H., & Anderson, R. C. (1998). Learning to read Chinese: The development of metalinguistic awareness. In J. Wang, A. Inhoff, & H. C. Chen (Eds.), *Reading Chinese script: A cognitive analysis* (pp. 1–18). Mahwah, NJ: Lawrence Erlbaum Associates.

Shu, H., Anderson, R. C., & Wu, N. (2000). Phonetic awareness: Knowledge of or-thography–phonology relationships in the character acquisition of Chinese chil-dren. *Journal of Educational Psychology, 92,* 56–62.

Shu, H., Anderson, R. C., & Zhang, H. (1995). Incidental learning of word meanings while reading: A Chinese and American cross-culture study. *Reading Research Quarterly, 30,* 76–95.

Shu, H., Chen, X., Anderson, R. C., Wu, N., & Xuan, Y. (2003). Properties of school Chinese: Implications for learning to read. *Child Development, 74,* 27–47.

Siegel, L. (1993). Phonological processing deficits as the basis of a reading disability. *Developmental Review, 13,* 246–257.

Singson, M., Mahony, D., & Mann, V. A. (2000). The relation between reading ability and morphological skills: Evidence from derivation suffixes. *Reading and Writ-ing, 12,* 219–252.

Stanovich, K. E. (1993). Does reading make you smarter? Literacy and the develop-ment of verbal intelligence. In H. Reese (Ed.), *Advances in child development and be-havior* (Vol. 24, pp. 133–180). San Diego, CA: Academic.

Taft, M. (1985). The decoding of words in lexical access: A review of the morphographic approach. In T. G. Waller & G. E. Mackinnon (Eds.), *Reading re-search: Advances in theory and practice* (Vol. 5, pp. 83–123). New York: Academic.

Treiman, R., Mullennix, J., Bijeljac-Babic, R., & Richmond-Welty, E. D. (1995). The special role of rimes in the description, use, and acquisition of English orthogra-phy. *Journal of Experimental Psychology: General, 124,* 107–136.

Tunmer, W. E., Herriman, M. L., & Nesdale, A. R. (1988). Metalinguistic abilities and beginning reading, *Reading Research Quarterly, 23,* 134–158.

Tyler, A., & Nagy, W. E. (1989). The acquisition of English derivational morphology. *Journal of Memory and Language, 28,* 649–667.

Tyler, A., & Nagy, W. E. (1990). Use of derivational morphology during reading. *Cog-nition, 36,* 17–34.

White, T. G., Power, M. A., & White, S. (1989). Morphological analysis: Implications for teaching and understanding vocabulary growth. *Reading Research Quarterly, 24,* 283–304.

Wu, X., Anderson, R. C., Li, W., Chen, X., & Meng, X. (2002). Morphological instruc-tion and teacher training. In W. Li, S. J. Gaffney, & J. L. Packard (Eds.), *Chinese lan-guage acquisition: Theoretical pedagogical issues* (pp. 157–173). Norwell, MA: Kluwer Academic.

Wu, X., Li, W., & Anderson, R. C. (1999). Reading instruction in China. *Journal of Curriculum Studies, 31,* 571–586.

Zhou, X., Marslen-Wilson, W., Taft, M., & Shu, H. (1999). Morphology, orthography, and phonology in reading Chinese compound words. *Language and Cognitive Processes, 14,* 525–565.

II

Literacy Development
Beyond the School Walls

6

Struggling Adolescent Readers: A Cultural Construction

Donna E. Alvermann
University of Georgia

Despite good intentions, reform-minded schools in the United States are coming to grips with the possibility that traditional school culture is *making* struggling readers out of some youth, especially the ones who have turned their backs on a version of reading and writing commonly referred to as *academic literacy*. Why might this be the case? I argued elsewhere (Alvermann, 2001) that in their effort to raise the bar by implementing high standards—a noteworthy goal by most people's reasoning—schools are promoting certain normative ways of reading texts that may be disabling some of the very students they are trying to help. The practice of constructing certain types of readers as "struggling"[1] is even more problematic when one considers that many such normative ways of reading are losing their usefulness, and

---

[1]The term *struggling* reader assumes various attributes depending on who is defining it and for what purpose. It is commonly used to describe students who for whatever reasons appear unable to keep up with the school-related reading that is required of them. Labels such as slow reader, low reader, disabled reader, and at-risk reader are often used interchangeably with struggling reader, though special educators prefer to put the person first and then the label in order to preserve the wholeness of the child (e.g., a reader with learning disabilities, or a reader who struggles). In the professional literature, as well, there is little agreement on what constitutes a struggling reader. For example, a cursory analysis of the table of contents of *Struggling Adolescent Readers: A Collection of Teaching Strategies* (Moore, Alvermann, & Hinchman, 2000) reveals that the term *struggling* is used to refer to youth with clinically diagnosed reading disabilities as well as to those who are unmotivated, disenchanted, or generally unsuccessful in school literacy tasks.

perhaps to some extent their validity, in the wake of new media and interactive communication technologies and the changing literacies they evoke (Chandler-Olcott & Mahar, 2001; Lankshear, Gee, Knobel, & Searle, 1997; Mackey & McClay, 2000; O'Brien, 1998).

Concurrent with the rhetoric on school reform is a mandate to implement *best practice*, as variously defined by researchers and policymakers with different views on what constitutes evidence of "best." Not so coincidentally, it is the case that one can observe in U.S. teacher education circles a growing number of literacy educators who are critical of a one-size-fits-all model of reading. This is particularly so for a group of us whose work is focused on reconceptualizing the literacies in adolescents' lives (e.g., Alvermann, Brozo, Boyd, Hinchman, Moore, & Sturtevant, 2002; Alvermann, Hinchman, Moore, Phelps, & Waff, 1998; Bean & Readence, 2002; Hagood, 2002; Hagood, Stevens, & Reinking, 2002; Hinchman & Lalik, 2002; Lewis & Finders, 2002; Moje, 2002; Moje, Young, Readence, & Moore, 2000; Mosenthal, 1998; O'Brien, 1998; Young, Dillon, & Moje, 2002). Building on the work of Gee (1996), Lankshear et al. (1997), Street (1995), and numerous others whose writings question an autonomous, one-size-fits all model of reading, we are coming to understand why some students' literacy development is every bit as dependent on access to discursive knowledge and socioeconomic and cultural resources as it is on skills instruction.

As researchers and teachers working in rapidly changing times and from a *new literacies* perspective (Gee, 2000; A. Luke & Elkins, 2000; New London Group, 1996; Willinsky, 2001), we are beginning to see how schools may unintentionally construct readers who struggle. This is indeed unfortunate given that improving academic literacy, while still a useful and valid goal, does not go far enough in educating youth for life in the 21st century. Finding new ways of seeing, thinking, talking, and writing about adolescents and their literacies in a digital world is a challenge worthy of our attention. It is also the purpose of this chapter. Toward that end, the chapter includes the following sections: (a) Assumptions Underlying the Research on Struggling Readers, (b) Various Approaches to Thinking About School Culture and Struggling Readers, and (c) Teaching for Critical Awareness Using New Media and Interactive Communications Technology.

ASSUMPTIONS UNDERLYING THE RESEARCH ON STRUGGLING READERS

Do all readers struggle? At some point? With certain texts? In different contexts? The answer to all of these questions is yes. It is the rare individual, indeed, who has never met a text (print or nonprint) that did not prove too challenging a read, at least momentarily. What distinguishes that kind of reader from the struggling adolescent reader discussed here is a whole set of assumptions underlying how the latter came to be viewed as struggling, at least as portrayed in the research literature. This literature covers a broad spectrum and varies in specificity according to the perceived reasons behind the struggle. For instance, reviews of research focusing on individuals with clinically diagnosed reading disabilities (Shaywitz et al., 2000) tend to see in their data a cognitive or neurological basis for the struggle. Reviews of research on second-language reading (Bernhardt, 2000; Garcia, 2000), on the other hand, consider the social, cultural, motivational, and linguistic factors that may account in part for the struggle and that vary according to the population of English language learners being studied. Similarly, the New London Group (1996), an assemblage of interdisciplinary scholars interested in literacy acquisition and learning, and McDermott and Varenne (1995), writing from an anthropological perspective, would have us concentrate on the social and cultural aspects of so-called reading disabilities. Clearly, there are differing views on what contributes to a reader's struggle to comprehend, but for the purposes of this chapter the focus is on the cultural construction of that struggle.

Contrary to what might seem to be the case, the cultural construction of struggling readers is not simply a school-related phenomenon. According to McDermott and Varenne (1995), it is society at large that produces the conditions necessary for some to succeed, others to struggle, and still others to fail outright at reading. In their words, everyone is involved—"school personnel, of course, and parents, and let us not forget the philosophers, curriculum designers, textbook publishers, testers, and educational researchers … in other words, 'Us'" (p. 331). To understand why this may be so, and in particular, how we as educators have established cultural norms for reading that construct certain adolescents as the strugglers and others as the achievers, it is instructive to examine the assumptions underlying those norms. In the next section, I use McDermott and Varenne's article on the development of disability as an institution and trope in American culture (and, most notably, in education in the United States) to provide a framework for discussing three approaches to thinking about culture and the struggling reader: (a) the deprivation approach, (b) the difference approach, and (c) the culture-*as*-disability approach.

VARIOUS APPROACHES TO THINKING ABOUT SCHOOL CULTURE AND STRUGGLING READERS

One way of conceptualizing how culture constructs readers who struggle is through H. G. Wells's (1979) short story "The Country of the Blind." In brief, it is a story about Nunez, a sighted man who miraculously survives a nasty fall from a peak in the Andes and lands, relatively unharmed, in an isolated valley populated exclusively by people who for generations have been born blind and have no words for *see* or for anything that can be seen. Nunez, being an opportunist of the worst kind, immediately senses he will have many privileges accorded him in a land where he alone can see. What he fails to consider, however, is that the people who live in "The Country of the Blind" have no need to see. They live a well-ordered life, moving about confidently in a culture that fits their needs precisely:

> Everything, you see, had been made to fit their needs; each of the radiating paths of the valley area had a constant angle to the others, and was distinguished by a special notch upon its [curbing]; all obstacles and irregularities or path or meadow had long since been cleared away; all of their methods and procedures arose naturally from their special needs. (Wells, 1979, p. 135)

Time passes, and the people of the valley grow weary of putting up with Nunez's pompous and clumsy ways. They turn to their surgeon to define the problem so that they may find a solution to this stranger's intrusive ways. After examining Nunez, the surgeon's diagnosis is *"diseased eyes"*: "They are greatly distended, he has eyelashes, and his eyelids move, and consequently his brain is in a state of constant irritation and destruction" (Wells, 1979, p. 142). On hearing this, the people decide that the only solution to the problem is to surgically remove Nunez's eyes—the thought of which sends Nunez scurrying back up the mountain from which he fell.

The Deprivation Approach

This approach might be thought of in Nunez's case as "I have eyes and you don't" or, as explained by McDermott and Varenne (1995), "We have culture, and you don't" (pp. 333–334). This way of thinking about culture and the struggling reader buys into the argument that adolescents develop differently enough that they can be shown to fall into reliably distinct categories of reader types (e.g., struggling, not struggling), at least as defined by standardized, performance-based, or informal tests and teacher observations.[2] There is usually a stable set of tasks, deemed *milestones* by a particular culture, to which all its members must respond if they are to qualify as developmentally competent on those tasks. Being able to decode, comprehend, and summarize information would qualify as one such set of tasks.

---

[2]The problem with thinking about culture in this way—as containing distinctive groups or categories of people—is that the container leaks. Rarely are cultures as isolated as the H. G. Wells (1979) short story would have us imagine. The leaky container metaphor also applies to the dynamic and permeable boundaries that separate the lifeworlds of struggling and non-struggling readers. Specifically, McDermott and Varenne (1995) emphasized the need to avoid educational practices that mark those who are different from the perceived norm as lacking something that is of their own doing—that they are being singled out for a reason and are in fact "disabled."

Low-level performances on these tasks by some members of the group would be viewed as evidence that these members had not yet developed the requisite set of skills necessary for reading competently at a particular grade level or in a particular set of texts.

By unpacking some of the assumptions underlying this argument, it is possible to see a culture's influence on a reader's self-perception and identity formation. Individuals who recognize and are recognized by others like themselves as being struggling readers often end up the recipients of what Finn (1999) called a *domesticating* education—that is, an education that stresses "functional literacy, literacy that makes a person productive and dependable, but not troublesome" (pp. ix–x). It is a second-rate kind of educational arrangement that typically leads to lower expectations and to social and economic inequalities. A further assumption of the deprivation approach is that adolescents who struggle with reading will have lowered self-esteem when they find they are unable to compete for the privileges that come with grade-level (or above) performance on reading-related tasks. To partially offset the negative fallout from these kinds of assumptions, schools and university clinics have been known to offer small-group or one-on-one remedial tutoring programs (e.g., Morris, Ervin, & Conrad, 2000). Still, as McDermott and Varenne (1995) noted, "there is a public assumption that, although society can care for those who lag behind, they are out of the running for the rewards that come with a full cultural competence" (p. 334).

The Difference Approach

Once again referring to the story of Nunez, the difference approach to thinking about culture and the struggling reader might be, as McDermott and Varenne (1995) phrased it, "We have culture, and you have a different one" (p. 335). This rather off-handed, tongue-in-cheek observation serves to point out one of the assumptions underlying the difference approach: Namely, it is assumed that an arbitrary set of reading tasks deemed important by one group of people may have little or no relevance for another group. Translated into classroom practice, this assumption is often the underlying rationale for culturally relevant teaching, such as that described in a study of Minerva Salazar's eighth-grade unit on Mexican American community life in the southwestern United States (Brozo, Valerio, & Salazar, 2000).

Proponents of the difference approach argue that the ways in which people develop competencies as literate beings will vary according to the demands of their particular cultures. Thus, it would follow that adolescents who struggle with school literacy tasks under the difference approach would likely be introduced to relatively few predefined reading tasks; instead, they would be encouraged to focus on the literacy activities that adults in their culture regularly perform as fully functioning members of that culture. A second assumption underlying this approach is that teachers will have the resources necessary—both personally and professionally, in terms of their own background and development—for instructing students from various cultural backgrounds with varying literacy practices. A corollary to this assumption is that adolescents exposed to such instruction would benefit from it in the long term. This is not a trivial consideration, for as McDermott and Varenne (1995) pointed out, "despite a liberal lament that variation is wonderful, those who cannot show the right skills at the right time in the right format are considered out of the race for the rewards of the larger culture" (p. 335).

The Culture-as-Disability Approach

This approach assumes that school culture (like other kinds of culture) is a historically evolved way of doing life. As such, it has certain norms that implicitly and explicitly teach students about what is worth working for, how to succeed, and who will fall short. According to McDermott and Varenne (1995), "cultures offer a wealth of positions for human beings to inhabit" (p. 336). Each position requires certain things. For example, to inhabit the position of "good reader," one must possess certain abilities that are verifiable and recognizable to others who occupy that same position. To McDermott and Varenne's way of thinking, how people end up inhabiting some positions and not others is more a matter of extenuating circumstances and/or differential treatment than any kind of innate ability. They argued, for instance, that culture disables some of its members by developing what is assumed to be a stable (although arbitrary) set of tasks against which individuals can be measured, perhaps remediated, but, if not, then pushed aside. In their words:

> It takes a whole culture of people producing idealizations of what everyone should be and a system of measures for identifying those who fall short for us to forget that we collectively produce our disabilities and the discomforts that conventionally accompany them. (McDermott & Varenne, 1995, p. 337)

One of the assumptions underlying the culture-*as*-disability approach is that, unlike the deprivation and difference approaches, it does not isolate groups so that one group stands apart from another; neither is one group marginalized in relation to another group. Instead, all groups—for example, good and not-so-good readers—stand in relation to the wider culture of which they are a part. Viewed from this approach, adolescents who struggle with reading are perceived as part of the same cloth from which good readers come. This has implications for instruction, as Dillon (1989) discovered in her microethnography of a high school English teacher who showed that he cared about all kinds of readers—including those who struggled—by encouraging them to stay in school and by holding equally high academic expectations for everyone.

Another assumption of the culture-*as*-disability approach is that politically charged arrangements presume certain levels of competence in an individual. But therein lies the rub for, as McDermott and Varenne (1995) argued, "Competence is a fabrication, a mock-up, and people … work hard to take their place in [a] hierarchy of competence displays" (p. 337). Speculating as to why many societies hold school literacy in high regard despite the fact there is little evidence to support the notion that it is difficult to acquire and that it is best learned in classrooms, McDermott and Varenne wrote:

- The more people believe that literacy is difficult to acquire, the more they find reasons to explain why some read better than others and, correspondingly, why some do better than others in the economic and political measures of the society; and
- The more people believe that literacy is best learned in classrooms, the more they ignore other sources of literacy, and the more they insist on bringing back to school those who have already "failed" to develop school literacy. (p. 341)

Whether or not one agrees with this speculation, it seems likely that struggling readers caught in a society that insists on treating school literacy as something that is hard to acquire (and thus possibly out of their reach) will indeed find it difficult to think of themselves as motivated and competent learners. Finally, although it is the case that literacy can be taught in classrooms, it does not follow that privileging school literacy over other forms of literacy is in the best interests of struggling readers; neither does such privileging take into account the multiple literacies in which these youth participate on a daily basis outside of school.

TEACHING FOR CRITICAL AWARENESS USING MEDIA AND INTERACTIVE COMMUNICATIONS TECHNOLOGY

Attending to critical literacy development in youth was described by Freebody and Luke (1990) as "crucial to an understanding of successful reading in our culture" (p. 14). Although referring to Australian culture in particular, their comments are no less relevant for literacy educators and researchers in the United States. Here, as elsewhere, everyday literacy practices are changing at an unprecedented pace, and speculation as to the impact of new media and interactive communication technologies on current conceptions of reading and writing is evident on many fronts. At the center of much of the discussion is the perceived need to develop adolescents' critical awareness of how all texts (print, visual, oral, and Internet mediated) position them as readers and viewers within different social, cultural, and historical contexts. This need, however, as Australian educator Wendy Morgan (1997) pointed out, should not be mistaken as a call for the type of critical literacy instruction that would have students searching for the villains or heroes in their texts, for the oppressors or emancipators among us, and the general labeling of oppositional categories such as "us" and "them." Rather, it is a summons to eschew these overly simplistic categories in order to develop, in her words, "a different view of how people may act, provisionally, at a particular time and within particular conditions" (p. 26). These conditions, though variable, are routinely affected by our views about what makes critical literacy "critical" and by the approaches we use to teach it (e.g., using interactive communications media).

What Makes Critical Literacy "Critical"?

Orienting students toward thinking, reading, and writing in ways that challenge the status quo for the purpose of promoting social justice in the world is a defining element in what makes critical literacy "critical." In Ira Shor's (1997) words:

> This kind of literacy—words rethinking worlds, self dissenting in society—connects the political and the personal, the public and the private, the global and the local, the economic and the pedagogical, for rethinking our lives and for promoting justice in place of inequity. (p. 1)

An orientation to effecting social change carries with it an invitation to rethink one's identity as a reader, and it was that thought that propelled me to write a proposal to the Spencer Foundation to fund a study that would eventually involve 30 struggling readers in an after-school media club for a period of 14 weeks in the local public library (Alvermann, 2001). Grady, a pseudonym for a struggling reader with whom I worked closely for those 14 weeks, participated in a series of critical literacy activities that involved him and 29 other adolescents in thinking not only about how popular media texts constructed them as readers, viewers, and listeners but also how they used those same texts in ways that gave them pleasure—ways, in fact, that were not always in sync with how the producers of the texts might have desired. According to Grady's teachers and his mother, he showed little interest in school reading, but his engagement with several *Pokémon* training manuals during media club was undeniably intense and long term. He would also leaf through video magazines hour after hour, looking for cheat codes that would make him a better *Pokémon* trainer. Although not prone to spend much time on the Internet during media club hours, Grady nonetheless was an astute critic of the video games his friends chose to play online. He displayed a keen sense of who produced the games, for what purpose, and with what audience in mind. For example, he was often critical of game producers who had only boys in mind as potential players, a point that he made repeatedly when the girls in the club refused to join in the games. As the weeks passed, Grady's mother, the research assistants on the project, and I noted a change in Grady's perception of himself as a reader. Though still not interested in academic texts, he became a frequent e-mailer in the club's closed discussion group, and he offered help to others in the club as they attempted to build home pages on the Web, read *Dragon Ball Z*[3] online, or search the Internet for lyrics written by their favorite rappers. In short, I had evidence that a club organized for the purpose of engaging struggling readers in critical literacy activities around media that they found pleasurable could serve as an invitation to helping them rethink their identities as readers. What the media club project also showed me was that without some guidance, struggling readers are apt to gain little from their forays into the world of new media and interactive communication technologies.

More generally speaking, adolescents' interests in video games, the Internet, and various interactive communication technologies (e.g., chat rooms where people can take on various identities unbeknown to others) suggest the importance of teaching them to read with a critical eye toward how writers (including textbook authors), illustrators, advertising executives, and the like represent people and their ideas—in short, how individuals who create texts make those texts work. Viewed from this standpoint, commonly referred to as a *media studies perspective* within education circles (Semali & Pailliotet, 1999), one might argue that critical literacy seeks to free people from coercive practices, that it recognizes how knowledge constitutes power, and that it is a process for emancipating and/or empowering readers. Teaching for critical awareness from a media studies perspective, then, would mean focusing on creating communities of active readers, viewers, and listeners capable of identifying the various ideological positions that print and nonprint texts offer them. It would also mean calling attention to how people typically have choices about which ideological positions they will accept or take up, which they will resist, and which they will attempt to

---

[3]*Dragon Ball Z*, created by Japanese animé expert Akira Toriyama, is about a group of warriors skilled in the martial arts who engage in death-defying battles to save the Universe. There are seven planets in the *Dragon Ball Z* Universe, each of which has 7 Dragon Balls that allow one to summon a mystical dragon that grants wishes. In *Dragon Ball Z*, the characters improve themselves through effortful training and can be brought back to life through wishes being granted by the mystical dragon. The battles between the warriors consist of physical contact and the deployment of various energy devices, such as energy balls, energy saws, and energy hand-cuffs (Johnny Gil's *About Dragon Ball Z*, n.d.). Originally based on a Manga comic strip, *Dragon Ball Z* requires considerable inferencing and tracking of character development—skills most literacy educators would recognize as marks of a competent reader.

modify. Viewed from a cultural studies perspective, however, one would find less concern for countering the media's so-called threatening and manipulative hold on audiences; instead, advocates of teaching critical literacy from this perspective (e.g., Hagood, 2002; C. Luke, 1997; Morgan, 1997) would focus on helping adolescents strike a balance between pleasure and critique. Teaching for critical awareness from this perspective would involve looking for ways to guide readers, viewers, and listeners through a self-reflexive process aimed at teaching them to question their own pleasures within their own set of circumstances and with texts of their own choosing. And, as anyone can attest to who has browsed the Web for media offerings of late, the choices are many, as are the meanings.

Because media texts are often hybrids of the images, language, and sounds they incorporate from television, video, multimedia, hypertext, the Internet, and other forms of new communication technologies (e.g., instant messaging, e-mailing), developing youth's critical awareness involves showing them how these polysemic texts are never inscribed with meaning that is guaranteed once and for all to reflect the intentions of their producers; instead, such meaning is negotiated by audiences—readers, viewers, and listeners such as themselves—and expressed differently within different contexts and at different moments in time (Hall, 1982; Storey, 1996). Just how polysemic text—in this case, hypertext—works to facilitate critical literacy is illustrated in an example offered by Morgan and Andrews (cited in Mackey & McClay, 2000):

> Hypertext allows for a move away from the monologic towards discrepancies. It can foreground debates, differences, dissensions. It's not necessarily about an already achieved harmony. So it encourages the taking of positions which aren't necessarily fixed ... A single, print text can be offered as something coherent and closed, finished and polished—a policy document, which has its own disembodied, authoritative voice from nowhere—the word from on high. To be able to break into that, create irruptions and eruptions—that's at the heart of critical literacy work. (p. 200)

Increasingly, as school-based programs for working with struggling adolescent readers are written up, it is clear that the authors of these programs are taking seriously the need to consider multiple forms of texts as entry points into teaching for critical awareness. For example, Ash (2002) incorporated a critical literacy component in her "Teaching Readers Who Struggle: A Pragmatic Middle School Framework." In addition to a synthesis of successful tutoring programs and critical literacy activities, this framework includes a program for managing five research-based literacy practices: (a) daily oral reading, (b) guided reading in flexible groups, (c) word study, (d) self-selected reading/writing, and (e) explicit comprehension strategy instruction. Activities for developing adolescents' critical competencies include analyzing the assumptions text authors make about their readers and, alternatively, the assumptions readers make about texts and their authors. Mackey and McClay (2000) extended this notion of examining reciprocal assumptions by problematizing situations in which some teachers working with adolescents mistakenly regard picture-books as being either too ambiguous and thus too challenging—as in the case of David Macaulay's (1999) *Black and White*—or too simple and thus insulting. As Mackey and McClay were quick to point out, "Dismissing these text forms ... underestimates the value of all forms of picture books as complex and polysemic texts in their own right, and also as routes to meeting the sophisticated reading demands of texts in new media and technologies" (p. 191).

Kist (2002), in his attempt to study and document the characteristics of new literacy classrooms in the Midwest, found that teaching for critical awareness includes embracing multiple forms of representation and engaging students in meaningful literacy tasks—practices thought to increase struggling readers' sense of competence as well (Guthrie & Davis, 2003). Although not specifically directed at teaching readers who struggle, Kist's research demonstrates that new literacy classrooms are places where students report being engaged in their work and experiencing a sense of achievement—two attributes of a learning environment that would seem to have potential for struggling readers as well. And, in fact, there is empirical evidence to show that this is the case. It is not surprising, as O'Brien (1998, 2001) has documented in his 4-year study of Midwestern working-class youth deemed at risk of failing their academic subjects because of poor reading skills, these same students were exceedingly adept at (and interested in) understanding how media texts work—in particular, how meaning gets produced and consumed. O'Brien reported that the adolescents with whom he worked over an extended period of time were quite successful in producing their own electronic texts (e.g., multimedia documentaries) and critiquing media violence using multiple forms of visual texts. Working alongside the students and their teachers in what came to be called the "Jeff Literacy Lab," O'Brien concluded that as a consequence of his research team's decision not to privilege print over other forms of literacy, the students appeared capable and literate.

Approaches to Teaching Critical Media Literacy

To begin developing youth's critical awareness of the media texts that figure prominently into their everyday lives may require a new set of metaphors for thinking about teaching struggling readers. Drawing on the work of Cole and Griffin (1986), who taught at-risk readers how to comprehend texts using dramatic role-playing techniques, A. Luke and Elkins (2000), in their introduction to a themed issue of the *Journal of Adolescent and Adult Literacy* on re/mediating adolescent literacies, noted how Cole and Griffin's work set up conditions in which students could rethink who they were in relation to texts (e.g., their strategy "Question Asking Reading" engaged at-risk readers in generating questions about texts as opposed to answering them). But what interested Luke and Elkins most about this work was that it provided an alternative vocabulary for talking about re/mediating adolescents' literacies, as they explained:

> The term *medium*—the forgotten and neglected singular of the ubiquitous noun *media*—was used in the early part of the 20th century to refer to psychics who purported to be able to communicate with spirits. The concept refers to communication technologies that we use to mediate, frame, and scaffold our social relations with one another and our material worlds. Language and literacy provide symbolic tools, resources, and means to conduct social and ecological relations. Cole and Griffin's view is that the teacher's task is to re/mediate struggling readers' relationships with texts, whether these are traditional print texts or those of new communications media. By this account, the aim of literacy is not to use methods to fix deficits, remediation in the traditional sense used by special educators and reading specialists. Rather, literacy education involves staging the conditions for students to rethink and reenact their social and semiotic relations. It is about changing the ecology. (A. Luke & Elkins, 2000, p. 397)

As Luke and Elkins go on to explain, teaching in new times with new media and communications technologies will require that literacy educators re/mediate struggling readers' relationships with the social and cultural aspects of these new texts by developing their critical awareness of the power dynamics operating within such relationships. Although there are undoubtedly numerous pedagogical approaches for doing so—with none being the single "best" way of accomplishing the task—the four described here and elaborated elsewhere (Alvermann, Moon, & Hagood, 1999) build on Carmen Luke's (1997) work pertaining to the politics of media, images, and text representation.

The first approach, based on false consciousness ideology, suggests that if students knew the detrimental aspects of most popular media, they would be wiser consumers. This is what Alvermann et al. (1999) referred to as the "I know more about you than you know about yourself" syndrome. Teachers who elect to use this approach in developing struggling readers' critical awareness may be well attuned to the race, class, and gender literature as well as to the injustices and inequalities contained therein. However, if by using this literature they turn students into what some critics refer to as "little Marxists," they should not be surprised to find that they may have created a group of less-than-forthcoming learners. As C. Luke (1997) reminded us, would any teacher expect to get an honest answer from youth who are asked to critique the very media they find most pleasurable and useful?

The second approach subscribes to the notion of teacher-as-liberating-guide. Teachers who use this approach might be said to be good role modelers; that is, they work hard at modeling the ways in which students can develop strategies for becoming the "ideal" (thus critically aware) reader, viewer, and listener. Although there is considerable support in the research literature for modeling effective strategy instruction when working with struggling readers (Guthrie & Davis, 2003), putting this research into practice was not as easy as my colleagues and I (Alvermann et al., 2000) had first imagined. In fact, the 30 adolescents with whom we worked for 14 weeks in an after-school media club resisted our initial attempts to model critical literacy strategies. Only after major adjustments were made in our weekly plans did we see the loopholes in the teacher-as-liberating-guide approach to helping youth become effective readers, viewers, and listeners of popular media texts.

The third approach, described as *pleasures without parameters*, takes a standpoint most teachers would recognize as *relativistic*; that is, those teaching from this point of view would argue that all media texts are equally good or useful. However, a major criticism of pleasures without parameters is that views and voices from everywhere become views and voices from nowhere. For example, in arguing that Robert's engagement with *Dragon Ball Z* was not a waste of time but rather a good example of how some struggling readers construct themselves as competent learners in out-of-school contexts when they are given choices in reading materials, Alvermann and Heron (2001) were forced to acknowledge the paradox of "free choice" in Robert's selection of texts. Clearly, "free choice" under the pleasures without parameters banner is a misnomer if one considers the economic investments made by U.S. and Japanese corporations to distribute the *Dragon Ball Z* series as part of an effort to target potential consumers of the series and its many related products.

The fourth approach, labeled *self-reflexive* and *balanced*, is an attempt to teach students the importance of weighing in on both pleasure and analysis. Unlike the pleasures-without-parameters approach, a self-reflexive and balanced approach underscores the importance of providing struggling readers with opportunities to examine how their interests and likes are bound up in the decisions they make about media text usage. Rather than asking youth to critique these texts as being too commercially oriented, too violent, too sexist, too racist, and so on, teachers using this approach would ask them to analyze what is in it for them as users. They would also ask students to consider alternative readings and alternative text productions, as Chandler-Olcott and Mahar (2001) did in their study of digital literacy classrooms. For example, in teaching adolescents how to analyze texts using alternative readings, they posed the following questions about various Web sites the students had visited:

- What assumption is it fair to make about the person whose sites are on this list?
- How might these bookmarked digital texts coincide with print genres?
- What do the digital texts allow them to do that print genres do not?

CONCLUSION

We are at a turning point in the field of adolescent literacy, one in which effective literacy instruction for struggling readers will need to take into account that youth who do not excel in academic literacy may still be capable and literate individuals in arenas outside the normative ways of doing school. It is a time of major shifts in cultural practices, economic systems, and social institutions on a global scale, a time when literacy educators from around the world are speculating about the ways in which new media and interactive communications technologies will alter people's conceptions of reading and writing. One might argue, as I do in this chapter, that it is also a time for taking stock of how well- intentioned school reform efforts may actually construct readers who struggle, especially among youth who have turned their backs on a version of reading and writing commonly referred to as *academic literacy*. Finally, in all four approaches to teaching for critical awareness using media and interactive communications technology there is an underlying assumption that access to such technology is a given. Because this may very well not be the case, it is important that we remain sensitive to individual differences. As Chandler-Olcott and Mahar (2001) remind us, "Teachers ... need to be aware that lack of digital literacy is for many students just as stigmatizing as the inability to read print."

REFERENCES

Alvermann, D. E. (2001). Reading adolescents' reading identities: Looking back to see ahead. *Journal of Adolescent & Adult Literacy, 44,* 676–690.
Alvermann, D. E. (2002). Effective literacy instruction for adolescents. *Journal of Literacy Research, 34,* 189–208.
Alvermann, D. E., Brozo, W. G., Boyd, F., Hinchman, K. A., Moore, D. W., & Sturtevant, E. G. (2002). *Principled practices for a literate America: Flexibility in learning and literacy instruction* (final report prepared for the Carnegie Corporation), University of Georgia.
Alvermann, D. E., Hagood, M. C., Heron, A. H., Hughes, P., Williams, K. B., & Jun, Y. (2000). *After-school media clubs for reluctant adolescent readers* (final report submitted to the Spencer Foundation), University of Georgia.

Alvermann, D. E., & Heron, A. H. (2001). Literacy identity work: Playing to learn with popular media. *Journal of Adolescent & Adult Literacy, 45,* 118–122.

Alvermann, D. E., Hinchman, K. A., Moore, D. W., Phelps, S. F., & Waff, D. R. (Eds.). (1998). *Reconceptualizing the literacies in adolescents' lives.* Mahwah, NJ: Lawrence Erlbaum Associates.

Alvermann, D. E., Moon, J. S., & Hagood, M. C. (1999). *Popular culture in the classroom: Teaching and researching critical media literacy.* Newark, DE: International Reading Association.

Ash, G. E. (2002). Teaching readers who struggle: A pragmatic middle school framework. *Reading Online, 5*(7). Retrieved March 16, 2002, from http://www.readingonline.org/articles/art_index.asp?HREF=ash/index.html

Bean, T. W., & Readence, J. E. (2002). Adolescent literacy: Charting a course for successful futures as lifelong learners. *Reading Research and Instruction, 41,* 203–210.

Bernhardt, E. (2000). Second-language reading as a case study of reading scholarship in the 20th century. In M. L. Kamil, P. B. Mosenthal, P. D. Pearson, & R. Barr (Eds.), *Handbook of reading research* (Vol. 3, pp. 793–811). Mahwah, NJ: Lawrence Erlbaum Associates.

Brozo, W. G., Valerio, P. C., & Salazar, M. M. (2000). A walk through Gracie's garden: Literacy and cultural explorations in a Mexican American junior high school. In D. W. Moore, D. E. Alvermann, & K. A. Hinchman (Eds.), *Struggling adolescent readers: A collection of teaching strategies* (pp. 66–73). Newark, DE: International Reading Association.

Chandler-Olcott, K., & Mahar, D. (2001). Considering genre in the digital literacy classroom. *Reading Online, 5*(4). Retrieved June 10, 2002, from http//www.readingonline.org/electronic/elec_index.asp?HREF=hillinger/ index.html

Cole, M., & Griffin, P. (1986). A sociohistorical approach to remediation. In S. deCastell, A. Luke, & K. Egan (Eds.), *Literacy, society and schooling* (pp. 110–131). Cambridge, England: Cambridge University Press.

Dillon, D. R. (1989). Showing them that I want them to learn and that I care about who they are: A microethnography of the social organization of a secondary low-track English classroom. *American Educational Research Journal, 26,* 227–259.

Freebody, P., & Luke, A. (1990). "Literacies" programs: Debates and demands in cultural context. *Prospect: The Australian Journal of TESOL, 5*(5), 7–16.

Garcia, G. E. (2000). Bilingual children's reading. In M. L. Kamil, P. B. Mosenthal, P. D. Pearson, & R. Barr (Eds.), *Handbook of reading research* (Vol. 3, pp. 813–834). Mahwah, NJ: Lawrence Erlbaum Associates.

Gee, J. P. (1996). *Social linguistics and literacies* (2nd ed.). London: Taylor & Francis.

Gee, J. P. (2000). Teenagers in new times: A new literacy studies perspective. *Journal of Adolescent & Adult Literacy, 43,* 412–420.

Gil, J. (n.d.). *About Dragon Ball Z.* Retrieved August 19, 2001, from http://www.members.tripod.com/~Gil/dbzabout.htm

Guthrie, J. T., & Davis, M. H. (2003). Motivating struggling readers in middle school through an engagement model of classroom practice. *Reading & Writing Quarterly, 19,* 59–85.

Hagood, M. C. (2002). Critical literacy for whom? *Reading Research and Instruction, 41,* 247–266.

Hagood, M. C., Stevens, L. P., & Reinking, D. (2002). What do THEY have to teach US? Talkin' cross generations! In D. E. Alvermann (Ed.), *Adolescents and literacies in a digital world* (pp. 68–83). New York: Lang.

Hall, S. (1982). The rediscovery of "ideology": The return of the repressed in media studies. In M. Gurevitch, T. Bennett, J. Curran, & J. Woollacott (Eds.), *Culture, society and the media* (pp. 56–90). London: Methuen.

Hinchman, K. A., & Lalik, R. (2002). Imagining literacy teacher education in changing times: Considering the views of adult and adolescent collaborators. In D. E. Alvermann (Ed.), *Adolescents and literacies in a digital world* (pp. 84–100). New York: Lang.

Kist, W. (2002). Finding "new literacy" in action: An interdisciplinary high school Western Civilization class. *Journal of Adolescent & Adult Literacy, 45,* 368–377.

Lankshear, C., Gee, J. P., Knobel, M., & Searle, C. (1997). *Changing literacies.* Buckingham, England: Open University Press.

Lewis, C., & Finders, M. (2002). Implied adolescents and implied teachers: A generation gap for new times. In D. E. Alvermann (Ed.), *Adolescents and literacies in a digital world* (pp. 101–113). New York: Lang.

Luke, A. (2002). What happens to literacies old and new when they're turned into policy. In D. E. Alvermann (Ed.), *Adolescents and literacies in a digital world* (pp. 186–203). New York: Lang.

Luke, A., & Elkins, J. (2000). Re/mediating adolescent literacies. *Journal of Adolescent & Adult Literacy, 43,* 396–398.

Luke, C. (1997). Media literacy and cultural studies. In S. A. Muspratt, A. Luke, & P. Freebody (Eds.), *Constructing critical literacies: Teaching and learning textual practice* (pp. 19–49). Cresskill, NJ: Hampton.

Macaulay, D. (1999). *Black and white.* Boston: Houghton Mifflin.

Mackey, M., & McClay, J. K. (2000). Graphic routes to electronic literacy: Polysemy and picture books. *Changing English, 7,* 191–201.

McDermott, R., & Varenne, H. (1995). Culture as disability. *Anthropology & Education Quarterly, 26,* 324–348.

Moje, E. B. (2002). Re-framing adolescent literacy research for new times: Studying youth as a resource. *Reading Research and Instruction, 41,* 211–228.

Moje, E. B., Young, J. P., Readence, J. E., & Moore, D. W. (2000). Reinventing adolescent literacy for new times: Perennial and millennial issues. *Journal of Adolescent & Adult Literacy, 43,* 400–410.

Moore, D. W., Alvermann, D. E., & Hinchman, K. A. (2000). *Struggling adolescent readers: A collection of teaching strategies.* Newark, DE: International Reading Association.

Morgan, W. (1997). *Critical literacy in the classroom: The art of the possible.* London: Routledge.

Morris, D., Ervin, C., & Conrad, K. (2000). A case study of middle school reading disability. In D. W. Moore, D. E. Alvermann, & K. A. Hinchman (Eds.), *Struggling adolescent readers: A collection of teaching strategies* (pp. 8–18). Newark, DE: International Reading Association.

Mosenthal, P. B. (1998). Reframing the problems of adolescence and adolescent literacy: A dilemma-management perspective. In D. E. Alvermann, K. A. Hinchman,

D. W. Moore, S. F. Phelps, & D. R. Waff (Eds.), *Reconceptualizing the literacies in adolescents' lives* (pp. 325–352). Mahwah, NJ: Lawrence Erlbaum Associates.

New London Group. (1996). A pedagogy of multiliteracies: Designing social futures. *Harvard Educational Review, 66*, 60–92.

O'Brien, D. G. (1998). Multiple literacies in a high-school program for "at-risk" adolescents. In D. E. Alvermann, K. A. Hinchman, D. W. Moore, S. F. Phelps, & D. R. Waff (Eds.), *Reconceptualizing the literacies in adolescents' lives* (pp. 27–49). Mahwah, NJ: Lawrence Erlbaum Associates.

O'Brien, D. G. (2001). "At-risk" adolescents: Redefining competence through the multiliteracies of intermediality, visual arts, and representation. *Reading Online, 4*(11). Retrieved June 2, 2002, from http://www.readingonline.org/newliteracies/lit_index.asp?

Semali, L., & Pailliotet, A. W. (1999). *Intermediality.* Boulder, CO: Westview.

Shaywitz, B. A., Pugh, K. R., Jenner, A. R., Fulbright, R. K., Fletcher, J. M., Gore, J. C., & Shaywitz, S. E. (2000). The neurobiology of reading and reading disability (dyslexia). In M. L. Kamil, P. B. Mosenthal, P. D. Pearson, & R. Barr (Eds.), *Handbook of reading research* (Vol. 3, pp. 229–249). Mahwah, NJ: Lawrence Erlbaum Associates.

Shor, I. (1997). What is critical literacy? *Journal for Pedagogy, Pluralism & Practice, 4.* Retrieved July 7, 2000, from http://www.lesley.edu/journals/ppp/4/shor.html#intro

Storey, J. (1996). *Cultural studies and the study of popular culture: Theories and methods.* Athens: University of Georgia Press.

Street, B. V. (1995). *Social literacies: Critical approaches to literacy in development, ethnography, and education.* New York: Longman.

Wells. H. G. (1979). *Selected short stories.* Baltimore: Penguin.

Willinsky, J. (2001). *After literacy.* New York: Lang.

Young, J. P., Dillon, D. R., & Moje, E. B. (2002). Shape-shifting portfolios: Millennial youth, literacies, and the game of life. In D. E. Alvermann (Ed.), *Adolescents and literacies in a digital world* (pp. 114–131). New York: Lang.

7

Family Literacy in Canada: Foundation to a Literate Society

Heather Sample Gosse
Linda M. Phillips
University of Alberta

Literacy is one of the most important goals of child development, the success of which is rooted in the family. It is the thesis of this chapter that literacy must be valued by the family, that the role of the family in literacy development must be valued by educators and others, and that family literacy must be acknowledged as the foundation to a literate society. If family literacy is not embraced as the foundation to a literate society, then many will continue to experience a dissatisfaction with the predominant approaches to literacy despite enormous investments and painstaking efforts by individuals, local communities, and governments (Jung & Ouane, 2001). It is widely accepted that literacy development is embedded in social and cultural practice. Despite the fact that people bring local and diverse interests and concerns to literacy learning and the problems they encounter, families—regardless of whether they live in a literate or becoming-literate society (Olson & Torrance, 2001)—want their children to be able to read and write.

We begin by presenting (a) a demographic overview of Canada as an example of a literate society coupled with (b) an updated profile of literacy development in Canada; (c) a rationale for the family as foundation for literacy learning; (d) the challenges to the family as the foundation for literacy learning; and (e) the nature of family literacy programs; followed by a discussion of (f) program, philosophy, and evaluation issues in family literacy. We go on to call for a familial perspective in family literacy programs and to specify some areas of much-needed research.

CONTEMPORARY PROFILE OF CANADA AND LITERACY DEVELOPMENT

Canada as a Nation

Canada, like other countries, is unique in its own way. It is a land with fascinating geography, demographics, a rich and varied literacy history; and it is a country that welcomes cultural and linguistic diversity. Although it is the second largest country in the world in terms of geographical area, Canada has a population of only 31.5 million people, distributed across 10 provinces and three territories. In Nunavut, for example, the total population is 28,000, compared to more than 12 million inhabitants in Ontario. Most of Canada's population is urban based, and there are enormous discrepancies in resources, services, literacy levels, and educational opportunities between rural and urban locations.

Urban centers attract immigrants. Eighteen percent of Canada's population is foreign born, which is second only to Australia (22%). In contrast, only 11% of the U.S. population is foreign born, although as in Canada and Australia, this proportion is the highest in 70 years. Approximately 1 in every 6 people in Canada speaks a language other than English or French as their first language (Statistics Canada, 2001). Canadians welcome immigrants and are proud of their tolerance and diversity ("Canada's new spirit," 2003, p. 13). Canada's ethnocultural portrait is changing. Half a century ago, most immigrants came from Europe, and now most newcomers are from Asia. Despite their proximity, the ethnocultural portraits of Canada and the United States are different. The United States, because of its history and geographical position, has large populations of African Americans and Hispanics. Immigration to Canada has resulted in Asians, East Indians, and Filipinos being the largest groups of visible minorities. In addition, the indigenous peoples of Canada (North American Indians, Métis, and Inuit) comprise approximately 5% of the population and are increasing rapidly in number (at a rate of 161% in the last 50 years, while the Canadian population as a whole has only doubled). One third of the indigenous population is aged 14 years and under.

Canada's openness to linguistic diversity is seen in its educational settings. Some Canadian children, while learning to speak one of two of our official languages (French and English), are also learning to read in their mother tongue, which is commonly a language other than English and French. Others, whose mother tongue is not English, the dominant language in North America, are learning to read in enrichment contexts and receive formal schooling in a second language. In a single school, for example, there may be as many as 35 different languages spoken. In Edmonton, Canada's sixth largest city, many schools are dedicated to a language other than, or in addition to, English as the language of instruction. Some of these languages include Arabic, Cree, French, German, Hebrew, Italian, Mandarin, Polish, Spanish, and Ukrainian.

Literacy Development in Canada

Within the past 20 years, there has been a heightened interest in literacy issues within Canada. Despite the wealth of the nation as a whole, a significant proportion of Canada's population have literacy challenges that affect every area of their lives, including health, employment, economic status, social status, and life chances. In 1996, Statistics Canada reported that 22% of adult Canadians had serious problems dealing with any printed materials and that an additional 24% of Canadians could deal only with simple reading tasks. Literacy levels have been found to vary across Canada, with the populations of western Canada and Ontario generally having higher literacy skills than those in Atlantic Canada and Quebec. In Canada, jurisdiction over education is provincial and territorial, not federal as in the United States. Provinces and territories across Canada may have different school entry ages, required numbers of teaching days, programs, and resource allocations. Perhaps, then, we ought not to be surprised at the variation in literacy levels across Canada.

Specific links between immigration and literacy at both the lowest and highest levels were identified by Statistics Canada (1996). There are proportionally more immigrants at the lowest level of literacy than those born in Canada. There are also, however, proportionally more immigrants at the highest levels of literacy. A strong relationship between educational attainment and literacy level has been identified. Residents with more education have higher literacy skills, and those with less education have lower literacy skills. On the other hand, about 20% of Canadians have lower literacy skills than their education might indicate, and 16% have higher skills than indicated by their education regardless of whether they are new Canadians.

Seventy-four percent of young Canadians who graduate from high school have strong literacy skills. The remaining 26% can complete simple reading and writing tasks. Those who leave school before graduation generally have lower literacy skills. Canadians with the lowest literacy skills have higher rates of unemployment (26%), and those with the highest skills have lower rates of unemployment (4%). Canadians with low literacy skills are more likely to have lower incomes than those with higher skills. Over

80% of Canadians at the lowest literacy level, and over 60% in the second lowest literacy level, have no income or incomes of less than $27,000 (Statistics Canada, 1996).

In December 2001, the Organization for Economic Co-Operation and Development (OECD) reported the results from the Programme for International Student Assessment (PISA) of the performance of Canada's youth (15 years of age) in reading, mathematics, and science. Overall, Canadian students performed well in reading compared with students in most of the other 31 participating countries. Students in Canada performed second only to students from Finland, although the Finnish students performed significantly better. Students from New Zealand, Australia, Ireland, and Japan performed on average the same as Canadian students.

The study also measured the impact of family characteristics and home environment on achievement. In half of the 14 countries examined, including Canada, students from two-parent families had higher levels of achievement than did students from single-parent families (OECD PISA, 2001, p. 31). Differences were linked to other important characteristics, such as family socioeconomic status. These differences held true for Canada, Finland, and Japan, with the other G8 countries including Germany, France, Italy, the United Kingdom, the Russian Federation, and the United States, showing greater variability in performance on the basis of socioeconomic factors. Home environment, including family possessions, home educational resources, and number of books, are all tied to socioeconomic status, and hence independent effects are difficult to separate. Regardless of socioeconomic status, however, families who are interested in and involved in their children's education and who provide a home environment that stimulates learning can positively influence their children's level of achievement. The report concluded that all Canadian parents ought to be aware of the positive influence they can have on the academic achievement of their children (OECD PISA, 2001, p. 47).

Many agencies within Canada are working to improve access to literacy. Some of these organizations are supported and directed by the private sector (e.g., ABC CANADA). The government of Canada supports the National Literacy Secretariat, which works in partnership with provincial and territorial governments, business, labor, and the volunteer community with the goals of increasing public awareness of literacy, helping to share information, improving access to literacy programs, developing learning materials, and advancing research on literacy. There is increasing recognition that although research conducted in Australia, the United Kingdom, the United States, and elsewhere is relevant to the Canadian scene, it is not always directly generalizable. In 2001, the Canadian Language and Literacy Research Network was funded to bring together Canadian experts from numerous sectors and backgrounds to focus on research aimed at improving the language and literacy development of all Canadian children. The diversity of Canadian society calls for a breadth of research that examines biological, cognitive, cultural, educational, linguistic, psychological, sensory, and social variables through cross-linguistic, intergenerational, multidisciplinary, and second-language perspectives.

THE FAMILY AND FAMILY LITERACY PROGRAMS

Family as Foundation

Recognition of the role of the family in learning has a long history in Canada. The first known Canadian family educator, Adelaide Sophia Hunter Hoodless, born in 1857, made the prescient statement "A Nation cannot rise above the level of its homes" (British Columbia Women's Institute, 1892). Hoodless saw education as a means of implementing social reform and worked tirelessly to promote the education of families. Known for her directness, she said (reflecting her own time, but perhaps appearing sexist today), "Educate a boy and you educate a man, but educate a girl and you educate a family" (British Columbia Women's Institute, 1892). Her point was that the home and what is learned there is central to education.

More than 100 years on, with a global surge in interest in how to best facilitate literacy development, attention is increasingly being paid to the contributions of the family. Sociologically, the family is the basic kinship group in all societies. Families provide support for their kin in the form of security, shelter, and food. They have an important role in caring for, educating, and socializing children. Over the past 20 years, there has been significant support for the idea that the family is the foundation for learning, particularly in the area of language and literacy development (Dickinson & Tabors, 2001; Heath, 1983; Moll & Greenberg, 1992; Morrow, 1989; Neuman & Dickinson, 2001; Nickse, 1989; Paratore, 2001, 2002; Phillips & Sample Gosse, 2005; Purcell-Gates, 2000; Purcell-Gates & Dahl, 1991; Sénchal, Thomas, & Monker, 1995; Sulzby & Teale, 1991; Taylor, 1982; Teale & Sulzby, 1986).

What infants and toddlers learn is not learned in isolation. Adult–child interactions encourage the gradual involvement of children in skilled and valued activities of the society in which they live. Parents arrange children's activities and facilitate their learning by regulating the difficulty of tasks and modeling mature performance during joint participation in activities (Bransford, Brown, & Cocking, 2002, p. 103), by guiding children's understanding of how to act in new situations through emotional cues and providing verbal labels to classify objects and events (Rogoff, 1990), and by framing their language and behavior in ways that facilitate learning by young children (Papousek, Papousek, & Bornstein, 1985). As children grow, parents continue to provide sensory stimulation, opportunities, models, and interactions that are critical to their language and literacy development.

Rodriguez-Brown and Meehan (1998) synthesized the research on the import of family literacy as the foundation for learning into four areas that support the relevance of parents' impact in children's education: (a) literacy opportunity, (b) literacy models, (c) literacy interactions, and (d) school–home relationships (p. 183). They defined *literacy opportunity* as a supportive home environment providing children with the opportunity to use literacy. They noted that most children who succeed in school literacy learning are familiar with a culture rich in literacy materials, including books, magazines, and tools for writing. These successful children also often have *literacy models*, defined by Rodriguez-Brown and Meehan as significant people within a child's environment who engage in literacy openly and obviously (p. 183). *Literacy interaction* refers to any exchanges between parents and their children that enhance children's literacy knowledge. Finally, Rodriquez-Brown and Meehan noted the importance of positive home–school relationships by commenting on the importance of parents understanding what their children's teachers are trying to accomplish and of teachers recognizing parents' concerns and aspirations (p. 185).

In addition to the four areas noted by Rodriguez-Brown and Meehan (1998), there is support for the contribution of language interactions within families. It has been suggested that specific types of language interactions in homes prepare children for the language demands of text comprehension and that these effects are seen after basic word-reading skills are in place (Snow, Barnes, Chandler, Goodman, & Hemphill, 1991). There is some evidence that the relationship between home language use and literacy development begins early in life. Watson and Shapiro (1988) identified patterns of discourse during book reading episodes that were related to the later emergence of print-related literacy skills such as understanding of story schemata, good oral language skills (Doiron & Shapiro, 1988), and sensitivity to the use of the language of books (Reeder & Shapiro, 1993).

Dickinson and Tabors (1991) found that preschoolers' engagement in oral extended discourse was related to their kindergarten and first-grade reading outcomes. Specifically, the results indicated that the more exposure 4 and 5-year-olds had to explanatory talk (e.g., explanations of people's actions or speech), the greater their ability to connect a word with the correct picture. The greater amount of narrative talk (e.g., the type that usually occurs at mealtimes, when there are several turns in the conversation about an event that has happened or will happen) resulted in higher receptive, expressive, and listening comprehension abilities (p. 90).

Monique Sénéchal, a Canadian researcher at Carleton University in Ottawa, and her collaborators have taken a closer look at the literacy interactions between parents and children in a longitudinal study. Sénéchal, LeFevre, Thomas, and Daley (1998) argued that children are exposed to two types of literacy activities in the home—(a) informal, message-focused ones, such as storybook reading, and (b) formal, print-focused ones related to specific teaching activities—and that the two are uncorrelated. On the basis of a longitudinal study, Sénéchal and LeFevre (2002) suggested that informal literacy experiences might not be sufficient to promote children's specific emergent literacy skills such as alphabet knowledge or early decoding. They suggested that the various pathways leading to fluent reading originate in different aspects of children's early experiences within the family. Language and literacy success was predicted by engagement in both storybook reading and home activities designed to support reading and writing.

Variation in the ways in which families create environments to foster young children's language and literacy skills and the amount of exposure to these supportive environments is inevitable. In some cases, families explicitly ask for help. We (Phillips & Sample Gosse, 2005) found that parents talked about wanting to move beyond what they were doing at home with their children. Families wanted to learn more about the school ways to engage in literacy experiences and ways to focus more on the print so that their children would be better prepared to understand and engage in reading. In other cases, families provide limited experiences with print and, for whatever reasons, do not ask for help.

Challenges to Family Literacy

When considering the family as the foundation for literacy learning, it is important to begin with an understanding of the challenges modern families face.

Language and Cultural Backgrounds

Returning to the Canadian scene, we have already discussed the increasing diversity of the population. This diversity influences literacy programs for children. For example, a Borrow-the-Book program needed to operate in up to 11 languages in order to meet the language needs of participants (Houston, 1995). We must remain cognizant of the potential impact on families of sending their children to English-language preschool programs when English is not the language of the family. Wong-Fillmore (1991) showed that second-language children usually learn English instead of their first language, a pattern referred to as *subtractive bilingualism*. These children may end up with diminished abilities to communicate with their parents, their extended family, and especially with their grandparents.

It has also been suggested that parents of different cultural backgrounds may hold perceptions of literacy learning that are inconsistent with an emergent literacy perspective. Anderson (1995) found from a sample of 30 families that Chinese-Canadian, Euro-Canadian, and Indo-Canadian families agree that encouraging children to discuss what is read helps them learn to read. The Indo-Canadian parents, however, did not endorse the idea that children be encouraged to engage in reading-like behavior, even though research suggests this stage is an important one in children's literacy development (p. 275).

Lifestyle

There are also lifestyle influences that affect all Canadian families regardless of language and ethnicity. Williams (2002) discussed data from the 1998 Statistics Canada General Social Survey (GSS) on time use, which was used in interviews with almost 11,000 people on how they spent their time during one day. In her report, Williams included survey information from individuals aged 25 to 54 years, "as they were the ones thought most likely to be in the labour force and to have families and significant demands on their time" (p. 7). For purposes of the GSS study, people were classified as high income if their total household income was equal to or greater than $80,000 and as low income if their total household income was $30,000 or less. Williams calculated that, using these definitions, approximately 2.4 million Canadians live in high-income households, and 1.9 million live in low-income households. The GSS study found that whereas virtually all working-age adults in high-income households were employed (97%), a notably smaller proportion (72%) of those with low incomes worked at a job or business. Regardless of income, most employed Canadians aged 25 to 54 spent the largest portion of their waking day doing paid work. Those with high income, however, spent an average of 15% more time on their paid job, 46 hours compared with 40 hours by those with low income. Unpaid work, such as housework and home maintenance, took up much of the time left after paid work was done.

Time

The vast majority of Canadians reported feeling rushed at least a few times a week (84% of Canadians with high incomes and 73% of individuals in low income households). Juggling responsibilities did not end with the traditional workweek. Nearly 60% of high-income and about 47% of low-income individuals reported feeling rushed every day, including Saturday and Sunday.

The time crunch was also found to significantly affect activities of family life. Williams (2002) noted that "much of childcare is done while engaging in other activities such as cleaning, cooking, or watching television," with "considerably less time devoted to exclusive interaction with children" (p. 10). In both low- and high-income households, parents reported spending under 5 minutes a day reading or talking with their children and less than 20 minutes a day playing with them. However, low-income parents devoted more time to teaching or helping their children, at about 9 minutes a day, than did parents with high income, who did so for approximately 4 minutes a day. Neither group of parents seemed to have much time to create literacy opportunities, to model literacy, or to engage in literacy interactions with their children.

One-Parent Families

In recent years, Western societies have seen an increase in the number of one-parent families, and Canada is no exception. These families may consist of an unmarried mother and her child or children, or a father or mother left without a partner through death or divorce and his or her children. Divorce has been noted to be a direct cause of poverty for many women and children. Kaye (2003) noted that poverty dramatically worsens children's achievement outcomes. Poor children often live in crowded or run-down housing in neighborhoods that may be noisy, polluted, or characterized by high crime rates. Single parents are often forced to work long hours, resulting in less attention to, direction for, and supervision of their children as they try to provide for them as best they can. Others are financially disadvantaged, socially isolated, and linguistically challenged. Family literacy programs address many of these challenges, at least for a short period.

Family Literacy Programs

Family literacy is an educational movement that acknowledges the importance of the family as the core environment for the promotion of literacy learning. A term meaning different things to different people (Durkin, 1966; Sticht & McDonald, 1989; Taylor & Dorsey-Gaines, 1988; Teale, 1986), *family literacy* has been notoriously difficult to define. Wasik, Dobbins, and Herrmann (2001) described family literacy as a broad agenda including (a) descriptive studies of families' literacy and language practices; (b) studies of family members' influences on children's literacy and language development; and (c) studies of family literacy programs, including literacy interventions with children, parents, and the whole family (p. 444). It is to the third aspect of family literacy programs that we now turn.

According to Neuman (1998), family literacy programs share common features in that they offer literacy instruction to members of families, involve participants in curriculum planning and development, create supportive learning environments, provide opportunities for the formation of family and social networks, and actively collaborate with other social and educational services. Purcell-Gates (2000) noted that these programs vary according to whom they deliver instruction. She pointed to a typology developed by Ruth Nickse in 1991 as capturing the array of programs currently in operation: "(1) instruction delivered directly to both adults and children, separately and together, (2) instruction delivered directly to adults only with benefits expected to impact children, and (3) instruction delivered directly to children only, with expected indirect impact on parents" (p. 860).

Wasik et al. (2001) referred to family literacy programs that incorporate early-childhood programming and adult education along with an element of parents and children working together as *comprehensive programs*. Based on the presumption that the skills learned and practiced by the adult and the child produce an intergenerational and/or reciprocal transfer of skills (Neuman, 1998), these programs vary in the relative emphasis on the child and adult components (Hendrix, 1999). Within the child-focused component, developmentally appropriate experiences are offered to promote language and literacy learning. The adult literacy instruction is typically geared to the goals of the individuals, either relating to parent–child learning or to employment (Brizius & Foster, 1993). Facilitators promote parents' awareness of their own knowledge and capabilities for helping their children (Rodriguez-Brown & Meehan, 1998). The joint parent–child activities are focused on families learning how to become a greater part of the world of print and are designed to promote interactions that lead to greater understanding, communication, and skill gains. Many programs also specifically seek to provide opportunities for parents to support parents, provide time for sharing of experiences, and discuss ways to overcome challenges to family literacy. The extent to which family literacy programs can claim success has been and continues to be extensively debated (see, e.g., Gadsden, 2000; Purcell-Gates, 2000). Our purpose in the next section is not to reiterate all the points of ongoing discussion but rather to demonstrate through Canadian examples how the family literacy movement is attempting to deal with such issues in two broad areas: (a) program philosophy and design and (b) program evaluation.

Challenges to Family Literacy Programs

Program Philosophy and Design Issues

Family literacy programs have often provided opportunities for lower income parents and children to learn and practice strategies demonstrated to be successful for middle-income parents and children. Wasik et al. (2001)

described the role of family literacy facilitators in these programs as one of encouraging participating families as they acquire new skills, such as techniques for book sharing, questioning, language facilitation, and providing positive feedback to children. These practices are supported by those who observe that lower income parents want to learn how to help their children and seek specific assistance to overcome the difficulties they have supporting their children's literacy development (Edwards, 1991, 1995; Newman & Beverstock, 1990; Phillips & Sample Gosse, 2005).

These types of family literacy programs, however, have been criticized for encouraging families to perform school-like literacy activities in the home instead of capitalizing on literacy activities that are already an integral part of families' daily lives (Auerbach, 1989). This criticism is related to the concept of *multiple literacies*, which recognizes the fact that literacy practices vary between groups within a society as well as between societies (Heath, 1980). A sociocultural theory of literacy arose that emphasized an understanding of family culture and worldview in developing interventions. Family literacy programs built on a sociocultural foundation were described as promoting the use of reading and writing to investigate family and cultural issues (Auerbach, 1989). An appropriate measure of the effectiveness of sociocultural family literacy programs was seen to be the extent to which they involved family members in determining their roles in their own literacy development (Gadsden, 1994). Family literacy programs that provide opportunities for families to engage in school-like literacy activities and those that acknowledge variant literacy practices between groups are sometimes seen to be mutually exclusive. It is our position that to perceive of these two approaches as mutually exclusive is to limit the very options requested by families.

We urge continued support for the importance of obtaining and using knowledge about and from families to refine literacy instruction and to improve learning (Gadsden, 1998) and a new recognition that both home literacy practices and school-like literacy practices can and should be supported (Wasik et al., 2001). It is acknowledged that when families become collaborators in their design, programs are often broader in perspective and better situated within the daily lives of the families (Rodriguez-Brown & Meehan, 1998), and retention rates in the programs are higher (Saracho, 1997) than if families are not involved in their design. The following Canadian examples attest to the utility of a familial perspective as a unifying force in family literacy program philosophy and design.

We are currently engaged in an extensive 6-year longitudinal study (Data collection will end December 2005) of the *"Learning Together"* family literacy program offered by the Centre for Family Literacy in Edmonton, Alberta. The 13-week program includes eight units with sessions for adult, child, and joint adult–child components. The units build on what the parents want to learn and focus on creative play; language for literacy; games to give parents alternative ways to interact with children; a beginning-with-books unit; and units on early reading, writing, and drawing, environmental print walks, and question-and-answer sessions for parents. A total of 183 urban and rural families of low income and low educational backgrounds with children aged 3 to 5+ years considered to be at risk of school failure are participating in the study. Although the *Learning Together* program facilitators adapt the program content as a result of observations of and discussions with the diverse families, the families themselves support the provision of information and activities to extend their ways of dealing with print. In addition to the standard measures, we conduct ongoing extensive parent interviews on what parents say they want to learn in order to help their children. Recently, we reported the results of these interviews to date and parents were unequivocal about wanting to learn specific ways to help their children to read and write and to succeed in school (Phillips & Sample Gosse, 2005). We firmly support the importance of taking a familial perspective and agree with Linder and Elish-Piper (1995) that family literacy programs that listen to and incorporate the wishes of the families are more responsive in design and evaluation.

The work of Vianne Timmons and her team provides another Canadian example of collaborative family literacy program design. A professor and researcher at the University of Prince Edward Island, Timmons has developed family literacy programs that provide a needed context to reading and writing interventions for marginalized families (Timmons, O'Donoghue, MacGillivray, & Gerg, 2003). The challenges faced by the families are many. They are isolated by distance and by a history of literacy failure, and they often do not identify with what their middle-class teachers read and write. In their first project, Timmons and her collaborators worked with 10 rural families who volunteered to develop a family literacy program specific to their needs. The project focused on providing families with an opportunity to participate in a program that incorporated the development of both literacy and parenting skills. The families worked with the researchers to develop a curriculum that reflected their life experiences and incorporated aspects of their family lives and experiences. Parents and children worked together to document their family histories. The program capitalized on the richness of the oral language tradition of the families by encouraging the development of children's books that portrayed stories of their children. As the program progressed, parents provided input on how it could be improved. Participating families claimed that the program enhanced their language and literacy skills and provided an opportunity for mutual support (Timmons et al., 2003). Buoyed by the positive anecdotal reports and high participation rates, Timmons and her colleagues have expanded the program to include aboriginal and nonaboriginal families in rural Prince Edward Island. This program provides more anecdotal evidence of the benefits of family-centered program design.

Evaluation Issues

The pedagogical debate in family literacy has also had an influence on discussions of appropriate evaluation practices. Evaluation of family literacy programs has long been problematic. Research into individual program components and positive anecdotal reports have too often been used to justify family literacy interventions. Calls for comprehensive studies of the efficacy of family literacy programs have been ongoing. Early studies were criticized for focusing more on the definition and description of programs than on assessing their influence on families (Paratore, 1993).

There have been many suggestions of how to structure an appropriately comprehensive evaluation of family literacy programs. Gadsden (1994) called for an intensive examination of the interaction of families, literacy opportunities, and institutional structures as well as the real or perceived obstacles to literacy education for family members. She proposed a research focus on the entire family and the effect of life circumstances and advocated taking a closer look at how literacy is used and program participation negotiated within families. Ryan, Geissler, and Knell (1994) supported the idea of measuring change in the context of the self-determined goals of family members.

Purcell-Gates (2000) reported that positive public perception, funding, and program implementations outpaced empirically based knowledge. She further suggested that most of the evidence currently supporting family literacy programs relied on reports of immediate outcomes for child participants with little consideration of whether the gains were sustained over time and of the impact of the programs on family literacy practices. She called for research directly exploring the many issues arising from attempts to change the ways parents interact with their children. She noted also the need to document program impact on the frequency and nature of parent–child interactions around print, and she noted the need for controlled studies using comparative groups to differentiate between development that occurs from typical experience and instruction and that which occurs as a direct effect of family literacy intervention. Primavera (2000) supported the need for longitudinal data to assess the longevity of the positive impact of family literacy interventions, and Gadsden (2000) continued the call for a careful consideration of the roles and relationships of families themselves.

There are acknowledged difficulties in conducting literacy research with very young children, with parents of low educational levels, and with second-language children. Obtaining reliable and valid measurements of the literacy of 2½- to 5-year-olds is difficult, because their understanding of literacy is still emerging and their progress is uneven (Phillips, Norris, & Mason, 1996). In addition, many parents with low levels of education have less than positive attitudes about schooling and literacy activities, so including evaluations of their reading in programs may deter their participation. When attempting to measure the outcomes of instructional practices in family literacy, direct observation of parent–child interactions may not be feasible, yet the veracity of self-reports of such interactions has been questioned (Purcell-Gates, 2000). Parents do have valuable insights into their preschool children's literacy development that could complement standardized tests results and teacher observations (Dickinson & DeTemple, 1998, p. 241). With refinement and validation, parents' reports could become a valuable assessment component of preschoolers' early literacy development.

Children learning a second language may not have oral language proficiency in that language, but Geva and Wade-Woolley (in press) reported that difficulties with processes such as phonological awareness, speed of naming, and verbal memory appear to be as much a matter of individual differences in reading development for children learning a second language as they are for first-language children. They went on to advise the use of test norms based on a child's first language and that assessments be conducted in both the second language and home language whenever possible.

There is evidence that family literacy programs are dealing with challenges in the areas of program philosophy and design and program evaluation. Other challenges are to be addressed as well; these include building on what is known about program participation, integrating the culture of participants, and creating ways of building capacity to sustain community programs.

RECOMMENDATIONS FOR FAMILY LITERACY PROGRAMS

Build on Past Knowledge

To further promote family literacy programs, we must consider how to best reach out to families. Primavera (2000) suggested that some parents may overestimate their reading and book-sharing competence. These parents were described as being more likely to volunteer for interventions that are advertised as being related to enhancing their children's competencies rather than those focused on their own literacy needs. Primavera's observations of the positive effect of advertising that emphasized helping children prepare for school is consistent with our own observations of keen parental interest in school literacy.

Regardless of the success of programs emphasizing children's needs, we cannot ignore the similarities between many parents who participate in family literacy interventions and the target group for adult basic literacy programs. Because of this similarity, family literacy organizations can learn from information collected by adult basic literacy and upgrading initiatives. In Canada, two extensive studies (Long, 2002; Long & Middleton, 2001) were conducted for ABC CANADA, a private literacy organization. In the first study, telephone surveys were conducted to follow up on the experience of callers who contacted literacy and upgrading groups about their programs. Although the great majority (88%) of callers who had completed or are still in a program reported high levels of satisfaction with the program level, content, and teaching structure, the study found that less than half of those who contacted a literacy group enrolled in a program. Of those who did enroll, 30% dropped out (Long & Middleton, 2001). Those who did not enroll frequently cited program and policy-related problems, such as not being called back by a program contact person, long waiting lists, inconvenient course times, wrong content or teaching structure, and unhelpful program contact because of message-managers rather than a person at the end of the line. Those who enrolled but dropped out also identified program and policy-related factors, which included wrong program level, content, or teaching structure and program cancellation. Financial problems and family and work responsibilities were major barriers to participation for both groups.

In the second study (Long, 2002), interviews and telephone surveys were conducted with Canadians without high school diplomas who had never contacted a literacy or upgrading program. Although close to 60% of those interviewed had thought about the idea of taking upgrading or completing their high school diploma, only 20% thought they would actually take a program in the next 5 years. It is interesting that work-related issues frequently were cited both as reasons for thinking about taking a program and as reasons for not being able to take a program. Women were more likely than men to cite family reasons for their lack of interest in taking a program. Nonetheless, female single parents were found to be more than twice as likely as male parents in households with partners to think they might take an upgrading program or complete a high school diploma in the next 5 years. The study also found that those who stated they might take a program in the next 5 years showed strong interest in studying one on one with a tutor or small group sessions of 5 to 10 students. The preferred site for programs was a classroom in a local school, college, or university.

In addition to describing the barriers to participation in literacy and upgrading programs, the ABC CANADA studies provided guidance to program planners. They were advised to consider smaller classes instructed by more knowledgeable teachers in more diverse program locations with more individual attention and more relevant materials. Attention to socio-economic and circumstantial barriers to program participation was recommended. Other recommendations included the establishment of stable and adequate program funding within a national infrastructure, the development of partnerships with other community agencies to provide effective child care options, and the formation of solutions to financial problems of program participants.

Integrate Cultural Diversity

Family literacy program providers need to understand not only the families but also the cultural groups represented. Throughout the world, specific cultural groups are involved in efforts to ensure the survival and revival of their cultural beliefs, values, and practices while simultaneously working to ensure that their community members have access to dominant culture settings.

The *generative curriculum model* used by the First Nations Partnership Program at the University of Victoria provides a Canadian example of how culturally specific training programs can be developed. The First Nations Partnership Program is a university diploma program focusing on early childhood care and development that is available to First Nations, Inuit, Métis, and other cultural communities in Canada and internationally (Ball, 2001). The model was developed through collaboration between University of Victoria professors Alan Pence and Jessica Ball and representatives of First Nations organizations across central Canada. Although the curriculum begins its life at the university in the form of scripts and supplementary materials, it is fully generated as locally recruited instructors and elders facilitate dialogue with learners about their own culturally based child care practices and about Euro-Western research and practices (Ball & Pence, 2001).

The generative curriculum model has been successful in meeting the needs of the participating communities as evidenced by the fact that a high proportion of participants complete the program and remain in the community to staff new or existing child care programs (Ball, 2001). Ball (2001) also reported that the program had a positive impact on the wider communities by promoting cultural healing, continuity, and pride, as well as increased parental effectiveness and advocacy for the well-being of children. The participants and community members attributed the impact of the program largely to the generative curriculum model and community program delivery.

Accommodating the diversity of program participants will continue to be a significant challenge to family literacy programs. As we seek to understand diverse populations, it is critical that we do not lose sight of individual differences within these populations. Neuman, Hagedorn, Celano, and Daly (1995) observed that family literacy participants with similar ethnic, educational, and economic status held varying beliefs about children's learning, ranging from more behavioral to more constructivist perspectives. They noted also that the African American teenage mothers valued the same considerations as did school professionals. Some of these included educational achievement, security, independence in learning, respect from and for teachers, and information that might enable them to enhance their children's learning.

Develop Capacity to Sustain Programs

Anderson, Fagan, and Cronin (1998) commented on the transiency of literacy programs initiated by university academics. They noted that such programs often are not sustained after the initial study period because of a lack of program ownership on the part of the parents and the community. They suggested that this lack of ownership occurred regardless of how involved parents were in the program. In recognition of the problem of program sustainability, Rodriguez-Brown and Meehan (1998) began enlisting parents who had previously participated in their family literacy program and lived in the community as trainers in delivery of the program. They found that this practice added even more relevance to the literacy topics and enhanced program outcomes for the participants and the trainers.

It is necessary to not only build capacity within the target community but also to train a new generation of practitioners and researchers. Nickse and Quezada (1994) argued persuasively for multidisciplinary preprofessional training in the collaborative process, human development, life span education, and multicultural issues (p. 233). Participation by undergraduate and graduate students in supervised development of family literacy projects was seen as necessary to encourage development of the joint planning, negotiation, conflict resolution, and communication skills necessary in the field. Unfortunately, the lack of such academic and practicum opportunities noted by Nickse and Quezada in 1994 remains the case today.

Needed Research and Concluding Remarks

While program developers work to assimilate current research understandings into the design of family literacy programs, researchers must continue to probe for new knowledge to support practice. Ongoing investigation of the efficacy of re-visioned family literacy programs is required. Specifically, there is a need for detailed explorations such as those outlined in 2001 by Wasik et al. of "program variables such as intensity, duration, teaching strategies, and integration of program components" (p. 453). To come to some conclusions about efficacy, however, professionals in the field of family literacy will need to work toward greater clarity regarding the desired outcomes of family literacy programs.

Although quantifiable outcomes for family literacy programs are considered essential, a familial perspective affirms the importance of considering qualitative information provided by the participants. Obtaining information about parents' personal goals, views about program design and content, and perceived benefits is critical to understanding how family literacy programs meet the needs of participants (Phillips & Sample Gosse, 2005). We contend that families have much to contribute to the success of family literacy programs. Moreover, they are the final arbiters of the success of any program. If they see value in it, they will attend whenever possible despite sometimes very difficult daily living circumstances.

Supporters of family literacy programs work toward programs that have a lasting and positive effect on the participating families. Researchers have a role in investigating longitudinally the impact of family literacy program participation over time. Cairney (1997) noted the importance of breaking down barriers between home and school. This breakdown would enable both teachers and parents to understand the way each defines, values, and uses literacy as part of cultural practices and to come to terms with differences between home and school literacy practices. Research directed at identifying ways that family literacy programs can best prepare parents to deal with this negotiation is needed; indeed, it may be necessary to expand family literacy research to investigate how schools are able to manage this negotiation, as Victoria Purcell-Gates pointed out in 2000.

In addition to the need to develop methods for empirically exploring the effect of programs on family dynamics, marital relationships, and interactions with older and younger siblings not directly involved (Wasik et al., 2001), we would add the need to research the dynamic of the power of friends. Many families in our study commented on the positive influence of friendships, formed with other program participants, on literacy development (Phillips & Sample Gosse, 2005). We concur with Primavera's (2000) observations of increases in personal efficacy and self-confidence among program participants and suggest further investigation of the possible impact of these changes.

Referring back to Wasik et al.'s (2001) definition of *family literacy* reminds us that studies of family literacy programs are only one component of a broad concept that includes studies of families' literacy and language practices and of influences on children's literacy and language development. Indeed, the success of family literacy programs ultimately depends on continuing research in these areas. To institute the family as the foundation of literacy, we must thoroughly understand the nature and challenges faced by modern families, their evolving literacy and language practices, and the precise nature of their influence on children's literacy and language development.

Throughout this chapter, we have argued for the acceptance of the role of family as a necessary condition for sustained progress in national literacy levels. Although we have used Canadian examples, we know that the same issues are being considered internationally with solutions generated that are locally amenable. We are buoyed by the univocal aspiration of all parents, regardless of language, education, socioeconomic status, culture, and political factors, to help their children to read and write. The impact of these factors on children's literacy development is mutable. J. Douglas Willms, a prominent researcher at the University of New Brunswick, suggested that Canada is an ideal place to study such factors, for several reasons: "It is possible to study variation across provinces in children's outcomes and in the policies and practices aimed to support children and there is an optimistic spirit prevailing among many Canadians that change is possible" (Willms, 1999, p. 92). We concur with Willms and see Canada as an ideal place to study many of the issues and concerns that face families, family literacy, and literacy globally.

REFERENCES

Anderson, J. (1995). How parents perceive literacy acquisition: A cross-cultural study. In W. M. Linek & E. G. Sturtevant (Eds.), *Generations of literacy: The seventeenth yearbook* (pp. 262–277). Harrisonburg, VA: College Reading Association.

Anderson, J., Fagan, W. T., & Cronin, M. (1998). Insights in implementing family literacy programs. In E. G. Sturtevant, J. Dugan, P. Linder, & W. M. Linek (Eds.), *Literacy and community: The twentieth yearbook* (pp. 269–281). Carrollton, GA: College Reading Association.

Auerbach, E. R. (1989). Towards a socio-contextual approach to family literacy. *Harvard Educational Review, 59,* 165–181.

Ball, J. (2001). *First Nations Partnership Programs Generative Curriculum Model: Program evaluation summary.* Victoria, BC: University of Victoria, First Nations Partnership Programs.

Ball, J., & Pence, A. (2001). A "Generative Curriculum Model" for supporting child care and development programs in First Nations communities. *Journal of Speech–Language Pathology and Audiology, 25,* 114–124.

Bransford, J. D., Brown, A. L., & Cocking, R. R. (2002). *How people learn* (expanded ed.). Washington, DC: National Academy Press.

British Columbia Women's Institute. (1892). *Modern pioneers.* Vancouver, BC: Evergreen Press.

Brizius, J. A., & Foster, S. A. (1993). *Generation to generation: Realizing the promise of family literacy.* Ypsilanti, MI: High/Scope.

Cairney, T. H. (1997). Acknowledging diversity in home literacy practices: Moving towards partnership with parents. *Early Child Development and Care, 127–128,* 61–73.

Canada's new spirit. (2003, September 27). *The Economist*, p. 13.

Dickinson, D. K., & DeTemple, J. (1998). Putting parents in the picture: Maternal reports of preschoolers' literacy as a predictor of early reading. *Early Childhood Research Quarterly, 13,* 241–261.

Dickinson, D. K., & Tabors, P. O. (1991). Early literacy: Linkages between home, school, and literacy achievement at age five. *Journal of Research in Childhood Education, 6,* 30–46.

Dickinson, D. K., & Tabors, P. O. (2001). *Beginning literacy with language.* Baltimore: Brookes.

Doiron, R., & Shapiro, J. (1988). Home literacy environment and children's sense of story. *Reading Psychology, 9,* 187–202.

Durkin, D. (1966). *Children who read early.* New York: Teachers College Press.

Edwards, P. A. (1991). Fostering early literacy through parent coaching. In E. Hiebert (Ed.), *Literacy for a diverse society* (pp. 199–213). New York: Teachers College Press.

Edwards, P. A. (1995). Combining parents, and teachers, thoughts about storybook reading at home and school. In L. Morrow (Ed.), *Family literacy connection in schools and communities* (pp. 54–69). Newark, DE: International Reading Association.

Gadsden, V. L. (1994). Understanding family literacy: Conceptual issues facing the field. *Teachers College Record, 96,* 58–86.

Gadsden, V. L. (1998). Family cultures and literacy learning. In J. Osborn & F. Lehr (Eds.), *Literacy for all: Issues in teaching and learning* (pp. 32–50). New York: Guilford.

Gadsden, V. L. (2000). Intergenerational literacy within families. In M. L. Kamil, P. B. Mosenthal, P. D. Pearson, & R. Barr (Eds), *Handbook of reading research* (Vol. III, pp. 871–887). Mahwah, NJ: Lawrence Erlbaum Associates.

Geva, E., & Wade-Woolley, L (in press). Issues in the assessment of reading disability in second language children. In I. Smythe, J. Everatt, & R. Salter (Eds.), *The international book of dyslexia: A cross language comparison and practice guide* (2nd ed., pp. 195–206). New York: Wiley.

Heath, S. B. (1980). The functions and uses of literacy. *Journal of Communication, 30,* 123–133.

Heath, S. B. (1983). *Ways with words.* Cambridge, England: Cambridge University Press.

Hendrix, S. (1999). Family literacy education—Panacea or false promise? *Journal of Adolescent and Adult Literacy, 43,* 338–346.

Houston, M. W. (1995, Spring). Tell me a story (then tell it again): Supporting literacy for preschool children from bilingual families. *Interaction.* Retrieved October 20, 2003, from http://www.cfc-efc.ca/docs/cccf/00001045.htm

Jung, I., & Ouane, A. (2001). Literacy and social development: Policy and implementation. In D. R. Olson & N. Torrance (Eds.), *The making of literate societies* (pp. 319–336). Oxford, England: Blackwell.

Kaye, M. (2003, November). Divorced? Protect your kids. *Homemakers,* 48–55.

Linder, P. E., & Elish-Piper, L. (1995). Listening to learners: Dialogue journals in a family literacy program. In W. M. Linek & E. G. Sturtevant (Eds.), *Generations of literacy: The seventeenth yearbook* (pp. 313–325). Harrisonburg, VA: College Reading Association.

Long, E. (2002). *Why aren't they calling? Nonparticipation in literacy and upgrading programs: A national study.* Don Mills, ON: ABC CANADA Literacy Foundation.

Long, E., & Middleton, S. (2001). *Who wants to learn? Patterns of participation in Canadian literacy and upgrading programs: Results of a national follow-up study.* Don Mills, ON: ABC Literacy Foundation.

Moll, L. C., & Greenberg, J. B. (1992). Creating zones of possibilities: Combining social contexts for instruction. In L. C. Moll (Ed.), *Vygotsky in education* (pp. 319–348). New York: Cambridge University Press.

Morrow, L. (1989). *Literacy development in the early years.* Englewood Cliffs, NJ: Prentice Hall.

Neuman, S. B. (1998). A social-constructivist view of family literacy. In E. G. Sturtevant, J. Dugan, P. Linder, & W. M. Linek (Eds.), *Literacy and community: The twentieth yearbook* (pp. 25–30). Carrollton, GA: College Reading Association.

Neuman, S. B., & Dickinson, D. K. (2001). *Handbook of early literacy research.* New York: Guilford.

Neuman, S. B., Hagedorn, T., Celano, D., & Daly, P. (1995). Toward a collaborative approach to parent involvement in early education: A study of teenage mothers in an African-American community. *American Educational Research Journal, 32,* 801–827.

Newman, A. P., & Beverstock, C. (1990). *Adult literacy: Contexts and challenges.* Newark, DE: International Reading Association.

Nickse, R. S. (1989). *The noise of literacy: Overview of intergenerational and family literacy programs* (Report No. CE-053-282). Boston: Boston University Press.

Nickse, R. S., & Quezada, S. (1994). Collaborations: A key to success in family literacy programs. In D. K. Dickinson (Ed.), *Bridges to literacy: Children, families, and schools* (pp. 211–235). Cambridge, MA: Basil Blackwell.

Organization for Economic Co-Operation, Programme for International Student Assessment. (2001). *Highlights—Measuring Up: The performance of Canada's youth in reading, mathematics, and science.* Ottawa, ON: Statistics Canada, Human Resources Development Canada, and Council of Ministers of Education, Canada.

Olson, D. R., & Torrance, N. (2001). *The making of literate societies.* Oxford, England: Blackwell.

Papousek, M., Papousek, H., & Bornstein, M. H. (1985). The naturalistic vocal environment of young infants. In T. M. Field & N. Fox (Eds.), *Social perception in infants* (pp. 269–298). Hillsdale, NJ: Lawrence Erlbaum Associates.

Paratore, J. R. (1993). Influence of an intergenerational approach to literacy on the practice of literacy of parents and their children. In C. Kinzer & D. Leu (Eds.), *Examining central issues in literacy, research, theory and practice* (pp. 83–91). Chicago: National Reading Conference.

Paratore, J. R. (2001). *Opening doors, opening opportunities.* Needham Heights, MA: Allyn & Bacon.

Paratore, J. R. (2002). Family literacy. In B. Guzzetti (Ed.), *Literacy in America: An encyclopedia of history, theory, and practice* (pp. 185–187). Santa Barbara, CA: ABC-CLIO.

Phillips, L. M., Norris, S. P., & Mason, J. M. (1996). Longitudinal effects of early literacy concepts on reading achievement: A kindergarten intervention and five-year follow-up. *Journal of Literacy Research, 28,* 173–195.

Phillips, L. M., & Sample Gosse, H. L. (2005). Family literacy: Listen to what the families have to say. In J. Anderson, M. Kendrick, T. Rogers, & S. Smythe (Eds.), *Critical issues in family, community, and school literacies: Intersections and tensions* (pp. 91–107). Mahwah, NJ: Lawrence Erlbaum Associates.

Primavera, J. (2000). Enhancing family competence through literacy activities. *Journal of Prevention and Intervention in the Community, 20,* 85–101.

Purcell-Gates, V. (2000). Family literacy. In M. L. Kamil, P. B. Mosenthal, P. D. Pearson, & R. Barr (Eds.), *Handbook of reading research* (Vol. III, pp. 853–870). Mahwah, NJ: Lawrence Erlbaum Associates.

Purcell-Gates, V., & Dahl, K. (1991). Low SES children's success and failure at early literacy learning in skills based classrooms. *Journal of Reading Behavior, 23,* 1–34.

Reeder, K., & Shapiro, J. (1993). Relationships between early literate experience and knowledge and children's linguistic pragmatic strategies. *Journal of Pragmatics, 19,* 1–22.

Rodriguez-Brown, F. V., & Meehan, M. A. (1998). Family literacy and adult education: Project FLAME. In M. C. Smith (Ed.), *Literacy for the twenty-first century: Research, policy, practices, and the national adult literacy survey* (pp. 175–193). Westport, CT: Praeger.

Rogoff, B. (1990). *Apprenticeship in thinking: Cognitive development in social context.* New York: Oxford University Press.

Ryan, K. E., Geissler, B., & Knell, S. (1994). Evaluating family literacy programs: Tales from the field. In D. Dickinson (Ed.), *Bridges to literacy: Children, families, and schools* (pp. 236–264). Cambridge, MA: Basil Blackwell.

Saracho, O. N. (1997). Perspectives on family literacy. *Early Child Development and Care, 127–128,* 3–11.

Sénéchal, M., & LeFevre, J. (2002). Parental involvement in the development of children's reading skill: A five-year longitudinal study. *Child Development, 73,* 445–460.

Sénéchal, M., LeFevre, J., Thomas, E., & Daley, K. (1998). Differential effects of home literacy experiences on the development of oral and written language. *Reading Research Quarterly, 32,* 96–116.

Sénéchal, M., Thomas, E., & Monker, J. (1995). Individual differences in 4-year-old children's acquisition of vocabulary during storybook reading. *Journal of Educational Psychology, 87,* 218–229.

Snow, C. E., Barnes, W. S., Chandler, J., Goodman, I. F., & Hemphill, L. (1991). *Unfulfilled expectations: Home and school influences on literacy.* Cambridge, MA: Harvard University Press.

Statistics Canada. (1996). *International Adult Literacy Survey (IALS), Reading the future: A portrait of literacy in Canada.* Ottawa, ON: Government of Canada.

Statistics Canada. (2001). *Census 2001.* Ottawa, ON: Government of Canada.

Sticht, T., & McDonald, B. (1989). *Making the nation smarter: The intergenerational transfer of literacy.* San Diego, CA: Institute for Adult Literacy.

Sulzby, E., & Teale, W. (1991). Emergent literacy. In R. Barr, M. L. Kamil, P. Mosenthal, & P. D. Pearson (Eds.), *Handbook of reading research* (Vol. II, pp. 727–758). New York: Longman.

Taylor, D. (1982). *Family literacy*. Exeter, NH: Heinemann.

Taylor, D., & Dorsey-Gaines, C. (1988). *Growing up literate: Learning from inner-city families*. Portsmouth, NH: Heinemann.

Teale, W. H. (1986). Home background and young children's literacy development. In W. H. Teale & E. Sulzby (Eds.), *Emergent literacy: Writing and reading* (pp. 173–206). Norwood, NJ: Ablex.

Teale, W. H., & Sulzby, E. (Eds.). (1986). *Emergent literacy: Writing and reading*. Norwood, NJ: Ablex.

Timmons, V., O'Donoghue, F., MacGillivray, T., & Gerg, B. (2003, June). *A comprehensive family literacy program in rural Atlantic Canada*. Paper presented at the second annual scientific conference of the Canadian Language and Literacy Research Network, Victoria, BC.

Wasik, B. H., Dobbins, D. R., & Herrmann, S. (2001). Intergenerational family literacy: Concepts, research, and practice. In S. B. Neuman & D. K. Dickinson, (Eds.), *Handbook of early literacy research* (pp. 444–458). New York: Guilford.

Watson, R., & Shapiro, J. (1988). Discourse from home to school. *Applied Psychology, 37*, 395–409.

Williams, C. (2002, Summer). Time or money? How high and low income Canadians spend their time. *Canadian Social Trends, 65*, 7–11.

Willms, J. D. (1999). Quality and inequality in children's literacy. In D. P. Keating & C. Hertzman (Eds.), *Developmental health and the wealth of nations* (pp. 72–93). New York: Guilford.

Wong-Fillmore, L. (1991). When learning a second language means losing the first. *Early Childhood Research Quarterly, 6*, 323–346.

8

Understanding the Everyday: Adult Lives, Literacies, and Informal Learning

Mary Hamilton
University of Lancaster

In their recent review of research studies that have investigated literacy in out-of-school settings, Glynda Hull and Katherine Schultz (2001) remarked that "Empirical, field-based research on out-of-school literacy has led to some major theoretical advances in how we conceptualize literacy ... when researchers examined literacy in out-of-school contexts they often arrived at new constructs that proved generative for literacy studies." (p. 578). Making the links between research on out-of-school literacies and educational practice is urgent in the context of adult literacy in England. Just as in Canada and other countries, increasingly formal, standardized, and narrow boundaries are being drawn around literacy. The understandings of literacy on which programs are based are backward looking, rather than forward looking and do not take account of the new theoretical insights referred to by Hull and Schultz, or of the new shape of literacies in diverse cultural and multimodal contexts. In this chapter, I draw from ongoing ethnographic work in everyday settings (Barton & Hamilton, 1998) to explore useful ways of thinking about the relationship between the lived experience of literacy and learning and to examine what is done in the name of literacy in formal educational settings.

A SOCIAL PRACTICE VIEW OF LITERACY

One of the central ideas behind a social practice view of literacy is to encourage a reflection on our own uses and learning of literacy in the everyday world. The focus is on all of us, not on someone else with a problem. So I shall start by asking you, the reader of this chapter, to think about your responses to these questions: Do you ever write or give poems to other people? In what context have you done so? Which languages have you spoken or read in the last two weeks? Do you keep family records? What do you keep, and where? Have you ever written a fan letter? Have you ever taken on the job of secretary or treasurer for a local organization? When was the last time you asked for help with reading or writing?

These activities are all things that people have told me and my colleagues about and that we have observed going on in our ethnography of literacy in the community. People talked about choosing verses in greetings cards they exchanged, songs they wrote for parties and other celebratory occasions; of the complex ways in which different languages and their associated written forms map onto their social relationships and activities; of the photograph albums, financial records, and souvenirs they have kept from their own childhood and their children's lives; of cherished letters and autographs from popular celebrities; of their many involvements in local groups and the literacy involved in organizing events, taking minutes, and writing newsletters. Finally, regardless of their formal achievements in literacy, everyone had stories of instances where they had made use of "brokers"—official agents or friends, colleagues or family members—to help with specialized literacy tasks such as financial, legal, or medical issues. Such activities all fall within our definition of literacy as social practice.

Literacy is part of social practices that are observable in literacy events or moments and are patterned by social institutions and power relationships. Within a social practice view of literacy, we are encouraged to look beyond texts themselves to what people do with literacy, with whom, where, and how; that is, we focus attention on the cultural practices within which the written word is embedded, the ways in which texts are socially regulated and used, and the historical contexts from which these practices have developed. The differentiated uses of literacy in varying cultural contexts are considered, which go beyond print literacy to include other mass media, including visual and oral ways of communicating (Kress & Van Leeuwen, 1996). Special attention is paid to the way that the use of these media, using both old (print) and new (electronic) technologies, is interlinked. Within a social practice perspective, writing becomes as central as reading, and other ways of interacting with print culture are identified.

A *social practice* view of literacy demands that we make connections with the community in which learners lead their lives outside the classroom, with a notion of *situated learning*—between learning and institutional power, between print literacy and other media, between our own literacies as teachers and researchers, and the theory presented here. Within a social practice view of literacy the focus shifts from literacy as a deficit or lack, something people do not have, to the many different ways that people engage with literacy, recognizing difference and diversity and challenging how these differences are valued within society. The new literacy studies involve us in looking beyond educational settings to informal learning and to the other official and nonschool settings in which literacies play a key role. Learning does not just take place in classrooms and is not just concerned with methods.

New literacy studies represent a significant change of perspective on literacy, a basic paradigm shift, in our understanding of reading and writing. The shift is from a psychological or cognitive model of a set of skills to one that includes the practices associated with reading and writing. It is a social view of literacy rather than a purely psychological one. It has to be historically and socially situated. As Brian Street (1995) put it, it is a shift from literacy as an autonomous gift to be given to people, to an ideological understanding of literacy, placing it in its bigger context of institutional purposes and power relationships.

MAIN ELEMENTS OF A SOCIAL PRACTICE VIEW

Theories have different building blocks. The elements of a cognitive theory of literacy include phonemes, words, sentences, comprehension skills, and metalinguistic awareness. The building blocks of a social practice theory include different elements, namely, participants (who is involved in an interaction with a written text); activities (what participants do with the text, which is not just reading or writing; activities can include displaying, passing it on to others, or even erasing the text); settings (where participants read, e.g., as in the kitchen, in bed, on the bus); domains (the institutional spaces that organize particular areas of social life and the literacy associated with it, e.g., work, religion, or health); and resources (these might be cognitive skills and knowledge; they might also be paper, a wall, or other surface on which to write; a computer; a printer; a set of colored pens or a can of spray paint, or a hammer and chisel). It is important to notice that these elements include the material technologies and physical circumstances within which literacy is accomplished as well as the cognitive and symbolic resources of the encoded linguistic, visual, and other semiotic systems.

Before I turn to the research evidence generated by this new view of literacy, I provide some more illustrations of literacy as social practice. To do this, I appeal to newspapers, where a range of public discourses of literacy can be found. For several years, I have been looking closely at both the text stories and the images of literacy that abound in the newspapers in the United Kingdom (there are parallels in Australia, Canada, the United States, and elsewhere in the world) and taking photos of literacy events. I think that pictures convey the notion of "literacy event" very vividly because they show the physical, material circumstances in which interactions with written language take place. They also point out the differences between a traditional educational perspective on literacy and what literacy may look like through the lens of everyday life (see Hamilton, 2000, for an account of this work).

Unfortunately, because of copyright restrictions, I cannot reproduce the pictures. However, I can describe some of them. First, I have examples of current educational discourses of literacy represented in newspaper photographs: the "model student" shown as a serious young boy, sitting alone at a table, reading, with bookshelves in the background; a reproduction of a classical painting of Edward Arnold, "the master," in cap and gown, holding a religious text and being held up to contemporary teachers as an icon, published on the front page of a leading educational newspaper. Other education-related images included a picture of an obese child slumped in front of the television, surrounded by videos and snack foods. This image was illustrating a story about the results of a recent international survey that showed the English as top of the league in television watching but near the bottom in terms of reading scores. The "Free Books for Schools" campaign enlisted the help of sports stars who are shown posing, rather unconvincingly, on the soccer field holding popular children's books, in an effort to counter traditional stereotypes of sport as an alternative world to the world of books. All of these images tell interesting tales about our assumptions and concerns about literacy.

A further set of pictures appears entirely unrelated to literacy, and yet they convey a great deal about common social practices of literacy through their incidental depictions of them. One picture shows Italian immigrants competing in a desperate physical fight to obtain work permits; another shows a pair of shoes autographed by a top English footballer and sold for thousands of pounds; a woman sits at a computer under the title "The Future is Fe-Mail"; an early morning graffiti squad is shown with their hoses, cleaning up a wall in London; and a story of a political demonstration is accompanied by a picture of a young woman wearing a headband prominently decorated with a political slogan. Stories of sudden death are accompanied by pictures of people laying messages of condolence and signing books; in another, a mother sews a letter for her daughter into the hem of a wedding dress, a message that is found many years later. Pictures of politicians, lawyers, and professionals of all kinds show these people carrying files and books and surrounded by reading matter: in these pictures, literacy becomes an attribute from which we "read off" the identity of the person depicted.

As you can see, this view of literacy leads us out from the school room or the adult college, to the streets, workplaces, homes, sports clubs, war zones, and shopping malls where people are using, and thereby often learning, literacy in rather different ways from those traditionally identified with the school classroom.

LITERACY IN EVERYDAY LIFE: EVIDENCE FROM RESEARCH WITH ADULT USERS AND LEARNERS OF LITERACY SURVEY

Research studies of adult literacy and numeracy typically find a mismatch between test scores and self-reports about learning needs, with individuals claiming to experience fewer problems with everyday literacy and numeracy than the test results suggest they should (see, e.g., Bynner & Steedman, 1995; Bynner & Parsons, 1997; Organization of Economic Co-Operation and Development, 2000). How are these differences to be explained? It was this question in part that led me to be interested in carrying out more qualitative, ethnographic studies of literacy and numeracy uses in everyday life.

The "Local Literacies" project has been a detailed study of the role of literacy in the everyday lives of people in Lancaster, England, and was reported by Barton and Hamilton (1998) and elsewhere. This was a project, funded by the Economic and Social Research Council, that lasted several years. The study used in-depth interviews complemented by observations, photography, and a collection of documents and records. It included a door-to-door survey in one neighborhood of Lancaster and detailed case studies of people in 12 households in the neighborhood, observing particular literacy events and asking people to reflect on their practices. Alongside the case studies were 30 interviews of people in what we called "access points" for literacy, such as bookshops, libraries, and advice centers. There were also interviews of 20 adults who had identified problems with their reading and writing and had been attending courses at the adult college. More than a year after the main part of the study, in a phase called the "Collaborative Ethnography" project, we took back transcripts of interviews and drafts of our interpretative themes to 10 of the people for further discussion. This discussion generated further data, as people elaborated and commented on the information they had given in the original interviews.

In Lancaster we have explored a small town, within which there are some close-knit, long-standing communities with multiple overlapping ties and concerns. There are also groups and individuals whose identities are not so closely anchored to one locality, who come and go and maintain relationships in a number of different communities outside of Lancaster.

There are enclaves of highly educated and geographically mobile people but a great majority who are, based on the evidence from our ethnography, still on the edges of accessing new technologies and their transformative potential. The United Kingdom has a population still highly differentiated in their access to and attitudes toward new technologies. Many older people may never move far into this new world. Many of their children will do so, to an extent unimaginable to their parents.

The literacy project we carried out in Lancaster investigated uses of reading and writing rather than taking "learning" as a starting point. Nevertheless, it can tell us a great deal that is relevant to learning issues: about the role of networks in sharing information and supporting new uses of literacy, the flexible use of different media to accomplish everyday goals, people's motivations for learning new literacies; their identities in relation to literacy; and the shifting uses of literacy across domains and across the life span that lead to new practices constantly being introduced.

Our own study built on the earlier work of Shirley Brice Heath (1983), Brian Street (1984), and Denny Taylor and Dorsey-Gaines (1988). Since we began this study, a number of other learning ethnographies have been published, especially in the United States. These include Victoria Purcell-Gates's *Other People's Words* (1995), Juliet Merrifield and her colleagues' book *Lives on the Margins* (Merrifield, Bingham, Hemphill, & de Marrais, 1997); Wendy Luttell's (1997) *School Smart, Mother Wise*, and Hannah Fingeret's and Cassie Drennan's (1997) *Literacy for Living*. In our study, (Barton & Hamilton, 1998) we proposed a typology of everyday literacies that we had observed: *organizing life* (e.g., using appointment calendars, paying bills, and responding to official letters), *personal communication* (e.g., sending and receiving greetings, condolences, and love letters), *private leisure* (e.g., pursuing hobbies, being a fan, reading for relaxation), *documenting life* (e.g., keeping a diary, collecting souvenirs and family histories), *sense making* (e.g., pursuing information to solve a problem posed by life circumstances, such as illness, or developing religious or spiritual understandings), and *social participation* (e.g., working with others to effect changes though self-help or community or political groups). In all of these areas, we found examples of people becoming expert in particular uses of literacy, consciously carrying out their own research on a topic of interest to them.

VERNACULAR AND INSTITUTIONAL LITERACIES

Ethnographies of literacy turn up many and diverse practices, but not all literacies are equal. We apply a hierarchy of values to them. Some we consider real, proper, or serious; others are considered marginal, trivial, or inappropriate. To account for this hierarchy in our study of local literacies we used the idea of vernacular and institutional literacies, a distinction based on the sociolinguistic notion of *vernacular* (mother tongue) and official languages used in public life. This distinction enabled us to start thinking about issues of power and unequal social relations in literacy practices and how these affect what we value and devalue. It was an attempt to characterize the learning that takes place outside of formal institutions where the roles people take on, the goals and procedures of literacy activities are often fluid and not explicitly named.

The concept of the *vernacular* is well established in the sociolinguistic literature as referring to mother-tongue languages or regional variants of the spoken language that are not supported in the public domains of schooling, government, media, and the legal system. Our notion of vernacular literacies is meant to capture something of the same distinction. It has a parallel with Jim Gee's (1990) notion of *primary* and *secondary discourses*. Gee referred to a *primary discourse* as the one first learned by the child at home, whereas *secondary discourses* are those encountered later in public domains, such as school. Our distinction also has parallels with Habermas's (1987) notion of the "lifeworld" and the "system" and at its root describes interactions with written texts from the perspective of the everyday understandings and purposes of individuals and collectives, rather than from the perspectives of the institutions that often generate and impose literacy practices. Of particular importance is the notion of *lifeworlds*, where we need a critique of educational programs and policies that are heavily focused on developing a narrow, system-oriented view of literacy and do not acknowledge the lifeworlds of learners that exist beyond their own boundaries. The distinction enabled us to think about how literacy gets patterned and organized by formal institutions, including educational ones, and how some forms of literacy become privileged over others.

We identified the characteristics of vernacular literacies. First, vernacular literacy practices are learned informally. They are acquired in homes and neighborhood groups, through the everyday perplexities and curiosities of our lives. The roles of novice or learner and expert or teacher are not fixed but shift from context to context, and there is an acceptance that people will engage in vernacular literacies in different ways, sometimes supporting, sometimes requiring support from others. Identities shift accordingly.

Second, the vernacular literacy practices we identified are rooted in action contexts and everyday purposes and networks. They draw on and contribute to vernacular knowledge, which is often local, procedural, and minutely detailed. Literacy learning and use are integrated into everyday activities, and the literacy elements are an implicit part of the activity, which may be mastering a martial art, paying the bills, organizing a musical event, or finding out about local news. Literacy itself is not a focus of attention, but is used to get other things done. Everyday literacies are subservient to the goals of purposeful activities and are defined by people in terms of these activities.

Specialisms develop in everyday contexts and are different from the formal academic disciplines, reflecting the logic of practical application. Vernacular literacies are as diverse as social practices. They are hybrid in nature, and often it is clear that a particular activity may be classified in more than one way, because people may have a mixture of motives for taking part in a given literacy activity. Preparing a residents' association newsletter, for instance, can be a social activity, or it can be part of a leisure or political activity, and it may involve personal sense making. Such an activity is part of a "do-it-yourself" culture that incorporates whatever materials and resources are available and combines them in novel ways, making do and working around practical constraints (see de Certeau, 1984, for a much more detailed discussion of this idea). Spoken language, print, and other media are integrated; literacy is integrated with other symbolic systems, such as numeracy and visual semiotics. Different topics and activities can occur together, making it hard to identify the boundaries of a single literacy event or practice. This is in contrast to many school practices, where learning is separated from use and divided into academically defined subject areas, disciplines, and specialisms, and where knowledge is often made explicit within particular interactive routines, is reflected on, and is open to evaluation through the testing of disembedded skills.

Many of the Lancaster people we interviewed had experienced situations in their day-to-day lives that had motivated them to develop a specialized expertise and launched them into a new area of learning in which they mustered all the resources they could find, including literacy. Often these activities involve encounters with social institutions and dealing with professionals, ways of communicating, acting, and understanding that were quite alien to people's previous experience. Literacy is a key tool for interacting with these institutions and to have access to the knowledge they control.

Deliberate investigations of unknown topics included those to do with *ill health*, where people became expert in the treatment and understanding of particular ailments, and encounters with schools, where *parents* were acting as advocates on behalf of their children and dealing with educational systems that they found quite mystifying and opaque. There were a number of examples in our data related to *employment-related* problems, such as searching for and applying for jobs, dealing with official bureaucracy when registering as unemployed, claiming welfare benefit entitlements or tax refunds; and setting up small businesses. Another common group of practical problems are *legal problems*, involving encounters with the police, courts, and insurance companies. A variety of legal problems and consumer grievances arise for individuals at different stages of their lives, and sometimes more general issues affect large groups of people, as in disputes over land ownership and use. In these cases, people may act together to pool resources and develop new kinds of expertise.

As well as these short-term responses to urgent practical needs, people have preoccupations and pastimes, which they pursue over lengthy periods, including quests for information about family history, correspondences, and leisure activities of various sorts. These lead to a wide variation in what people know about, and it is revealing to look across a community to investigate the types of vernacular knowledge that exist. In Lancaster, the areas of vernacular knowledge that we have identified include home economics and budgeting, repair and maintenance, child care, sports, gardening, cooking, pets and animal care, and family and local history. Some people had also developed knowledge of legal, political, health, and medical topics.

UNDERSTANDING COMMUNITY
AND INFORMAL LEARNING

In going beyond a descriptive account of these ethnographic findings, I have found it is important to link up with wider theories of the everyday, particularly to make connections with theories of learning that might be able to illuminate what we have found. Traditional theories about community or informal learning are built on individualized notions of adult learning (see, e.g., Knowles, 1979; Merriam & Cafferella, 1991; Rogers & Freiberg, 1993; Tough, 1982). These theories have been extremely important in identifying the experiential dimensions of learning and the power of reflection in the learning cycle (Boud, Keogh, & Walker, 1998; Kolb, 1984; Schön, 1983). They make important distinctions, such as that between tacit and propositional learning (Eraut, 1994, 2000), where *tacit knowledge* comprises the taken-for-granted assumptions embedded in action, whereas *propositional knowledge* is explicitly encoded in verbal or other symbolic systems.

Recently, new waves of theorizing have incorporated a more social perspective into ideas of learning. In particular, the notion of *situated learning* has shifted the focus from the individual learner to the communities of practice within which learning happens (Lave & Wenger, 1991; Wenger, 1998). Learning is seen in terms of initiation into a community of practice involving apprenticelike relationships between expert and novice members of that community. Learning and change are therefore inherently social processes, intimately tied up with formation of identities, communication, and developing common understandings and meanings (see also Holland, Lachicotte, Skinner, & Cain, 1998). In addition, those engaged in looking at the informal aspects of organizational learning (see Blackler,

1995; Gherardi, Nicolini, & Odella, 1998) have noted the many aspects of learning beyond cognition, including the emotional and social dimensions that are integral to it.

In short, when we review these related areas we discover that the new literacy studies are just one part of a growing recognition that learning and "knowing" is not simply the product of individualized skills and understandings but a relational, social process. Neither is knowing simply a cognitive matter; it simultaneously involves other modes of engaging with the world. We can, for example, identify at least the following four types of knowing (adapted from Blackler, 1995): (a) *embodied knowing* is experiential and action oriented, dependent on peoples' physical presence, on sensory processes, physical cues, and may be only partially explicit; (b) *symbolic knowing* is mediated by conceptual understandings that are explicit, propositional, and encoded through a variety of semiotic technologies (spoken language and other symbol systems, print and electronic communications); (c) *embedded knowing* is procedural, shaped, or ingrained by practical routines that are configurations of material, technological, and social symbolic resources through which knowing is accomplished; and (d) *encultured knowing* is the use of the shared understandings that are achieved through social relationships and initiation into communities of practice. Some of these modes of knowing are more explicit, abstract, and portable; some are much more closely tied to physical localities and individual subjectivities and vary enormously in the relative value that is accorded to them in different contexts. However, they are all present and affect eventual outcomes.

DEVELOPING PRACTICE IN ADULT LITERACY

How can we build on community and informal learning in developing practice in adult literacy? This part of the chapter is not intended to offer a recipe. It is, rather, a challenge to you as the reader to engage with the ideas presented here and to go beyond them. The challenge (at least in the United Kingdom at the present time) is to turn around perceptions of what literacy is and to do this by helping people (all of us) to reflect on our own practices, to see ourselves as learners and users of literacy in a changing society and through our changing biographies. There is a crucial role for new vocabularies and discourses of literacy. I have three immediate suggestions as to how we might build on community and informal learning in developing practice in adult literacy:

> 1. Carry out ethnographies of literacy with learners that enable mutual reflection on the literacy practices of the group, including the teachers themselves. This is the first way to make an opening for "ver-

nacular practices" to enter the classroom or learning group, as Shirley Brice Heath suggested many years ago (see the final chapters of Heath, 1983). In programs at Lancaster, we are beginning to experiment with ways of doing this with a range of learners (see David Barton's chapter in Barton, Hamilton, & Ivanic, 2000) for an example of this.

2. Pay attention to the social relations and organizational contexts of learning (including those of schooling) and how these can help or hinder learning, how they match or are mismatched to the community contexts to which learners belong.

3. Acknowledge the many dimensions of learning—and the multiple ways of expressing these through the different media available to us as educators. Be broad in interpreting what *literacy* means and help learners connect across their experiences of different media and to capitalize on their strengths.

There are already a number of projects in which these ideas are being tried out. Comparing these experiences will be an important next stage for working out how theory can meet practice. Some references to projects with which I am familiar with are given in the Appendix. They include the "Read on Write Away!" project, which works through a partnership of many local community groups and services to embed literacy in the ongoing concerns of learners, and a recent project in Nepal, where a variety of literacy support systems have been established only after an extensive audit of literacy practices and needs among local people.

UNSOLVED ISSUES FOR INFORMAL LEARNING AND A SOCIAL PRACTICE THEORY OF LITERACY

Although we have learned a great deal already from looking at the uses and learning of literacies outside of school, important issues remain for further study and theorizing. The following are just two:

1. What is the relationship between the vernacular and forms of literacy supported and demanded by formal institutions? As a starting point, the distinction between *vernacular* and *institutional knowing* has been useful, but it needs to be further developed, especially in terms of the dialogic relationship between the two, how the one influences and articulates the other. The polarity between dominant and vernacular literacies was a useful heuristic for developing our thinking when we wrote 'Local Literacies' (Barton & Hamilton, 1998). The relationship between them is actually a complex one that needs to be further conceptualized. It is certainly not the case that vernacular literacies can be imported unproblematically into classroom activities, because this recontextualizes them and thereby changes their meaning.

2. What is the nature of informal learning a at different stages of the life cycle? For example, how does such learning vary between younger and older people, what are the strengths and weaknesses, possibilities and limitations, of vernacular learning strategies at these different ages and stages, in terms of willingness to take risks, breadth of experience, and so on? This is especially important to understand in terms of promoting community development and political participation. A range of representation is needed not just for social justice reasons but because different sections of the community offer the potential contributions of different strengths and a balance of resources. Similarly, what is the nature of informal learning in different domains of social activity? How does such learning manifest itself in the workplace or the domains of religious or community activity? In social action groups? How does informal learning vary within and between different community settings and structures, especially where the nature of social networks is different? Some communities are more dispersed; others have deeply embedded and stable networks reaching back into generations. Some are riven with conflicts or disrupted through war or migration. We need a much better characterization of these community types, the corresponding social capital to which they have access, and how this affects possibilities for informal learning. Finally, how does informal learning interact with changing technologies? We have the possibility of researching the impact of new computer technologies and many examples already of how the Internet reveals the submerged iceberg of informal learning practices in relation to literacy. Some examples include the huge popularity of family history Web sites, many self-help groups, and innumerable Web sites created by fans of popular culture, that include extensive writing, posting of personal written diaries on the Web, and accounts of day-to-day life through video diaries (see Lankshear & Knobel, 2001). Such examples attest not only to the ways in which new technologies are mobilized by people to support their existing day-to-day activities and literacy practices but also to how these technologies can extend these practices through the new opportunities they give for communicating.

CONCLUSION

I hope that I have been able to convey my excitement about the new insights that research into everyday literacies is able to contribute to educational practice. I hope also to have given a sense that this is still a new endeavor that has identified many questions that remain to be resolved. This chapter is intended as an invitation to readers—especially teachers of literacy—to engage with these ideas and questions and to join in the process of creating more effective and more inclusive ways of understanding and working with literacy learners of all ages.

REFERENCES

Barton, D. (2000). Researching literacy practices. In D. Barton, M. Hamilton, & R. Ivanic (Eds.), *Situated literacies* (pp. 167–179). London: Routledge.

Barton, D., & Hamilton, M. (1998). *Local literacies: Reading and writing in one community*. London: Routledge.

Barton, D., Hamilton, M., & Ivanic, R. (Eds.). (2000). *Situated literacies*. London: Routledge.

Blackler, F. (1995). Knowledge, knowledge work and organizations: An overview and Interpretation. *Organizational Studies, 16,* 1021–1046.

Boud, D., Keogh, R., & Walker, D. (1998). *Reflection: Turning experience into learning.* London: Kogan Page.

Bynner, J., & Parsons, S. (1997). *It doesn't get any better.* London: Basic Skills Agency.

Bynner, J., & Steedman, J. (1995). *Difficulties with adult basic skills.* London: Basic Skills Agency.

de Certeau, M. (1984). *The practice of everyday life.* Los Angeles: University of California Press.

Eraut, M. (1994). *Developing professional knowledge and competence.* Lewes, UK: Falmer.

Eraut, M. (2000). Non-formal learning and tacit knowledge in professional work. *British Journal of Educational Psychology, 7,* 113–136.

Fingeret, H., & Drennan, C. (1997). *Literacy for life: Adult learners, new practices.* New York: Teachers College Press.

Gee, J. (1990). *Social linguistics and literacies: Ideology in discourses.* Lewes, UK: Falmer.

Gherardi, S., Nicolini, D., & Odella, F. (1998). Toward a social understanding of how people learn in organizations: The notion of situated curriculum. *Management Learning, 29,* 273–297.

Habermas, J. (1987). *The theory of communicative action: Vol. 2. Lifeworld and system: A critique of functionalist reason.* London: Heinemann.

Hamilton, M. (2000). Using media photographs to explore literacy as social practice. In D. Barton, M. Hamilton, & R. Ivanic (Eds.), *Situated literacies* (pp. 16–34). London: Routledge.

Heath, S. B. (1983). *Ways with words.* New York: Cambridge University Press.

Holland, D., Lachicotte, W. S., Skinner, D., & Cain, C. (1998). *Identity and agency in cultural worlds.* Cambridge, MA: Harvard University Press.

Hull, G., & Schultz, K. (2001). Literacy and learning out of school: A review of theory and practice. *Review of Educational Research, 71,* 575–611.

Knobel, M., & Lankshear, C. (2002). Cut, paste, and publish: The production and consumption of zines. In D. Alvermann (Ed.), *New literacies and digital technologies: A focus on adolescent learners.* New York: Peter Lang.

Knowles, M. S. (1979). *Androgogy in action: Applying modern principles of adult learning.* San Francisco: Jossey-Bass.

Kolb, D. A. (1984). *Experiential learning: Experience as the source of learning and development.* Englewood Cliffs, NJ: Prentice Hall.

Kress, G., & Van Leeuwen, T. (1996). *Reading images: The grammar of visual design.* London: Routledge.

Lave, J., & Wenger, E. (1991). *Situated learning: Legitimate peripheral participation.* Cambridge, England: Cambridge University Press.

Luttrell, W. (1997). *School smart motherwise: Working class women's identity and schooling.* New York: Routledge.

Merriam, S. B., & Cafferella, R. S. (1991). *Learning in adulthood.* San Francisco: Jossey-Boss.

Merrifield, J., Bingham, M. B., Hemphill, D., de Marrais, K. (1997). *Life at the margins: Literacy, language and technology in everyday life.* New York: Teachers College Press.

Organization of Economic Co-Operation and Development. (2000). *Literacy in the information age.* Paris: Author.

Purcell-Gates, V. (1995). *Other people's words: The cycle of low literacy.* Cambridge, MA: Harvard University Press.

Rogers, C., & Freiberg, H. J. (1993). *Freedom to learn* (3rd ed.). New York: Merrill.

Schön, D. A. (1983). *The reflective practitioner: How professionals think in action.* New York: Basic Books.

Street, B. V. (1984). *Literacy in theory and practice.* Cambridge, England: Cambridge University Press.

Street, B.V. (1995). *Social literacies: Critical approaches to literacy in development, ethnography and education.* London: Longman.

Taylor, D., & Dorsey-Gaines, C. (1988). *Growing up literate: Learning from inner-city families.* Portsmouth, NH: Heinemann.

Tough, A. M. (1982). *Intentional changes.* Chicago: Follett.

Wenger, E. (1998). *Communities of practice: Learning, meaning and identities.* Cambridge, England: Cambridge University Press.

APPENDIX

Web Sites and Resources for Projects Referred to in the Chapter

The evaluation report of the Read on Write Away! (ROWA!) project has now been published and can be ordered from the Director, Read On Write Away!, c/o County Hall, Matlock, Derbyshire DE4 3AG. The ROWA! Web site, with information on its projects, is http://www.rowa.co.uk/

Information about this and other partnership projects going on in the United Kingdom can be found on the National Literacy Trust Web site: http://www.literacytrust.org.uk/. Searching on their site for *ROWA* produces a result called "cross-sector literacy partnerships -case studies," and ROWA! is described here along with other projects that might be of interest.

The Web site for the Nepal project is www.eddev.org/Hosted/clpn or, if the URL will not work, their e-mail is clrc@wlink.com.np (address it to the information officer there). The contact person is Dr. Anna Robinson-Pant, Centre for Applied Research in Education, School of Education and Professional Development, University of East Anglia, Norwich NR4 7TJ. E-mail: a.robinson-pant@uea.ac.uk

III

Changing Literacy Practices

9

Literacy and Diversity: Challenges of Change

Seok Moi Ng
Faculty of Education, University of Auckland, New Zealand

The term *literacy* has been increasingly extended to include domains other than reading and writing. There is now talk of *mathematical literacy, media literacy, musical literacy, computer literacy*, and so on. Janks (1997, p. 249) observed that the concept of multiliteracies "deprivileges the print-based verbal sign and makes way for oracies, visual semiotics, multimodal literacies." In a discussion of electronic literacy, Topping (1997) predicted that traditional skills of reading and writing are likely to lose their place in today's world of advanced technology, with many new ways of disseminating knowledge through interactive multimedia services. He hypothesized that basic literacy skills may not be relevant when a computer can transform speech directly into writing and that, one day very soon, books may be cherished as antiques and people will forget what they were used for.

However, there is still a lot of information in print, and this vast amount of information is not accessible to the nonreader either through a standard or electronic format. For now and into the foreseeable future, increasing levels of print literacy are required to tap into the mass of information afforded by computer technology and to cope with the daily demands of society. For a start, imagine the literacy skills required to read newspapers, tax returns, traffic manuals for drivers, mail-order catalogs, and insurance policies and rental agreements, not to mention e-mails, computer manuals (and the accompanying software), and ways of dealing with new computer viruses. Reading has, to date, remained the foundation of basic education and the main tool for independent learning throughout the world. This is particularly true of highly literate societies, but even for developing countries, there is a growing international recognition of literacy's direct benefit. International agencies like Rotary International are standing alongside the United Nations Educational, Scientific, and Cultural Organization to make basic literacy a priority on their agendas in parts of Africa and Asia, where there is a great need for basic necessities, such as food, clean water, and adequate health care.

Reading has been the most researched of school subjects in countries like the United States, with thousands of research studies and scholarly discussions conducted since the turn of the century. One of the International Reading Association publications, *The Reading Teacher*, published nearly 3,000 articles on reading in its first 20 years (Larrick, 1992). International comparison studies, such as the recent Organization for Economic Cooperation and Development Programme for International Student Assessment, have always measured reading alongside mathematics and science (Organization for Economic Cooperation and Development, 2000). This last study, similar in scope to a previous one (Elley, 1992; Lundberg & Linnakyla, 1993), surveyed the reading achievements of some 265,000 schoolchildren in 32 countries ("PISA survey," 2002). In the following sections I explore some of the issues that have dominated the literacy field and discuss some reasons for the dominance of reading in educational research.

EMERGENT LITERACY

Emergent literacy has continued to receive a fair amount of attention from reading educators (Cassidy & Cassidy, 2002; Pearson, 1992), partly because of research evidence indicating that failure in early literacy can limit school achievement. Studies have found that children reading at the lowest levels in early grades generally continued to read at lowest levels in later grades, whereas those reading at average or above-average levels in early grades tended to continue to read well over time (Clay, 1991; Juel, 1988). There are also longitudinal studies indicating that disadvantaged third graders who have failed one or more grades are extremely unlikely to complete high school (Kelly, Veldman, & McGuire, 1964; Lloyd, 1978). This means that children's achievement at the end of their first year in school predicts with alarming accuracy who will succeed and who will fail in school. Children who can't read grow into adults who can't read, and the costs of low literacy levels can be high, not only for the individuals but also for society (Benseman, 1989; Hartley, 1989; Johnston, 1985; McGill-Franzen & Allington, 1991; Slavin, Karweit, & Wasik, 1992).

Interest in emergent literacy has been accompanied by a lot of controversy about the best instructional methods. Although early studies (Auckerman, 1971; Bond & Dykstra, 1967) found that there is no single superior method, the American field has traditionally divided itself into two main camps: (a) those who advocate direct instruction of skills, particularly those related to letter–sound correspondences (commonly referred to as *phonics instruction*) and (b) those who favor more holistic (and often more natural) methods. American educators have continued to argue about the best way to introduce reading to children (Adams, 1990; Adams et al., 1991; Anderson, Hiebert, Scott & Wilkinson, 1985; Shanahan, 2002).

Recently, there appears to have been some resolution, and a position paper from the International Reading Association (1999) recommended balanced instruction. It seems logical that beginners receive instruction in word identification skills and letter–sound correspondences, because English is an alphabetic language in which there are many consistent, although not entirely regular, relationships between letters and sounds. Knowing the sound of a word however, is only part of reading; the reader needs to know the meaning of the words that he or she is sounding out.

Therefore, although phonics instruction is important, it is insufficient for full reading and language development. The smaller bits of language, such as letters, words, and their spelling patterns, are only one part of the total body of linguistic information with which the learner must come to grips. Even in the simple stories of early language lessons there are other important language features, including plot and dramatic effect, sequence of events, climax and endings, the many meanings contained in the story, sentence structures, discourse, layout, and other print features. Although some researchers have maintained that the larger features should be delayed for later instruction, others claim that if the child does not also have some understanding of the larger features from the beginning, language learning will be more difficult. The claim is based on an observation that letters and individual words do not have much meaning by themselves and are thus more difficult to learn. They should be easier to learn when set in the context of larger meaningful units such as sentences and stories. In any case, learning a language and learning to read involve more than merely knowing letters and their corresponding sounds, and it is to some of the more global aspects of literacy that I turn next.

COMPUTER LITERACY AND INFORMATION LITERACY

There is a lot of confusion about the relationship and role of technology in education. For example, in New Zealand, much of the discussion about information communication technology in the mass media is about allocating physical resources and machines (Skerman, Billany, Just, & Stove, 2000).

Likewise in Britain, many discussions focus on the technical level, for example, whether one equipment brand is better than another (Conlon, 2000). Findings from some studies challenge the assumption that the provision of and access to new technology will necessarily mean that teachers and students are able to use it effectively (M. Brown, 1995; Knapp & Glenn, 1996; Matthew, 1996; Reinking, 1997; Topping, 1997). Likewise, many are confused about the roles of information literacy and computer literacy in education.

Gawith (1992), once the New Zealand national coordinator of information studies, made the following distinction between computer literacy and information literacy: Computer literacy involves the technological skills for using computers, wordprocessing, interactive fiction, and creating simple databases; information literacy, however, is the ability to retrieve, process, and produce information effectively for independent lifelong learning. To work with information, students may use computers or other technologies, but the key processes are cognitive ones, directed by the brain, not by technology. The cognitive skills Gawith identified as important for dealing with the enormous amount of information are (a) deciding on the information needed in view of existing knowledge; (b) locating information sources and resources; (c) using information selectively, analytically, and critically, recording and organizing relevant information; (d) presenting information using relevant media; and (e) evaluating the process formatively and summatively.

It is well recognized that students pick up technological aspects faster than their teachers do. Toddlers exposed to technological tools can fast become adept users of scanners and webcams while their parents are still figuring out where the "on" button is. What is more difficult to develop are thinking skills and cognitive processes that deal with ideas, not merely information, because information only becomes knowledge once a person constructs new understandings from the information (M. Brown, 1995). Like the United States, Singapore has invested heavily in providing its schools with technological equipment such as computers. At the same time, Singapore also pushed strongly for the promotion of cognitive development in the school curricula (Baumfield, 1997; Chua & Leong, 1997). The country adopted the slogan "Thinking nation, thinking schools" in the 1990s. Since then, the education reforms have involved experimentation with thinking programs, with an aim of teaching children how to think and to apply the knowledge and skills they acquire to deal with ideas, to evaluate and extend them and to adapt them to new uses for the country's development, survival, and success (Ministry of Education, Singapore, 2001).

LITERACY AND THINKING SKILLS

Thinking skills are no strangers to literacy research; cognitive processes involved in literacy have been researched intensively in the last few decades

(Farstrup & Samuels, 2002; Pearson, 1992; Pressley et al., 1992; Pressley et al., 1995; Ruddell & Ruddell, 1994; Tierney, Readence, & Dishner, 1990). This is a well-established field, sometimes subsumed under content area of reading and reading comprehension (see, e.g., Vacca, 2002). As a result of this research, reading educators have developed and validated specific cognitive strategies, such as question generation or summarization, that students could use to help improve their reading comprehension. Examples can be found in the well-known teaching techniques of retelling (H. Brown & Cambourne, 1987), reciprocal questioning (King, 1990), and KWL (Ogle & Blachowicz, 2002; Olson & Gee, 1991). *KWL*, the *K*now, *W*ant to know, and *L*earn strategies, include brainstorming, categorization of ideas, generating questions before reading, and reviewing after reading. In other areas, such as writing, students are taught to use "think sheets" that contain a number of prompts that students can use to help them organize their thinking and revise their writing (Pressley et al., 1995).

An international project, coordinated by the Open Society Institute and the International Reading Association, contains many of these teaching strategies. Operating in 20 countries of central and eastern Europe and the former Soviet Union, the Reading and Writing for Critical Thinking methods are also designed to help students think reflectively; take ownership of their personal learning; understand the logic of arguments; listen attentively; debate confidently; and become independent, lifelong learners (Cretu, 2000; Markuckiene, 2000). These goals reflect the trend of linking thinking skills to language and of the growing interest in metacognitive skills.

Metacognition refers to people's knowledge about their cognitive resources, about task demands, and about strategies required to perform a task (Paris, Lipson, & Wixson, 1983). In developing metacognitive skills, the emphasis is on getting students to take responsibility for their own learning, to reflect on and regulate their own thinking processes (e.g., Chamot & O'Malley, 1994; Dickinson & Carver, 1980; Donhower, 1999; Pereira-Laird & Deane, 1997; Wenden, 1997). There is a keen interest in metacognitive skills because of a New Age demand for reasoning using higher order thinking skills. Applied to reading, metacognitive strategies are used to help individuals comprehend what they read, to plan and monitor what they read, to evaluate, and to know when and how to use particular strategies to improve reading comprehension (Currie, 1999). An example is the application of think-alouds that can be used by young children. Baumann, Jones, and Seifert-Kessell (1993) developed some simple procedures for teaching students to think aloud during reading as a way of helping them monitor reading comprehension and to work on comprehension breakdowns. The procedures involved strategies that included "asking questions, drawing on prior knowledge, assessing comprehension by asking, 'Is this making sense?' predicting and verifying, inferring unstated ideas, retelling, and reading on to clarify meaning"(p. 187).

Educators working in this field point out that cognitive and metacognitive strategies are not direct procedures to be followed precisely; instead, those strategies are heuristics: They support or facilitate learners as they develop internal procedures that enable them to perform the higher level operations. Teaching students to generate questions about their reading is an example of a cognitive strategy. Generating questions does not directly lead, in a step-by-step manner, to comprehension; rather, in the process of generating questions, students need to search the text and combine information, and these processes help students comprehend what they read. Teaching arrangements for developing thinking and metacognitive skills require a democratic environment that will be difficult to develop if the teacher adopts traditional didactic and prescriptive approaches to classroom teaching.

Despite the many studies about cognition and metacognition, teaching practices have not caught up with research findings. For example, it has been noted that reading comprehension instruction is not widely taught in the United States (Pressley & Wharton-McDonald, 1998). Educational improvement does not come easy; I discuss this further in the last sections of this chapter.

CRITICAL LITERACY

The study of *critical literacy* involves an analysis of what literacy is, an evaluative perspective of text and wider social practices, arrangements, and power relations that are mediated by literacy practices (Lankshear, Gee, Knobel, & Searle, 1997; Luke, 2000; Muspratt, Luke & Freebody, 1997; Wallace, 1992). Janks (1997) used the term *critical language awareness* as an umbrella term for different positions of critical literacy proponents. She identified the main goal of its study as making students aware that linguistic structures and forms are not neutral communication tools but are situated in social practices. Students are encouraged to examine language with questions such as "Whose interests are served by the way language is used? Who benefits? Who loses?"

One school of thought bases its critical-literacy work on systemic functional linguistics, criticizing traditional teaching practices as being narrowly focused on certain texts (e.g., literary narratives) and thus failing to provide students with explicit knowledge of how particular genres of intellectual and political power work. Six dominant genres (e.g., reports and exposition) are identified, and the proponents maintain that the scrutiny and construction of such texts raises awareness and gives mastery of genres in order for increased access to the dominant culture (Halliday & Martin,

1996). Others, such as Luke (2000), argue that having students understand and construct the dominant genres will only maintain their dominance and that of the dominant culture. Luke wants to go further and have students challenge the social conditions that uphold the use and practice of dominant genres and so lead to the construction of new texts and genres.

There is general agreement amongst the different theorists that development and use of critical literacy knowledge and skills are based on an equity and social justice agenda (Janks, 1997). This agenda is similar to that of other cultural critics who claim that the vital questions of the Information Age are not those related to the efficiency with which technology can improve literacy learning. They would ask fundamentally different questions of technology in language education: whether it is altering our conception of learning, whether it undermines social practices and relations, and whether it changes our conception of reality or the power relationship between the "haves" and "have-nots." Others argue that these very issues should be the fundamentals of all educational endeavor (see, e.g., Forester, 1992; Hawisher & Selfe, 1996; Oppenheimer, 1997; Postman, 1993, for a fuller discussion of these issues). The marginalization of diverse minority groups and the unequal distribution of power within economic and social groups have continued to plague both traditional and computer-supported literacy classrooms.

DIVERSITY IN THE CLASSROOMS

Cultural diversity confronts the individual as the world becomes increasingly smaller in the global village. Robertson (1981), a social psychologist, remarked on the different foods we eat: "Americans eat oysters but not snails. The French eat snails but not locusts. The Zulus eat locusts but not fish. The Jews eat fish but not pork. The Hindus eat pork but not beef. The Russians eat beef but not snakes. The Chinese eat snakes but not people. The Jale of New Guinea find people delicious" (p. 63).

Cultural differences affect myriad other behaviors—we differ in what we drink, how we dress and behave, what we believe, and the way we use language. This point is strikingly illustrated in a study of classroom discourse in a section of San Diego, one of the cities ranked lowest in terms of income and school achievement in the United States, with a high proportion of African American and Mexican American children in the first three grades (Cazden, 1988). The initial observation, supported in a follow-up experimental study, was that there was a difference in the way diverse groups responded to some of the children's stories related during sharing time, when children were allowed to talk for some length of time. The White adults responded rather negatively to a story told by a Black child, with remarks such as "terrible story, incoherent," and "this kid hops from one thing to the next" (Cazden, 1988, p. 18). The child's academic standing was rated as low. In contrast, the Black adults' reaction to the same story was very different. They found the story "well formed, easy to understand, and interesting with lots of detail and description," and the child was rated as very bright (Cazden, 1988, p. 18)!

Cazden (1988) argued that different cultures have different ways of telling a story and that there could be a "cultural mismatch between the narrative themes and styles of the children and the knowledge and expectations of their white teachers" (p. 17). Surface manifestations of cultural differences may evoke interest and amusement or feelings of discomfort, but this study has more serious implications: The impact of teachers' responses to children's different narrative styles can either restrict or foster children's language growth (Cazden, 2001). The sum effect of negative responses can prevent children from using their own effective ways of learning and from using language from their home background; it can also reduce children's opportunities for developing language in school. The cumulative effect of appreciation or disapproval was found in several other examples in this study, indicating that cultural differences can have profound influences on literacy development (see also Delpit, 1988).

CULTURAL DIFFERENCES: SOCIAL CLASS

Students can differ in one or more dimensions of ethnicity, nationality, socioeconomic status, language, age, sexual orientation, and so on. There has been a strong interest in social class as a significant factor for the generation of educational differences in education.

In a New Zealand study of almost 1,400 families with children aged between 5 and 15, Nash and Harker (1992) explored processes they believed are responsible for differential achievement of children from different social class origins. They obtained a scale based on occupations of both marital partners, ranging from professional to working class. They were interested in a family's level of involvement with the products of "a culture of literacy and its associated class-marked preferences for textual and broadcast media" (Nash & Harker, 1992, p. 6).

In brief, their study shows that the level of production and consumption of literacy varies in the different social classes. Take the working class for example: Literacy does not occupy a prominent position in working-class families, especially those in manual occupations where little reading is required:

> Working class men ... often say that they are too busy to find time to read for pleasure ... As for their children, working class families recognise the need for them to have access to books but often believe that, given a home encyclopedia, the public library and the school can meet their needs. There is little sense

that reading should be developed as a habit and rarely are children able to acquire that habit from their parents' example … reading is only rarely demonstrated to their children as an integral part of family life. Not only is literacy
not central—it is often barely even peripheral. As one mother replied to our
question whether she read much herself (she has told us of the care she took to
listen to her child's school-set reading), "Oh, no, I've got no patience for reading myself." (Nash & Harker, 1992, pp. 16–17)

In contrast, professionals need to be in regular contact with the professional literature to meet the demands of their employment. Reading occu-
pies not only a great deal of professionals' lives at work but also at home,
where literacy is valued and practiced. Professionals appear to deliberately
develop in their children a reading habit and "even an actual sense of joy in
language" (Nash & Harker, 1992, p. 14). The literacy activities found in
Nash and Harker's (1992) professional homes are similar to those found for
children who are early readers. A well-known group of literacy studies has
identified home variables important for fostering early reading success and
engagement with reading as a leisure pursuit (see, e.g., Guthrie & Greaney,
1991; Teale, 1984; Teale & Sulzby, 1987). The main variables found included
the following: (1) Children with early experience with books tend to have
an increased interest in reading and begin to read early. (2) These children
also have a ready access to books. (3) They are more likely to have books of
their own. (4) There is regular provision of space and opportunity for reading in the home. (5) Parents of enthusiastic readers are those who are more
likely to set aside time for reading themselves, thus acting as models.

Other studies have attempted to identify the key factor for success. From
an in-depth longitudinal study of 32 families, Wells (1985, 1987) concluded
that, of all the preliteracy activities monitored, the mere act of listening to
stories at home bore a strong correlation with children's reading success at
age 7. More recently, evidence was found of another useful literacy activity:
adult–child conversations about past events in children's personal lives
(Reese, 1995).

Early success in literacy skills could mean a cumulative advantage for
vocabulary growth and skill development—the "rich get richer" phenomenon. Researchers (Stanovich, 1986; Stanovich & Cunningham, 1998) have
argued that good readers have opportunities to accumulate good vocabularies that will help them to read more, learn more word meanings, and
hence read even better. Children with inadequate vocabularies—who read
slowly and without enjoyment—read less and as a result have slower development of vocabulary knowledge, which inhibits further growth in
reading ability (Stanovich, 1986).

Early reading success and good reading habits, both important prepara-
tions for schoolwork, are not the only advantages bestowed on profes-
sional-class children. Other important school behaviors have been found.

In another New Zealand study, Jones (1987) worked with two groups of 15-year-old schoolgirls. One was labeled 5 *Simmonds*, a top-stream class with mainly professional parents. Through classroom interaction, the teachers showed that they expected these girls to express themselves and apply ideas and concepts, confronting them with questions that demanded interpretation and thought. These girls regarded their schoolwork seriously and discussed their schoolwork with teachers and among themselves, inside the classroom and out. They were labeled as having brains, and they demonstrated independent work habits.

In contrast, 5 *Mason* was a middle-to-low stream class, not expected to pass many subjects in the end-of-year school certificate examinations:

> The girls spent a lot of their time "doing nothing"—like just sitting, or staring out the window or into space ... They also spent a lot of time copying from the blackboard, textbooks, or the teacher's dictation ... They often listened silently to the teacher talking. They didn't talk to each other about their work, and rarely asked the teacher questions. Their teachers asked them a great number of simple rote questions, which demand no interpretation, just a short memorised reply. These students rarely used their own words in any extended way either verbally or in written work, and were constantly told by their teacher what and how to do it. (Jones, 1987, p. 2)

This observational study shows one group of girls learning and practicing useful forms of thinking—the interpretative, searching ways of thinking that are needed to pass examinations and proceed to tertiary education. Although the other group seems to be also working hard, they are not learning and practicing the thinking skills necessary for school success.

CAUSAL EXPLANATIONS
AND EDUCATIONAL IMPLICATIONS

Social theorists generally agree that schools appear to be preparing students for different positions in the economic hierarchy by providing different experience and curriculum knowledge—one group for the professional class, the other for the working class. But there is less agreement on the determining factor.

In explaining the differences, Nash and Harker (1992) referred to Bordieu's (1986) concept of *cultural capital*. This refers to an advantage experienced by people who belong to certain groups, particularly certain social classes, such as the professional and managerial middle classes. Nash and Harker's basic assumption is that certain social class differences are associated with literate cultural capital that is a part of family resources and are significantly associated with pupils' reading attainment. They maintain that cultural capital is usually owned by dominant groups who are in a position to prescribe norms for identity, behavior, social relationships, and lifestyle that puts them at an advantage and helps them gain an edge over other children. Their norms, values, and ways of thinking and doing things are presented as universal and worthwhile in a range of institutions, including schools. Through their control of education, the dominant group's culture becomes the culture of the schools. This means that those who do not share the dominant culture stand a good chance of being failed at school, because valuable knowledge is not made available to them. Ultimately, this means that the social and economic hierarchy is maintained, partly through cultural domination (Jones, 1987). Corson (1998) identified language as a main vehicle for power and discussed ways in which it can be used to "repress, dominate, and disempower diverse groups whose practices differ from the norms that have been established" (p. 5).

In examining causal factors for different achievement of diverse students, a lot of educational research focuses on the goings-on in classrooms, looking at teaching-and-learning interactions or asking questions about curriculum content, different teacher styles, and students' abilities and motivation (Block & Pressley, 2002; Farstrup & Samuels, 2002; Jacobs, 1997; National Reading Panel, 2000; Pressley & Wharton-McDonald, 1998; Pressley et al., 1995). A sociological approach suggests a different perspective—that differential achievement may not be individually determined. Jones (1987) argued that sociological studies suggest that socioeconomic class factors may be at play and that "they provide another way of understanding classroom interaction: as part of a larger, political process—that of reproducing the existing unequal power relations in our society" (p. 5).

Nash and Harker (1992) took painstaking care to point out that they have avoided the traditional construct of *causal sociology*—for example, accusing working-class people of having low aspirations for their children. They acknowledged that all of the parents in their study seemed to provide a supportive learning environment but that the significant differences lie in literacy practices. "What we do say is that given the resources they have, working class families, on the whole, cannot compete with the superior resources of the middle class and in all probability would not be able to compete on equal terms no matter what changes might be made to the educational system" (Nash & Harker, 1992, p. 18).

Nash and Harker's (1992) study also showed that Maori ethnicity in New Zealand is strongly associated with poor educational performance but that the negative effects of social class on educational performance are actually stronger in the case of Maori than of non-Maori children. Another New Zealand study (Hill & Hawk, 1997) demonstrated a number of other powerful influences over which schools have little control. Many of these influences—jobless parents or caregivers, poor housing, poor student health, family dysfunction, and a general lack of money to provide the basic equipment that middle-class students take for granted—are associated with poverty. Hill and Hawk (1997) attributed these poor conditions partly to the result of policy in areas such as health, employment, housing, and social policy and partly to education policies. Most students live in five or six worlds (e.g., world of family, their own ethnic culture, world of church, world of school, peer world), but most parents and teachers are familiar with only a few of these worlds. Difficulties for students arise when values, customs, and expectations from two or more of these worlds are in conflict (Hill & Hawk, 1997). This seems a pessimistic scenario for minority groups (i.e., for those with different language, ethnicity, and socioeconomic status from the majority), not to mention those with special needs and others with special abilities. There are many records of minority groups being marginalized, disadvantaged, and, in extreme cases, discriminated against and persecuted. Is there any hope for these diverse students, or will the poor forever get poorer?

Jones (1987) argued that people are not merely passive pawns of social forces and found interesting evidence in her study of students' intentional behavior that contributed to those teaching methods and influenced what happened in the classroom. When a 5 Mason teacher attempted to encourage discussion, she was met with uncooperative behavior; girls would chat, go to sleep, and so on. If, however, copying work was provided, the teacher could be assured of a quiet and attentive class. This reflected a 5 Mason girls' belief that schooling is "getting the teacher's knowledge" (p. 4) and that the most efficient way of doing that is to copy it. If a teacher asked the 5 Simmonds girls to copy more than a line or two, she was met with complaints and requests for handouts (Jones, 1987). It appears that both groups of girls could be responsible for constructing their learning environment through their system of reward and punishment for the teachers for what they considered to be appropriate or inappropriate schoolwork.

This perspective is shared by social psychologists who, like the sociologists, examine social influences on people. Myers (2002) summarized that position thus: "Persons and situations interact in at least three ways. First, individuals vary in how they interpret and react to a given situation. Second, people choose many of the situations that influence them. Third, people help create their social situations. Thus power resides both in persons and in situations. We create and are created by the social worlds" (p. 200).

This more positive position paves a way for recommendations for educational improvement. Hill and Hawk (1997) studied students in low-achieving areas and used their findings to make recommendations for improving secondary school students' learning. Some of the recommendations are at the school and community level (e.g., relating to easing the transition from primary to secondary school and better communication and collaboration with parents to strengthen the home–school network). There is also a major focus on the key teacher qualities that are thought to be conducive to student success. Student opinion showed that a high level of the teacher's knowledge of subject content and teaching skills were favored, along with the teacher's positive personal attitudes and attributes. According to Hill and Hawk (1997), some of these personal attitudes and attributes are:

- Showing respect for students and treating them as individuals.
- Being able to relate to cultures other than their own.
- Being able to relate to them as young adults.
- Showing kindness and caring.
- Maintaining confidentiality.
- A commitment to preparing well for lessons.
- A sense of humour. (p. 3)

Corson (1998), in his book, *Changing Education for Diversity*, drew from a range of studies and described education reforms for diverse groups of students, outlining policies and practices that have worked in schools and what we can learn from them. Although many of his recommendations were at the structural level for institutional change in the school, he also recognized the teacher's central role in change. In his concluding chapter, he identified two things to make the world a safer place for diverse groups. The first was a supply of well-trained and widely educated teachers who can challenge, change, and reform schools as a direct result of the high-quality curriculum provided in their teacher education. The second was a critically informed knowledge base for teachers to work from. Corson suggested the following ways for teachers to help bring about change:

- In place of a didactic teaching style ... a flexible and self-directed approach to diverse students rooted in the use of natural language.
- In place of a methods-based approach ... a readiness to meet unusual classroom situations in imaginative and ingenious ways.
- A person oriented approach, sensitive to the different values and norms of diverse students.
- A curriculum that builds critical thinkers who are in control of their lives.
- An evaluation system that builds, extends, and challenges students to higher levels of achievement.
- A professional engagement with diversity that celebrates difference.
- A willingness to look at the school as a source of educational failure. (p. 215)

Educational improvement clearly requires attention to the teacher's role, whether it be for better teaching methods in emergent literacy, teaching cognitive or metacognitive skills, infusing critical literacy into the curricula, or redressing social inequities for diverse groups of students. Involvement in innovative project work, however, has been a humbling learning experience for me; more than a decade ago, I started work in the field of introducing educational change to literacy classrooms. In the next section I describe some of that experience in three Asian educational systems.

THE CHALLENGES OF EDUCATIONAL CHANGE: SOME ESOL EMERGENT LITERACY PROJECTS

In the mid-1980s, the Singapore Ministry of Education commissioned an interdisciplinary team from the local teacher education institute to develop an effective primary reading and English acquisition program for children learning English as speakers of other languages (ESOL). Pedagogical recommendations were derived from the findings of a longitudinal research study and nationally implemented for Singapore ESOL children (Ng, 1988).

This first project was closely followed by a similar project in Brunei and, more recently, in Hong Kong. Extensive evaluation exercises over several years consistently showed that, compared with nonproject children, the Singapore and Brunei project children not only learned English faster but also had more positive attitudes toward reading and learning. Those results have been obtained in follow-up studies for thousands of primary school children in Singapore, Brunei and Hong Kong (Ng, 2001a, 2001b; Ng & Sullivan, 2001). It was observed that the projects not only affected children's language learning; there was also evidence of changes in teachers' behavior and beliefs. To understand the nature of the changes, a background of the traditional classroom culture prior to these projects is required.

TRADITIONAL CLASSROOM PRACTICES

In the 1980s, Singapore teachers faced many external constraints (e.g., relatively large classes averaging 40 students, inflexible time-tabling, rigid syllabi, limited curriculum time for English language teaching, and the heterogeneity of students' backgrounds). The ethnic majority is Chinese, and the main minority groups are Malay, Indian, and Eurasian. Instructional methods were governed by parental expectation of success in examinations. As a result, children were subjected to daily doses of preexamination practice, and English lessons consisted mainly of written work based on prescribed textbooks, workbooks, and past examination papers. Prior to project implementation, the classroom learning environments in Brunei (Ng, 2001b) and Hong Kong (Ng, 2000; Ng, 2001a) were similar to those in Singapore, except for some differences in the ethnic mix.

In these traditional classrooms, oral work comprised mainly reading flash cards of words and sentences, reading aloud selections from textbook readers (often in unison), and factual recall of answers to comprehension questions (Khoo & Ng, 1985). These activities did not promote much meaningful teacher–student interaction, and children rarely asked questions or initiated discussion in the classroom. The following transcript is typical of classroom interactions found in many classrooms prior to project implementation (Ng, 2003):

Teacher:	Where's the ruler? Sally. (Teacher points to a ruler placed on a box.)
Sally:	The ruler on the box.
Teacher:	Can you repeat? The ruler …
Sally:	The ruler in the box.
Teacher:	Is
Sally:	Is
Teacher:	In or on
Sally:	In or on
Teacher:	In or on? (Teacher points to helping words on the board.)
Sally:	In or on the box.

Although the exact content differs from lesson to lesson, many will be familiar with the "guess what's in the teacher's head" game, in which classroom interactions are geared solely toward discovering the correct answer the teacher has in mind. In this lesson, the stated objective was to get children using the prepositions *in* and *on* accurately in a sentence after the teacher had provided a few examples. This is congruent with the traditional method of teaching aimed at covering one language item at a time, based on a structural syllabus.

CHANGES IN PROJECT CLASSES

After an extensive literature search, the interdisciplinary team of project developers in Singapore recommended the more flexible *shared book* and *language experience* approaches to replace traditional teaching methods. The recommendation runs counter to those who advocate that children, especially ESOL students, should be able to decode the text and make sense of the words before the introduction of other global strategies and skills (e.g., predictions in reading or process writing). The Singapore ESOL project incorporated many of the most useful ideas in language teaching based on psychological principles of learning through interest and motivation. Continued reference to new literature has not found a need to revise many of the Singapore project recommendations for the later projects in Brunei and

Hong Kong. For example, many of those recommendations are similar to ones found in a recent extensive study on effective literacy teaching in the United States (Pressley, Rankin, & Yokoi, 1996). The United Kingdom's National Literacy Strategy implemented nationally since 1998 (with a budget of £565 million over 3 years) has incorporated similar teaching methods in its curriculum (Department for Education and Skills, 1998).

There was also an important supplementary aim of providing a more flexible framework in the project to cater to a more diverse and heterogeneous population and for coping with children from different levels of progress. To facilitate differentiated instruction for diverse students, small group and paired work were introduced in addition to the usual whole-class teaching. In addition to learning to manage a variety of groupings, project teachers also had to learn to generate more meaningful interactions between teachers and children and among children themselves. The teachers were introduced to a whole range of question forms in the workshops, learning how to use different questions in language teaching. Instead of the usual closed questions requiring no more than yes/no answers in the classroom, they were to ask "who" and "where" questions and "why" questions that demand richer resources of vocabulary and more imagination (Stevick, 1982). They were to encourage children to talk about their experiences, whether they were personal responses to a book introduced in the class or their own life experiences. Children's own writings and drawings were to be hung on walls for display and reading.

It can be seen that a dramatic and radical change had been demanded of teachers in the project—demands that required not merely physical arrangement of chairs and tables or the learning of a few new teaching tips (Cheah, 1997; Ng, 2001a). Classroom management for interactive teaching is very different from that for the traditional teaching style. In place of the traditional ideal of a quiet and well-behaved class, the project teacher had to manage the active and noisy participation of more than 40 children. At another level of management, these recommendations led to a change in the interaction patterns and power relationships in the classroom, whereby the teacher was no longer seen as the sole purveyor of knowledge; children's voices and opinions were heard, and their contributions were encouraged and valued.

Some project teachers were able to achieve such a different kind of classroom (Cheah, 1997; Ng, 2001a). In the more flexible and relaxed learning environment of some project classrooms, teachers were not the only ones asking questions; the children also asked many questions to initiate discussion. The following questions were taken from transcripts of Hong Kong Year 1 ESOL children during shared readings of a story (Ng, 2003).

- When we change the *d* to *s* in dog, does it say *sog*?

- Why is there an *s* after *monster* in the sentence "No more monsters" when there are no more?
- Why are some books written by Chinese authors and some by English authors?
- Why is *panda* on our spelling list when it is not in the Big Book story?

These questions reflect engagement at different levels of language learning. The first two questions relate to some teacher-stated lesson objectives; they were questions about letter–sound relationships and grammatical rules. The third question was not one that had been specifically introduced by the teacher, and the last question can be perceived as a challenge to the teacher's set curriculum. Although these 7-year-old ESOL children were not yet competent in English (only the first question was asked in English), they seemed capable of complex thinking about their English instruction in their dominant language.

Baker (1997), in an article on literacy practices and classroom order, discussed the analysis of discourse to raise awareness of the effect of interaction styles in the classroom. Using her system, the last two questions of the preceding transcript can be classified as ones that question the terms of the pedagogy and rock the classroom boat—ones that may be construed to be problematic because they deviate from the teacher set targets and plan of that particular lesson. The ensuing class discussion of the last two questions reflected a willingness of the teacher to relinquish her set lesson plan and agenda and to involve young learners in a process where they tried to make sense of the project lesson and relate it to their understanding of their worlds. In this way, the teacher used children's contributions to help them create knowledge by evaluating and extending their own conceptual frameworks. The departure from teacher-controlled lesson objectives signaled a shift in the balance of power and authority in the classroom with a move to a more democratic, in comparison to the usual autocratic, classroom environment. Such a radical shift, indicating commitment to an open and egalitarian agenda, demands accompanying changes in the teachers' fundamental beliefs regarding their roles as teachers and their expectations of the children and of classroom discipline.

Old habits die hard, and the project teacher advisers who regularly visited schools found that in the early stages, many project lessons contained preproject teaching styles, and many teaching interactions were aimed at guessing correct teacher answers. This is not a feature peculiar to Asian classrooms; such interactions were also found in Australian shared reading lessons (Baker 1997; Talty, 1995). New initiatives involving changes such as these would seem impossible if teachers continue to adopt the traditional didactic approach to classroom teaching. In southeast Asia, teachers are often part of bureaucratic systems that are traditionally autocratic in style of management and were not nurtured in the liberal humanistic tradition of the West (Ho, 1991). They were more used to working with children in teacher-fronted, teacher-controlled situations. What we were asking teachers in the projects to do was to provide an experience for learning that was markedly and dramatically different from their own recollections of 20+ years. Other constraints, such as large classroom sizes and inflexible timetabling, added to the difficulties inherent in developing liberal teaching styles.

THE TEACHER IN EDUCATIONAL CHANGE

Challenges are common to most educational innovative projects; they are not particular to Asian classrooms or to literacy programs and practices. The following advice relates to innovative technological projects: "Looking back on the 1980s, we see that most countries followed quite 'simplistic' introduction strategies, based upon the assumption that the provision of hardware and software might result almost automatically in fundamental changes in instructional practices. For real changes, more sophisticated strategies need to be developed, taking into account that ultimately it is the teacher who determines changes in the classroom practice" (Pelgrum & Plomp, 1993, pp. 238–239).

Other project implementers have also recognized the important role of the teacher in educational change (DuFour & Eaker, 1998; Hoffman et al., 1998; Hurst, 1983; Reinking, 1997; Whitehead, 1991). Beeby (1986), a prominent New Zealand educator made this observation:

> It has taken a long time for us to learn that no fundamental change can be brought about in schools on a national scale unless the average teachers understand the change, believe in it and, above all, accept it as their own idea. Without that, the teaching profession has a remarkable defensive skill at going on doing the same old things under a fancy new name. (p. 28)

The price for ignoring teachers is huge, and the implementation literature is replete with records of dismal failures of projects that did not take the teacher factor into account. If we need teachers to change, then we will have to consider, among other things, whether our schools have provided adequate and appropriate professional development opportunities for teachers and the infrastructure to support the new innovation.

There was enough evidence in the literature in the early 1980s to convince the Singapore project developers that teachers are critical to educational change; consequently, they were invited to be part of the project team (Ng, 1988; Ng & Sullivan, 2001). Teacher preparation was considered to be as important as the development of the instructional program. At all stages of planning, the project team members tried to anticipate the problems that teachers would face when using the new teaching methods in the classroom, and they developed appropriate professional development opportunities for the teachers. Teacher workshops and advisory classroom visits were spread over the school year to allow practice and consolidation for each main technique. Professional development proceeded through school-based practice demonstrations, participant interaction, provision of general and detailed guideline notes for lesson planning, and on-call resource persons for participating schools. All these provisions had been described in the literature current at that time (see Joyce & Showers, 1980; Walter & Marks, 1981). In this way, teachers gained greater understanding of teaching principles that had previously only been remote theories confined to lectures and academic texts.

SUPPORT THROUGH ADVISORY VISITS

A different kind of practicum supervision, comprising lesson observations and conferencing, was deployed to monitor classroom implementation in the Asian ESOL projects. In professional practice, the aim of supervision is usually to get valid and reliable information to assess quality or level of teaching for rehiring, dismissal, or promotion. Another purpose, which was the project's main aim, is to help teachers improve their professional performance. Unfortunately, many teachers do not welcome supervision because it is associated with past experiences that were accompanied by a sense of threat or anxiety (Husen & Postlewaite, 1985; Wood & Thompson, 1980). Many teachers have reported an anxiety of being judged, and that anxiety precluded the likelihood of their approaching supervisors with real problems. Additionally, teachers already feel a lot of pressure in their work (e.g., tight time-tabling, heavy workloads, and an environment of negativism), and they often feel that they are at the bottom of the status ladder (DuFour & Eaker, 1998; Husen & Postlewaite, 1985). Past educational innovations have failed mainly because the implementers underestimated the difficulty of teaching, and project involvement adds to that pressure.

An important part of teacher adviser development was aimed at raising the advisers' awareness that project advisory visits could be perceived as a threat by teachers and that the tension created could hinder efficient learning. To alleviate the inevitable stress of lesson observations, the teacher advisers were to establish a strong rapport with their teachers. In their interactions with the teachers, they were to make a deliberate effort to demonstrate that the project advisory role was different from traditional supervision. Teachers were reassured that the visits and lesson observations were intended to be supportive; they were used to evaluate the project, not the teacher. All project personnel were primed to: (a) ensure that the teacher was comfortable during the visits and observations, (b) explain that project supervision was solely for professional teacher development (i.e., to obtain understanding of teaching behaviors and to problem solve during the conferencing process), and (c) display the concept of mutual learning and respect and good practices that they could share with other teachers.

The project advisory service therefore consisted of a two-way process. There were opportunities not only for project advisers to offer teachers feedback but also for the teachers to give feedback to the teacher advisers. In this way, a learning partnership was formed, a partnership that was non-threatening and nonjudgmental. Efforts were made to create an administrative support system at the school level and, when necessary, confidentiality was observed about the supervisory visits and classroom observations. After some initial apprehension, most teachers expressed appreciation for these advisory visits, saying that they had benefited from the teacher advisers' feedback and support.

SUPPORT FROM SCHOOLS AS LEARNING COMMUNITIES

In the Singapore and Brunei projects, the primary school teachers, as part of the project team, worked alongside other educators, such as education institute lecturers; school inspectors; and curriculum specialists in planning, advising, and working on project implementation. They proved to be an invaluable asset but, once seconded to the project team, they were no longer perceived to be part of the school. In Brunei, some project schools started having their own teacher leaders, developing a school-based mentoring system (Ng, 1996). The project team encouraged that initiative by providing additional workshops for those teacher leaders. Those workshops introduced the teacher leaders to effective methods of working with other teachers in their own schools.

In the Hong Kong project, a mentor's course is being developed from the experience of the previous two projects and the growing literature about mentors and effective schools (e.g., DuFour & Eaker, 1998; Garmston, 1987; Ng, 2001a; Raywid, 1993). Concepts about coaching, mentoring, and learning communities (DuFour & Eaker, 1998; Joyce & Showers, 1995, 1996) have been discussed in some of the sessions. Other sessions in the course focus on skills required to facilitate meetings and workshops, communication skills, and teaching demonstrations. The mentors are given information and advice on how to lead regular school meetings among their colleagues to share ideas about teaching methods and materials, teaching aids, assessment ideas, and school administration. They also facilitate sessions in which the teachers collaboratively discuss practice and inform and critique one another. Although seconded to the project team, these mentors are still based in their own schools with some teaching duties as part of their workload.

Feedback from the teacher advisers, principals, and the mentors' journals on the mentoring system has been very encouraging (Ng, 2001a). For one thing, project implementation has generally been strongest in the mentors' schools. These schools have reported that the greatest achievement in the project has been the development of professionalism among teachers in their own schools, a spirit of cooperation and camaraderie. These features signal the beginnings of a learning community, a community motivated toward continuing improvement (DuFour & Eaker, 1998; Joyce & Showers, 1995, 1996). The most successful schools are those that have provided for collaboration in the following ways: Time is allocated in the school schedule for meetings and discussion; clear, explicit purposes are defined for collaboration; mentors help the training for collaboration; and team members are encouraged to work together as true professional colleagues.

It is exciting to witness the development of these schools toward a new teaching and learning culture, where there is a deliberate effort to identify helpful knowledge and spread its use within the school (DuFour & Eaker, 1998). Another gratifying feature is that, despite the heavy workload brought on by project work, many project teachers have expressed a willingness to persist in the new teaching approaches. This can be seen as an indication of a *discretionary* commitment—a commitment generated by the best of those in the learning community, the commitment to go the extra mile for improvement (DuFour & Eaker, 1998).

Yet implementation experts have warned that it takes decades for a small proportion of successful ideas to filter through the system and become common practice. This is rather disheartening, because most education studies are of a short duration. The National Reading Panel (2000) found few studies longer than 1 school year. The evaluation study for the Singapore project went on for 6 years, and the Brunei project for 10 years. It is hoped that having school-based teacher leaders in the Hong Kong project will help sustain and improve on teaching practices when schools are no longer monitored by the implementation team in a few years' time. Whether these projects will take hold as part of the educational culture in the long term remains to be seen. Besides, there are other considerations.

CONTINUING CHALLENGES OF CHANGE

The 1984 Report of the Commission on Reading concluded that "America will become a nation of readers when verified practices of the best teachers in the best schools can be introduced throughout the country" (Anderson et al., 1985, p. 120). Despite countless expensive attempts at education reform since 1984, that statement has not become a reality in U.S. schools. More needs to be done to find out what conditions are favorable for implementing and sustaining educational changes. Veteran reformers such as Beeby (1986) throw some light on the matter:

The first thing I learnt as an impatient young reformer is that real change to education is slow, often maddeningly slow. Society is constantly changing and, in theory, the schools that serve it should be changing just as rapidly. At first glance this looks simple. It seems as if all you have to do is to agree on a new curriculum and new syllabuses, and pass regulations. Put up better buildings, buy new equipment, produce new textbooks and train teachers to use them. If all you are trying to do is to find new ways of achieving old objectives, you might reach something like your goal in five or 10 years.

But if you want to go deeper than that and change the very objectives of education, change the kind of students who emerge from the school system, then you have at least a generation of work ahead of you. That calls for changes of attitudes, not just in the teaching profession but also in the parents of the students, the employers, and the country as whole. Changing attitudes is a vastly slower business than changing the tricks of the teachers' trade. (p. 28)

Would larger scale interventions speed up the reform process? New Zealand has recently attempted such large-scale changes, undergoing massive reforms and restructuring for its whole educational system. New Zealand, traditionally based on a welfare state system, has gone faster and further than any other country in realizing the blueprint of a market society (Lauder, Hughes, & Watson, 1999). In the late 1980s, market principles were introduced into education with the view that markets will appropriately select students and distribute resources equitably between schools. It was thought that educational improvement would result with schools ("providers") having to compete for "customers" and "consumers" all wanting the best for their children. Open competition in markets was therefore thought to promote greater equality of educational opportunities. A large longitudinal study conducted between 1992 and 1997, to study the impact of market-style policies on schools, has yielded rather disappointing results. Lauder et al. (1999) observed the following: "Successive governments in New Zealand have acknowledged that not all has been well with their market experiment and have made a number of responses including changes to the policy" (p. 94). Years after the first policies were made, New Zealand educators are still surveying and debating the losses and gains in the education system (e.g., Thrupp, 1999).

Implementing change for a whole country's educational community is indeed very complex. New ideas, however brilliant, and blueprints, however carefully constructed and researched, are only a start. The change agenda is difficult because the educational community is a dynamic complex of people, their cultures, processes, equipment, materials, and ideas. But there is a clear indication in the implementation literature of the necessity for widespread involvement of all sectors in the various educational establishments and community affected by the innovation, not only other teachers and senior members of the project schools. In the concluding sections I look at two of these sectors.

SUPPORT FROM THE HOME

In the Singapore and Brunei projects there were deliberate attempts to publicize the project through the public media (i.e., newspapers, radio, and television). In both projects, voluntary professional associations for reading and literacy were established to draw interested members from different sectors of the community. Through their activities and celebrations, these nongovernmental organizations can help inform and raise public awareness about important literacy issues. This has only just started in the most recent project in Hong Kong.

In Hong Kong, schools that indicated their readiness for change complained about the constraining influence of parental demands for traditional teaching methods. The Standing Committee on Language Education and Research (2003) acknowledged parents as a significant factor in the promotion of innovative educational projects. As a start to address this issue, the Hong Kong project team is developing a parent project to be delivered through the existing school network. This project includes training of supervisors, principals, and librarians from primary schools and preschools to facilitate workshops for fostering parental awareness about the educational innovation currently being carried out in ESOL teaching. A secondary aim is to disseminate research-related findings about sound literacy practices for parents and caregivers of young children.

This initiative has aims similar to those in other countries, for example, the well-established Reading Is Fundamental (1992) initiatives in the United States. Projects such as these have promoted the findings in many reading projects and staged campaigns to provide guidelines for parents and community to build up a literacy-rich environment for their children. In the Hong Kong project, the facilitators' workshops are supported by locally developed materials consisting of a booklet, an educational video compact disc, and other information materials. The team is exploring whether school staff, rather than volunteers, would provide a more stable support network for working with parents. The pilot project, currently in its second year, aims for 200 workshops conducted all over Hong Kong. The team is hoping to extend this project to look at culturally responsive ways of instruction that do not require students to give up the values of their home cultures (see Au, 2002).

SUPPORT FROM THE EDUCATIONAL COMMUNITY

In an attempt to reach out to the wider educational community, the three Asian ESOL projects disseminated project information, rationale, and workings through regular seminars to educators such as principals and senior staff members, supervisors, inspectors, tertiary education lecturers, and policymakers. Is there room for more involvement? In a World Assembly of the International Council on Education for Teaching, Shulman (1991) concluded his keynote address by asking that educators reflect on the nature of their involvement in educational improvement:

> As members of the world teacher education community, we can certainly lay claim to an abundance of troubles. I fear that we have sometimes tended to respond to these troubles by selecting neat, well formed puzzles and pursuing them. Our puzzles have followed the traditional disciplines—a history of education course here, a method of reading instruction course there, student teaching experience neatly placed at the top. The puzzles are discrete, often detached from one another, too rarely well-connected to the persistent demands of practice. (p. 20)

To be effective in educational improvement, Shulman (1991) advised tertiary lecturers to link their education courses more closely to teaching practices. The other important component of tertiary educators' work is research, yet it is well known that classroom teachers are often disappointed when they look to academic research to lead practice. Apparently, it is an illusion that the work of researchers is to study classroom problems, pose questions, find answers, and then recommend things to do in the classroom. Clay (1991), a leading authority in language education and whose research findings have been applied in international settings, observed that researchers rarely ask questions that teachers want answered and educators rarely work to implement the implications of particular research findings. Pica (1992), working in the area of second-language acquisition and language teaching methods, agreed with this view. She found that researcher concerns are shared primarily within a research community and are applied not to classroom decisions but to the interpretation of previous investigations and the design of follow-up studies.

A probable reason that few tertiary educators have ventured into implementation work is that it is messy, uncertain, and full of unintended consequences (Whitehead, 1991). As well, the implementer has to deal with conflict, compromise, and negotiation. Yet substantial educational change can come about only with a greater level of commitment and participation from educational researchers through joint projects with practicing teachers. There should be a willingness to form partnerships within the educational community, partnerships involving curriculum developers, text material writers, teacher educators, media experts, and so on, with a main focus on the teacher as one of the most important factors in promoting change. Instead of rewarding academic publications only, institutions should encourage participation by recognizing and honoring the innovation and ingenuity displayed in implementation work.

There is a lot of talk in the educational community about the inequities in society, but the widening gap can be reduced only through active involvement of educators to begin the process of reforming education for diversity. Instead of only participating in intellectual exchanges within the research community, they must at least start to engage in meaningful conversations with policymakers and practitioners about strategies to address literacy and diversity issues, such as: (a) employing best-teaching practices in emergent literacy to ensure that all children have quality-first teaching; (b) implementing catch-up programs for children needing a second (or third) chance; (c) developing classrooms that are conducive for collaborative work for the fostering of cognitive and metacognitive skills and independent learning, infusing critical literacy into the curriculum to empower learners to reconstruct their literacy agendas and lives; and (d) rebuilding an educational system to accord fair treatment to students from diverse backgrounds and/or with diverse abilities, to achieve social justice.

Delpit (1988), well known for her work with minority groups, maintains that it is those with the most power who must take the greater responsibility for initiating the communication process, with a particular focus on listening:

> To do so takes a very special kind of listening, listening that requires not only open eyes and ears but open hearts and minds. We do not really see through our eyes or hear through our ears, but through our beliefs. To put our beliefs on hold is to cease to exist as ourselves for a moment—and that is not easy. It is painful as well, because it means turning yourself inside out, giving up your own sense of who you are, and being willing to see yourself in the unflattering light of another's angry gaze. It is not easy but it is the only way to learn what it is to be someone else and the only way to start a dialogue. (p. 297)

As members of the dominant and powerful group in society, tertiary educators should bear a substantial share of this responsibility and burden.

REFERENCES

Adams, M. J. (1990). *Beginning to read: Thinking and learning about print.* Cambridge, MA: MIT Press.

Adams, M. J., Allington, R. L., Chaney, J. H., Goodman, Y. M., Kapinus, B. A., McGee, L. M., et al. (1991). Beginning to read: A critique by literacy professionals and a response by Marilyn Jager Adams. *Reading Teacher, 44*(6), 370–395.

Anderson, R. C., Hiebert, E. H., Scott, J. S., & Wilkinson, I. A.G. (1985). *Becoming a nation of readers.* Washington, DC: National Institute of Education.

Au, K. H. (2002). Multicultural factors and the effective instruction of students from diverse backgrounds. In A. E. Farstrup & J. Samuels (Eds.), *What reading research has to say about reading instruction* (3rd ed., pp. 392–413). Newark, DE: International Reading Association.

Auckerman, R. C. (1971). *Approaches to beginning reading.* New York: Wiley.

Baker, C. D. (1997). Literacy practices and classroom order. In S. A. Muspratt, A. Luke, & P. Freebody (Eds.), *Constructing critical literacies* (pp. 243–261). Cresskill, NJ: Hampton.

Baumann, J. F., Jones, L. A., & Seifert-Kessell, N. (1993). Using think alouds to enhance children's comprehension monitoring abilities. *Reading Teacher, 47*(3), 184–192.

Baumfield, V. (1997, June). *Thinking skills: Identifying generic principles and supporting effective implementation.* Paper presented at the 7th International Conference on Thinking, Singapore.

Beeby, C. E. (1986). The place of myth in education change. *Listener, 114*(2436), 53–57.

Benseman, J. (1989). *Taking control over their lives.* Auckland, New Zealand: Auckland Adult Literacy Scheme.

Block, C. C., & Pressley, M. (Eds.). (2002). *Comprehension instruction: Research-based best practices.* New York: Guilford.

Bond, G. L., & Dykstra, R. (1967). The cooperative program in first grade instruction. *Reading Research Quarterly, 2,* 5–141.

Bordieu, P. (1986). *Distinction.* London: Routledge.

Brown, H., & Cambourne, B. (1987). *Read and retell.* North Ryde, NSW: Metheun Australia.

Brown, M. (1995). *What is the role of information and communication technology in the New Zealand curriculum?* Retrieved March 3, 2001, from http://www.massey.ac.nz/~wwedpsy/t&sres/mark1.htm

Cassidy, J., & Cassidy, D. (2002). What's hot, what's not for 2002. *Reading Today, 19,* 1, 18–19.

Cazden, C. B. (1988). *Classroom discourse: The language of teaching and learning.* Portsmouth, NH: Heinemann.

Cazden, C. B. (2001). *Classroom discourse: The language of teaching and learning* (2nd ed.). Portsmouth, NJ: Heinemann.

Chamot, A., & O'Malley, J. M. (1994). Language learner and learning strategies. In N. C. Ellis (Ed.), *Implicit and explicit learning languages* (pp. 371–392). London: Academic.

Cheah, Y. M. (1997). Shaping the classrooms of tomorrow: Lessons from the past. In G. M. Jacobs (Ed.), *Language classrooms of tomorrow: Issues and responses* (pp. 16–35). Singapore: South East Asian Ministers of Education Organization Regional Language Centre.

Chua, M. H. P., & Leong, H. (1997, June). *The thinking programme in Singapore—an overview.* Paper presented at the 7th International Conference on Thinking, Singapore.

Clay, M. M. (1991). *Becoming literate: The construction of inner control.* Auckland, New Zealand: Heinemann Education.

Conlon, T. (2000). Visions of change: Information technology, education and post modernism. *British Journal of Educational Technology, 31,* 109–116.

Corson, D. (1998). *Changing education for diversity.* Buckingham, England: Open University Press.

Cretu, D. (2000). Critical thinking at the university. *Thinking Classroom, 2,* 13–16.

Currie, L. A. (1999). "Mr Homunculus the reading detective": A cognitive approach to improving reading comprehension. *Educational and Child Psychology, 16,* 37–41.

Delpit, L. D. (1988). The silenced dialogue: Power and pedagogy in educating other people's children. *Harvard Educational Review, 58,* 280–298.

Department for Education and Skills. (1998) *The National Literacy Strategy: framework for teaching.* London: Her Majesty's Stationery Office. (Also available from http://www.standards.dfes.gov.uk/literacy/about/?a=fwa&art_id=81)

Dickinson, L., & Carver, D. (1980). Learning how to learn: Steps towards self-direction in foreign language learning in schools. *English Language Teacher Journal, 35,* 1–7.

Donhower, S. L. (1999). Supporting a strategic stance in the classroom: A comprehension framework for helping teachers help students to be strategic. *Reading Teacher, 52,* 672–688.

DuFour, R., & Eaker, R. (1998). *Professional learning communities at work.* Bloomington, IN: National Education Service.

Elley, W. B. (1992). *How in the world do students read?* Hamburg, Germany: International Association for the Evaluation of Educational Achievement.

Farstrup, A. E. & Samuels, J. (Eds.). (2002). *What reading research has to say about reading instruction* (3rd ed.). Newark, DE: International Reading Association.

Forester, T. (1992). Megatrends or megamistakes? Whatever happened to The Information Society? *The Information Society, 8,* 133–146.

Garmston, R. J. (1987). How administrators support peer coaching. *Journal of the Association for Supervision and Curriculum Development, 44*(5), 18–26.

Gawith, G. (1992, June). *Information technology and learning.* Paper presented at the National Conference on "Teacher Education: An Investment for New Zealand's future," Auckland, New Zealand.

Guthrie, B. J., & Greaney, V. (1991). Literacy acts. In R. Barr, M. L. Kamil, P. B. Mosenthal, & P. D. Pearson (Eds.), *Handbook of reading research* (Vol. II, pp. 68–96). New York: Longman.

Halliday, M. A. K., & Martin, J. R. (1996). *Writing science.* London: Longman.

Hartley, R. (1989). *The social costs of inadequate literacy: A report for International Literacy Year.* Canberra, Australia: Australian Government Publishing Service.

Hawisher, G., & Selfe, C. (1996). Reflections on research in computers and composition studies at the century's end. *Australian Journal of Language and Literacy, 19,* 291–304.

Hill, J., & Hawk, K. (1997). Aiming for student achievement. *Set: Research Information for Teachers, 2,* 1–4.

Ho, W. K. (1991). Theoretical influences on educational practice in Singapore. *Singapore Journal of Education, 11,* 21–34.

Hoffman, J. V., McCarthey, S. J., Elliot, B., Bayles, D. L., Price, D. P., Ferree, A., Abbott, J. A. (1998). The literature-based basals in first grade classrooms: Savior, Satan, or same-old, same-old? *Reading Research Quarterly, 33,* 168–197.

Hurst, P. (1983). *Implementing educational change—A critical review of the literature.* London: Institute of Education, University of London.

Husen, T., & Postlewaite, T. N. (1985). *The international encyclopaedia of education* (Vol. 8). Oxford, England: Pergamon.

International Reading Association. (1999). *Using multiple methods of beginning reading instruction: A position statement of the International Reading Association.* Retrieved December 17, 2003, from http://www.reading.org/pdf/methods.pdf

Jacobs, G. M. (Ed.). (1997). *Language classrooms of tomorrow: Issues and responses*. Singapore: South East Asian Ministers of Education Organization Regional Language Centre.

Janks, H. (1997). Teaching language and power. In R. Wodak, & D. Corson (Eds.), *Language policy and political issues in education* (pp. 241–251). Boston: Kluwer.

Johnston, P. H. (1985). Understanding learning disability. *Harvard Educational Review, 55*, 153–177.

Jones, A. (1987). What really happens in the classroom. *Set: Research Information for Teachers, 2*(7), 1–6.

Joyce, B., & Showers, B. (1980). Improving inservice training: The message of research. *Educational Leadership, 37*, 379–385.

Joyce, B., & Showers, B. (1995). *Student achievement through staff development: Fundamentals of school renewal* (2nd ed.). White Plains, NY: Longman.

Joyce, B., & Showers, B. (1996). The evolution of peer coaching. *Educational Leadership, 53*(6), 12–16.

Juel, C. (1988). Learning to read and write: A longitudinal study of 54 children from first through fourth grades. *Journal of Educational Psychology, 59*, 243–245.

Kelly, F. J., Veldman, D. J., & McGuire, C. (1964). Multiple discrimination prediction of delinquency and school dropouts. *Educational and Psychological Measurement, 24*, 535–544.

Khoo, M., & Ng, S. M. (1985). Reading instruction in the lower primary classes: A second observational study. *Singapore Journal of Education, 7*, 55–64.

King, A. (1990). Enhancing peer interaction and learning in the classroom through reciprocal questioning. *American Educational Research Journal, 27*(40), 664–687.

Knapp, L. R., & Glenn, A. D. (1996). *Restructuring schools with technology*. Boston: Allyn & Bacon.

Lankshear, C., Gee, J. P., Knobel, M., & Searle, C. (1997). *Changing literacies*. Buckingham, England: Open University Press.

Larrick, N. (1992). A 40-year celebration of *The Reading Teacher*. *Reading Teacher, 45*(5), 340–341.

Lauder, H., Hughes, D., & Watson, S. (1999). The introduction of educational markets in New Zealand. In M. Thrupp (Ed.), *A decade of reform in New Zealand: Where to now?* (pp. 86–98). Hamilton, New Zealand: Waikato University.

Lloyd, D. N. (1978). Prediction of school failure from third-grade data. *Educational and Psychological Measurement, 38*, 1193–1200.

Luke, A. (2000). Critical literacy in Australia: A matter of context and standpoint. *Journal of Adolescent and Adult Literacy, 43*, 448–461.

Lundberg, I., & Linnakyla, P. (1993). *Teaching reading around the world*. The Hague, The Netherlands: International Association for the Evaluation of Educational Achievement.

Matthew, K. I. (1996). Using CD-ROMs in the language arts classroom. *Computers in the School, 12*(4), 73–81.

Markuckiene, S. (2000). Philosophical props for the classroom: Critical thinking in an ethics lesson. *Thinking Classroom, 1*(1), 10–12.

McGill-Franzen, A. & Allington, R. L. (1991). Every child's right: Literacy. *Reading Teacher, 45*(2), 86–90.

Ministry of Education, Singapore. (2001). Mission statement. Retrieved January 26, 2005, from http://www.moe.gov.sg/corporate/mission_statement.htm

Muspratt, S. A., Luke, A., & Freebody, P. (Eds.). (1997). *Constructing critical literacies: Teaching and learning textual practice.* North Bergen, NJ: Hampton.

Myers, D. G. (2002). *Social Psychology* (7th ed.). New York: McGraw-Hill.

Nash, R., & Harker, R. (1992). Working with class: The educational expectations and practices of class-resourced families. *New Zealand Journal of Educational Studies, 27,* 3–20.

National Reading Panel. (2000). *Teaching children to read: An evidence-based assessment of the scientific research literature on reading and its implications for reading instruction* (National Institutes of Health Publication No. 00-4769). Washington, DC: National Institute of Child Health and Human Development.

Ng, S. M. (Ed.). (1988). *Research into children's language and reading development.* Singapore: Institute of Education.

Ng, S. M. (1996). Innovation, survival and processes of change in the bilingual classroom in Brunei Darussalam. *Journal of Multilingual and Multicultural Development, 17*(2–4), 149–162.

Ng, S. M. (2000). *Young Hong Kong children learning English as speakers of other languages.* Hong Kong: Council of Early Childhood Education & Services.

Ng, S. M. (2001a). Annual report submitted to the Quality Education Fund (2000–2001), Hong Kong.

Ng, S. M. (2001b). The Brunei Reading and Language Acquisition project. *International Journal of Educational Research, 35,* 169–179.

Ng, S. M. (2003). Classroom talk in Hong Kong elementary schools. Unpublished raw data.

Ng, S. M., & Sullivan, C. (2001). The Singapore Reading and English Acquisition programme. *International Journal of Educational Research, 35,* 157–167.

Ogle, D., & Blachowicz, C. L. Z. (2002). Beyond literature circles: Helping students comprehend informational texts. In C. C. Block & M. Pressley (Eds.), *Comprehension instruction: Research-based best practices* (pp. 259–274). New York: Guilford.

Olson, M. O., & Gee. T. C. (1991). Content reading instruction in the primary grades: Perceptions and strategies. *Reading Teacher, 45*(4), 298–307.

Oppenheimer, T. (1997). The computer delusion. *The Atlantic Monthly, 280*(1), 45–62.

Organization for Economic Cooperation and Development. (2000). Programme for international student assessment. Retrieved January 26, 2005, from http://www.pisa.gc.ca/pisa2000_e.shtml

Paris, S., Lipson, M., & Wixson, K. K. (1983). Becoming a strategic reader. *Contemporary Educational Psychology, 8,* 293–316.

Pearson, D. P. (1992). *RT* remembrance: The second 20 years. *Reading Teacher, 45*(5), 378–385.

Pelgrum, W. J., & Plomp, T. (1993). *The use of computers in education worldwide.* Oxford, England: Pergamon.

Pereira-Laird, J. A., & Deane, F. P. (1997). Development and validation of a self-report measure of reading strategy use. *Reading Psychology, 18*(3), 185–235.

Pica, T. (1992). Language-learning research and classroom concerns. *FORUM, 30*(3), 2–9.

PISA survey accents teacher role. (2002). *Reading Today, 19*(4), 1, 6. (Also available from http://www.oecd.org)

Postman, N. (1993). *Technopoly: The surrender of culture to technology.* New York: Vintage.

Pressley, M., El-Dinary, P. B., Gaskins, I., Schuder, T., Bergman, J. L., Almasi, J., & Brown, R. (1992). Beyond direct explanation: Transactional instruction of reading comprehension strategies. *Elementary School Journal, 92,* 513–555.

Pressley, M., Rankin, J., & Yokoi, L. (1996). A survey of instructional practices of primary teachers nominated as effective in promoting literacy. *Elementary School Journal, 96,* 363–383.

Pressley, M., & Wharton-McDonald, R. (1998). The development of literacy, Part 4: The need for increased comprehension strategies in upper-elementary grades. In M. Pressley (Ed.), *Reading instruction that works: The case for balanced teaching* (pp. 192–227). New York: Guilford.

Pressley, M., Woloshyn, V., Burkell, J., Carigli-Bull, T., Lysynchuuk, L., McGoldrick, J. A., et al. (1995). *Cognitive strategy instruction that really improves children's academic performance.* Cambridge, MA: Brookline.

Raywid, M. A. (1993). Finding time for collaboration. *Educational Leadership, 15,* 30–34.

Reading Is Fundamental (1992). *Choosing good books for your children: Infancy to age 12. A guide for parents presented by Reading is Fundamental.* Washington, DC: Author.

Reese, E. (1995). Predicting children's literacy from mother–child conversations. *Cognitive Development, 10,* 381–405.

Reinking, D. (1997). Me and my hypertext:) A multiple digression analysis of technology and literacy (sic). *Reading Teacher, 50*(8), 626–643.

Robertson, I. (1981). *Sociology.* New York: Worth.

Ruddell, M. A., & Ruddell, R. B. (1994). *Theoretical models and processes of reading* (4th ed.). Newark, DE: International Reading Association.

Shanahan, T. (2002). What reading research says: The promise and limitations of applying research to reading education. In A. E. Farstrup & J. Samuels (Eds.), *What reading research has to say about reading instruction* (3rd ed., pp. 8–24). Newark, DE: International Reading Association.

Shulman, L. S. (1991). Pedagogical ways of knowing. In W. K. Ho (Ed.), *Improving the quality of the teaching profession* (pp. 9–21). Singapore: Institute of Education.

Skerman, J., Billany, T., Just, D., & Stove, S. (2000). An open letter to the Minister of Education: Paving the road ahead. *Computers in NZ Schools, 12*(3), 9–13.

Slavin, R. E., Karweit, N. L., & Wasik, B. A. (1992). Preventing early school failure: What works? *Educational Leadership, 50*(4), 10–17.

Standing Committee on Language Education and Research. (2003). *Action plan to raise language standards in Hong Kong: Consultation document.* Hong Kong: Hong Kong Special Administrative Region Government.

Stanovich, K. E. (1986). Matthew effects in reading: Some consequences of individual differences in the acquisition of literacy. *Reading Research Quarterly, 21,* 360–407.

Stanovich, K. E., & Cunningham, A. E. (1998). What reading does for the mind. *American Educator, 22,* 8–15.

Stevick, E. (1982). *Teaching and learning languages.* Cambridge, England: Cambridge University Press.

Talty, F. (1995). Small talk around big books: Interaction or conversationalism? *Australian Journal of Language and Literacy, 18*(1), 5–18.

Teale, W. (1984). Reading to young children: Its significance for literacy development. In H. Goelman, A. Oberg, & F. Smith (Eds.), *Awakening to literacy* (pp. 110–121). London: Heinemann Educational.

Teale, W., & Sulzby, E. (1987). Literacy acquisition in early childhood. In D. Wagner (Ed.), *The future of literacy in a changing world* (Vol. 1, pp. 120–129). New York: Pergamon.

Thrupp, M. (Ed.). (1999). *A decade of reform in New Zealand: Where to now?* Hamilton, New Zealand: Waikato University.

Tierney, R. J., Readence, J. E. & Dishner, E. K. (1990). *Reading Strategies and Practices: A compendium* (3rd ed.). Boston: Allyn & Bacon.

Topping, K. J. (1997). Electronic literacy in school and home: A look into the future. *Reading Online,* International Reading Association. Retrieved July 25, 1997, from http://www.readingonline.org/international/future/index.html

Vacca, R. T. (2002). Making a difference in adolescents' school lives: Visible and invisible aspects of content area reading. In A. E. Farstrup & J. Samuels (Eds.), *What reading research has to say about reading instruction* (3rd ed., pp. 184–204). Newark, DE: International Reading Association.

Walter, G. A., & Marks, S. E. (1981). *Experiential learning and change.* New York: Wiley.

Wallace, C. (1992). Critical literacy awareness in the EFL classroom. In N. Fairclough (Ed.), *Critical language awareness* (pp. 59–92). London: Longman.

Wells, C. G. (1985). Pre-school literacy-related activities and success in school. In D. R. Olson, N. Torrance, & A. Hildyard (Eds.), *Literacy, language and learning: The nature and consequences of reading and writing* (pp. 229–255). Cambridge, England: Cambridge University Press.

Wells, C. G. (1987). *The meaning makers: Children learning language and using language to learn.* Portsmouth, NH: Heinemann Educational.

Wenden, A. L. (1997). Designing learner training: The curricular questions. In G. M. Jacobs (Ed.), *Language classrooms of tomorrow: Issues and responses* (pp. 238–262). Singapore: SEAMEO (South East Asian Ministers of Education Organization) Regional Language Center.

Whitehead, C. (1991). Implementation: The challenge to educational planning in the 1990s. *International Journal of Educational Development, 11,* 315–319.

Wood, F. H., & Thompson, S. R. (1980). Guidelines for better staff development. *Educational Leadership, 37,* 374–378.

10

Literacies Within Classrooms: Whose and for What Purpose?

Ileana Seda-Santana
Universidad Nacional Autónoma de México

> *What we resolve to do in school only makes sense when considered in the broader context of what the society intends to accomplish through its educational investment in the young.* (Bruner, 1996, p. ix)

Multiple literacies have been addressed in the literature from various perspectives that represent different understandings by different people and contexts. One view addresses the ability to read and comprehend effectively different texts and types of texts. Another addresses the reader's knowledge base given his or her background, experience, abilities, gender, and the like (Rasinsky et al., 2000). Still another view is centered on the diverse ethnic, linguistic, and socioeconomic understandings of individual literacies (e.g., Heath, 1991; Taylor, 1983).

The focus of this chapter represents yet another view of multiplicity of literacies, that is, the specific conceptions individual students and teachers may have about literacy, or how individuals conceive of and understand literacy, their own and that of others, as well as the roles these understandings play in learning and promoting literacy in particular contexts. This chapter is intended to address issues of how conceptions, beliefs, and sense of identity may play out in students' approach to literacy learning tasks in schools and teachers' approaches to help students become competent readers and writers for life.

Bruner (1996) pointed out that our processes of learning and comprehending are engrained in our culture; that is, our interpretations and understandings are determined by a cultural context that shapes the mind. In this sense, learning is considered to be situated in a cultural context and although it takes place "inside the head ... that mental life is lived with others, is shaped to be communicated, and unfolds with the aid of cultural codes, traditions and the like" (p. xi).

Classrooms represent diverse communities that comprise individual players within an entire classroom community, which are in turn promoted and created within a larger school community. In this sense, concepts/conceptions and beliefs are developed and learned through our life experiences and, in the case of literacy, as lived in and out of school. Conceptions and beliefs acquired through our culture, both within and outside of school, influence our literacies, school and others.

In the literature, this idea appears under different names such as cultural representations, symbolic representations, symbolic constructions, beliefs, and conceptions. That is, " ... a group of constructs that name, define, and describe the structure and content of mental states that are thought to drive a person's actions. Other constructs in this set include conceptions, perspectives, perceptions, orientations, theories and stances" (Richardson, 1996, p. 102).

According to *Merriam-Webster's* Dictionary, a *conception* is a formulation of ideas, a mental impression or image, whereas a *concept* is defined as a thought, a general notion, especially a generalized idea of a class of objects. In this chapter it refers to everyday knowledge (often called *common sense*) that individuals construct through their life experiences, in the different communities in which they participate. Everyday experiences, and the knowledge constructed along with them, become the individual's external reality as he or she constructs meaning from personal experiences within those communities and/or groups (Berger & Luckmann, 1967).

This knowledge emerges from the specific sociocultural context in which individuals are immersed, and it is instrumental in interpreting contexts and the events that make up such contexts, whether historical, social, political, or everyday actions (Jodelet, 1988; Moscovici, 1988; Popkewitz, 1985; Shutz, 1974). Knowledge is thus constructed through a series of social and cultural referents both by members of a group as a whole and by individuals; that is, it reflects the individual's external reality as interpreted and understood by the individual and his or her community (Berger & Luckmann, 1967; Cole & Wertsch, n.d.; Schutz, 1974). At the same time, interpretations and constructed knowledge are not identical for all members of a community; rather, they are individually constructed in response to accumulated cultural knowledge as triggered by some phenomena from the person's unique reality or context.

In the case of school and schooling, events and phenomena from the individuals' or group's reality are curricular contents, educational practice, the particular approach to schooling, as well as educational institution's societal mission. School and schooling are complex constructions that represent both formal (i.e. curriculum, educational policy) and informal (often implicit) everyday educational actions, processes, and practice. In this sense, educational practice is a complex fabric of social elaborations reflected in the actions of those individuals who participate in educational processes, be it students, teachers, parents, school administrators, politicians, employers, or the public in general. It is made up of a conglomerate of social practices and common knowledge that influences educational practice through our life experiences in school (Heller, 1977).

During the 1980s, educational researchers turned their interests toward teachers and teaching. Particular foci were teachers' knowledge about teaching and the subject matters they taught, as well as about their conceptions of teaching and children's learning. Stakeholders notwithstanding, one reason for this turn was the scant information available in the literature about what took place in classrooms that could account for educational investment and efforts (Connelly & Clandinin, 1990; Floden & Klinzing, 1990; Gage, 1989; House, Mathison, & McTaggart, 1989; Lampert & Clark, 1990).[1]

Previously, during the 1960s and 1970s, because of the influence of Jean Piaget, studies of children's knowledge and their conceptions proliferated in the domains of science and mathematics (e.g., Burton & Brown, 1978; Ginsburg, 1977; Lochhead, 1979). Educational researchers turned their efforts toward students' and teachers' minds in an attempt to understand their conceptions and the effects these had on learning and teaching. In the case of children and students, the general intent was to understand their conceptions and misconceptions in order to modify, expand, or change them through appropriate instruction. In the case of teachers, research was geared toward understanding teachers' conceptions/beliefs with the intention of modifying those considered important to improving educational practice and the overall quality of education. All of this led researchers to take a closer look and to view not only children but also teachers as active agents in learning and teaching. Consequently, they moved away from the perspective of passive teachers who implemented the curriculum (technician) and of passive children who were recipients of knowledge and information (Sacristán, 1989).

In the 1990s, the search for sound philosophies and appropriate pedagogical strategies to support and facilitate student learning promoted research on teachers' change processes (Cochran-Smith & Lytle, 1990; Fullan & Miles, 1992; Fullan & Steigelbauer, 1991; Lytle & Cochran-Smith, 1990;

---

[1]It is interesting that Philip Jackson's book *Life in Classrooms* was first published in 1968 by Teachers College Press but did not become well known until after a later printing in 1990.

Richardson, 1990). General conclusions indicate that if change is to be effective and affect teaching practice it has to: part from teachers' conceptions about their own practice, invite teachers to critically analyze their own practice, allow teacher participation in decision making processes and implementation of change, and respond to the particular needs of teachers and students.

Knowles (1994) and Pajares (1992) have emphasized that beliefs about school and teaching are established very early in life through school experiences and thus are difficult to change. Earlier, Hollingsworth (1989) and Lortie (1975) had pointed out that lack of knowledge about beliefs could be one of the main factors in perpetuating outdated, ineffective teaching practices; that is, in order to change teaching practices, research addressing teachers' beliefs was necessary if actions to promote change were to be effective.

In Mexico, Macotela, Flores, and Seda (2001) studied teachers' conceptions about school by means of self-reports. They concluded that teachers tend to conceive of school as a provider institution and of students as recipients of what school provides. The views reflected in teachers' self-reports differ from national educational policy and its mission to promote active learners and a problem-solving citizenry. They pointed out that the situation is worrisome and merits analysis, given the social and national missions ingrained in the nature of teaching and schools.

In this sense, to specifically address multiple literacies within classrooms requires addressing teachers' and students' conceptions of literacy. That way, our attempts to effect changes that promote and facilitate students' literacy learning should be more encompassing in nature. More important, given the resilient and lasting nature of beliefs regarding teachers' practice, as Knowles (1994) and Pajares (1992) have pointed out, these need to be taken into consideration when change is necessary and/or desirable.

BECOMING LITERATE IN SCHOOL

As a professor and lecturer, I often ask my audience where and how they learned to read and write and where and how they feel they became literate. Although responses vary, audience members usually point to life experiences outside of school in answer to both questions, particularly in response to the second question. School is usually identified as the place where they learned to recognize the letters and to decode; mainly, the mechanics of reading and writing. In contrast, becoming literate was something beyond school that involved family and community. Sometimes they identified exceptionally dedicated teachers who were good mediators and who had encouraged and challenged them in meaningful and interesting ways.

Rockwell (1991), in a study of literacy instruction in Mexican public schools, considered that most school tasks are functional only in and for school; that is, instructional tasks are geared to prepare children to perform present and future school tasks well. She gathered evidence of the opportunities children have to become literate in school, that are not due to instruction. These comprised a variety of literate experiences to which children were exposed within the context of school, albeit instructionally unintended, or what she called *extra-instructional*.

These literate experiences occurred mainly through non curricular activities, such as student's underground literacy, and by observing teachers and other school personnel engaged in literacy events, such as receiving and responding to memos and sending and receiving notes. Rockwell (1991) further concluded that, in this sense, children appropriate themselves of the necessary skills and knowledge about reading and writing in spite of instruction.

In this sense, to discuss multiple literacies means to address both individual and collective issues when the role of conceptions is acknowledged in instruction and learning. Furthermore, in agreement with Lortie (1975), Richardson (1991) and Hollingsworth (1989), efforts to improve education entail change, and can only occur through the life experiences of teachers and students that help shape or reshape their minds in the sense Bruner points out (Bruner, 1996).

CONCEPTIONS ABOUT LITERACY

In what follows, I share findings of several recent studies from the Universidad Nacional Autónoma de Mexico of teachers' and students' conceptions about reading and writing (Mocotela, Seda, & Flores, 1997).[2] Multiple conceptions of literacy, as reflected in teachers' and students' discourse, may shed some light regarding how it may possibly be enacted in literacy instruction and learning. Beyond the specific results and context, these studies are illustrative of the nature and strength of conceptions as they permeate teaching practices and of the tacit learnings children acquire through them. After that, I share some thoughts about instruction and models of change in educational settings, particularly as they refer to teacher change and in-service education.

In the studies to be discussed, reading and writing were addressed separately. The intent was to try to gain some insights about teachers' and students' conceptions about each, reading and writing, and the specific

[2]Project # 23369-H, *Development and evaluation of a collaborative program between classroom and resource teachers and its relation to academic achievement*, funded by the National Council of Science and Technology, Sylvia Macotela, Ileana Seda & Rosa del Carmen Flores, co-investigators, Universidad Nacional Autónoma de México.

instructional and learning actions they may entail. We reasoned that if there were a good alignment between educational policy and what students and teachers declared reading and writing to be, commonalities in the contents of their self-reports for reading and writing would be clear.

Participants in the studies were third-grade students and teachers from Mexican urban public schools. They responded to one self-report questionnaire about reading or about writing that were developed for each participant group (Aguirre-Alquicira, 2002; Arciniega-Olvera, 2001; Lara-Benítez, 2000; Lozada-Martínez, 2000).

Student questionnaires were administered by members of the research team in third-grade classrooms. Third grade was selected because Mexican educational policy identifies third grade as the consolidation year for reading and writing skills and abilities. Also, by then most students are able to respond to written questions. Teacher questionnaires were distributed to third-grade and resource special education teachers who worked with third graders.

Tables 10.1 through 10.4 show some of the questions and the most frequent responses given to them. Questions are synthesized according to purpose for both groups, and responses are organized according to categories of analyses. For each question, n refers to number of participants, and % (percentage) refers to the percentage of responses in the category, as most participants wrote two or more responses to each question.

Responses by students and teachers to the first set of questions (i.e., "What is reading" and "What is writing"?) represent desirable conceptions that are in agreement with the national educational framework for literacy (see Table 10.1). At the same time, there is agreement between students' and teachers' responses, which should be encouraging in terms of its instructional implications, if conceptions are indeed reflected in educational practice. In the case of the children's response to the reading question, "the text to be read" is a reflection of the common terminology used in language class, where *texts* are referred to as *the reading*. This may be an indicator of the power of both the implicit messages as well as the explicit messages that classroom communication and discourse conveys (Cazden, 1988).

Responses to the second set of questions (i.e., reading and writing activities you do in school) raise concerns about the nature and source of the responses to the first question (see Table 10.2). Although the issue is not whether they authentically reflect conceptions, the question is whether instructional actions concur with declared conceptions. In the first questions, both children and teachers seem to have based their responses on prior knowledge and the senses of identity they each had as literate beings in their literate environments. However, the mismatch between what they report they do in classroom activities is troublesome, more so in writing than in reading.

TABLE 10.1
Responses by Students and Teachers to the First Set of Questions

What Is Reading?[a]	*What Is Writing?*[b]
Children ($n = 132$) • The text to be read (46%) • Helps learn about other things (29%) • Something pleasant (14%)	Children ($n = 149$) • Something you learn (23%) • Writing (19%) • Something I like (19%) • Reading (16%) • Express ideas (16%) • Draw letter (15%) • A subject (9%)
Teachers ($n = 56$) • Process of comprehension (64%) • Decoding (26%) • Tool (7%) • Something pleasant (3%)	Teachers (2 groups: resource/classroom) • Communication with signs (25/51%) • Representing ideas and thoughts (38/42%) • Graphemes and phonemes (43/28%) • Letter–sound association (4/22%)

Note. [a]Macotela et al. (1997), Aguirre-Alquicira (2001), Lara-Benítez (2000). [b]Macotela et al. (1997), Arcieniega-Olvera (2001), Pérez-Sánchez (2002).

TABLE 10.2
Responses by Students and Teachers to the Second Set of Questions

Reading Activities You Do in School?[a]	*Writing Activities You Do in School?*[b]
Children ($n = 132$) • Copying and decoding (58%) • Reading and assessment questions (23%)	Children ($n = 149$) • Daily exercises (65%) • Mathematics (30%) • Oral expression (20%) • Cursive writing (15%)
Teachers ($n = 56$) • Comprehension and production of texts, summaries, etc. (22%) • Use of materials (21%) • Decoding (13%)	Teachers (2 groups) • Readings (34/31%) • Pasting activities (27/37%) • Written exercises (20/32%) • Games (13/29%) • Letter-sound association (4/22%)

Note. [a]Macotela et al. (1997), Aguirre-Alquicira (2001), Lara-Benítez (2000). [b]Macotela et al. (1997), Arcieniega-Olvera (2001), Pérez-Sánchez (2002).

One may be inclined to question teachers' honesty in their responses to the questionnaire; however, a more productive question is whether teachers believe that their instructional actions promote literacy (reading and writing abilities) in their classrooms. That is, both teachers and children seem to conceptualize reading and writing as constructive and productive processes. However, when it comes to activities to promote those processes, teachers seem to resort to the well-known routines and exercises that they and those before them have traditionally implemented. The fact that 30% of the students included mathematics and oral expression as part of their writing activities is interesting in itself. Either children have broad conceptions of what writing is, or again, the terminology used in school in reference to writing may be an important influence.

Responses to the third set of questions (i.e. what is assessed in reading and writing?) may serve to reinforce comments about the previous items (see Table 10.3). They suggest that teachers may not yet have the know-how to instruct and assess those abilities that they desire to promote in children.

What does all of this suggest about multiple literacies? There seem to be competing conceptions about literacy operating in the context of instruction for both groups. Children may be responding to implicit as well as explicit messages embedded in instruction and school, whereas teachers may be responding to ideas they consider to be politically correct and, at the same time, holding to their own conceptions. Overall findings of the various studies demonstrate that teachers have different theories about reading and writing as abilities and about the necessary instruction to promote their development. Their views about instructional practice are framed in the archaic (traditional) notions probably espoused by their predecessors. Teachers accurately recite the official discourse and educational policy; however, on the basis of their responses to questions about practice and assessment, its translation to instructional practice seems to be alien to them. This was

TABLE 10.3
Responses by Students and Teachers to the Third Set of Questions

What Is Assessed in Reading?[a]	What is assessed in writing?[b]
Children ($n = 132$)	Children ($n = 149$)
• Decoding (44%)	• Handwriting (60%)
• Handwriting and spelling (39%)	• Spelling (36%)
	• Neatness (19%)
	• Contents (16%)
Teachers ($n = 56$)	Teachers (2 groups)
• Comprehension (32%)	• Dictation and copying (40/34%)
• Decoding (26%)	• Other (34/26%)
• Verbal expression (13%)	• Tests (32/15%)
	• Class participation (14/13%)

Note. [a]Macotela et al. (1997), Aguirre-Alquicira (2001), Lara-Benítez (2000). [b]Macotela et al. (1997), Arcieniega-Olvera (2001), Pérez-Sánchez (2002).

so even though it may have required only recitation of some of the instructional activities suggested in their textbooks and teachers' manuals.

Teacher resistance is often blamed for the lack of implementation of educational policy into instructional practice. Far from trying to point to teachers as sole culprits in this situation, the intention here is to highlight the nature and strength of conceptions as they permeate teaching practices. Similarly, the tacit learnings of children, as triggered through teachers' actions, are both meaningful and powerful, so are the tacit learnings acquired by the teachers themselves as they experienced life as students in elementary school. Furthermore, if we abide by Tatto's (1998) stance that teachers' conceptions about their role molds their educational practice, it follows that children's conceptions about school literacy tasks mold their learning in school (Lara-Benítez, 2000).

The fourth set of questions in the questionnaires addressed the difficulties respondents encountered in learning/teaching reading, writing, or both, and how they were solved (see Table 10.4). In general, students did not feel they had difficulties, and whatever difficulties they mentioned were related to mechanics such as decoding and drawing letters (school demands). Teachers' responses in both the reading and the writing questionnaire groups were quite revealing (only one set of responses, reading or writing, is included in Table 10.4 because answers were, for most practical purposes, identical). Their views about where the problems lay, as well as their source and possible solution, indicate that teachers believed them to be beyond their realm of personal and professional possibility.

Responses from teachers and students to the fifth set of questions (i.e., "What does your teacher do to help you?" and "How do you solve these problems?") reflected optimism about teachers' commitment to and interest in their students (see Table 10.5). What is still pending are the specific targets of their good intentions and positive interventions. In response to

TABLE 10.4
Responses by Students and Teachers to the Fourth Set of Questions

Difficulties in teaching/learning Reading/Writing?

Children (*n* = 149)	Teachers (2 groups)
• Rules of grammar (18%)	• Other (34/33%)
• Handwriting-pretty (17%)	• Family (25/31%)
• Making stories (15%)	• Related to Teaching (12/9%)
• Math (14%)	• Other teachers (9/7%)
• Cursive writing (11%)	

Note. Responses varied from lack of motivation in children, television and video games, to lack of literacy promotion in the nation. Sources: Macotela et al. (1997), Arcieniega-Olvera (2001), Pérez-Sánchez (2002).

TABLE 10.5
Responses by Students and Teachers to the Fifth Set of Questions

What Does Your Teacher Do to Help You?/How Do You Solve These Problems?

Children (*n* = 132)	Teachers (*n* = 56)
• Helps me	• Written strategies
• Explains how to do it	• Reading strategies
• Punitive response	• Motivate them
• Other	• Get other material
	• Talk with parents
	• Provide support
	• Other

Note. Sources: Macotela et al. (1997), Aguirre-Alquicira (2001), Lara-Benítez (2000).

the fifth set of questions most students identified teachers as helpful and attentive to their needs (Lara-Benítez, 2000). Punitive responses consisted mostly of "repeat until I get it right," "do it again," and the like. Although for the most part teachers are helpful and attend to their students' needs, they do so according to the specific targets of their instruction as responses are good news if in-service education is geared toward change processes. These specific findings suggest that teachers would do what they consider necessary to help children achieve their instructional goals. Even in the category of punitive responses, teachers may authentically believe that repetition and not accepting "just anything" from their students helps them improve.

Thus, pre- and in-service education programs need to address teachers' prior conceptions about literacy, to understand them, to build new understandings from them, and to promote change. Most teachers who are active today did not live first hand in school the experiences that current research and educational policy may be promoting. Political caveats notwithstanding, in terms of educational policy, young generations need skills and knowledge that help them cope with the world in which they will live. School and schooling need to promote experiences that foster appropriate implicit and explicit messages within the school and community culture for a good fit into their world. Again, Bruner's (1996) words are helpful here:

> Mind could not exist save for culture. For the evolution of the hominid mind is linked to the development of a way of life where "reality" is represented by a symbolism shared by members of a cultural community, but conserved, elaborated, and passed on to succeeding generations, who by virtue of this transmission continue to maintain the culture's identity and way of life. (p. 3)

CONCLUSION

The power of conceptions is not to be underestimated. If we as educators assume that children and teachers acquire conceptions about school and literacy mainly from the school culture itself, a culture in which all of us are participants, we can also consider changes that are necessary. In essence, and for the sake of discussion, we may want to maintain the overall identity of school culture and its mission while addressing instruction as a key source of change. But effective change can occur only with teachers and students; thus, we need to bring conceptions to the forefront in our change processes, instructional and otherwise.

For a good many years now, research has shed light on the importance of students' conceptions in school learning (e.g., Burton & Brown, 1978; Ginsburg, 1977) as well as the effects of teachers' conceptions in instructional practice (e.g., Hollingsworth, 1989; Lortie, 1975). Educational systems have to invest in the right kinds of actions for the young and, most important, teachers will be expected to fulfill those actions. Teachers need to be aware of their own conceptions in addition to having the necessary knowledge and expertise to help children develop the kinds of conceptions that promote their literacy learnings, learnings that enable them to become literate beings in the various communities in which they participate.

In order for teachers to help create and promote interesting and stimulating learning communities in their classrooms, they need depth and breadth of understanding about students' and their own knowledge bases (conceptions of the world), of students' learning actions, and of their own instructional practice. As teachers, any less will only result in actions to administer the curriculum but not in effective mediation for their students (Paris & Ayres, 1994).

After my lecture at the University of Calgary, one of the teachers who had been in the audience shared with me an experience from her elementary school that may help illustrate the effects of conceptions in instruction. The school is facing serious problems with a group of students whose first-year teacher approached literacy instruction as all fun and games. The children had fun all year, because she wanted them to enjoy school, but apparently they did not learn the fundamentals of literacy as was expected. I consider this an example of the teacher conceiving good instruction and appropriate educational philosophy as children having fun, rather than as substantive learnings that make sense to them. The teacher inadvertently sidestepped the curriculum, its philosophy, and objectives, all the while believing that she was implementing it in ways that were appropriate for the children and that made sense to her.

In the case of our particular interest, literacy, the educational practice of schools, as well as in pre- and in-service teacher education programs, need to be filled with actions that promote and capitalize on what children and teachers seem to know and how they know it. Multiplicity of literacies and conceptions of instruction coexist within schools, and they may serve as stepping stones to diversify, enhance, and enrich the contents of school literacy—that is, rather than dichotomizing literacy into the school's type versus other types, the problem-solving individuals of tomorrow's world need to know, be aware of, understand, and effectively use multiple literacies within and outside of school in order to function well in life.

REFERENCES

Aguirre-Alquicira, N. A. (2001). *Las creencias de los maestros de educación primaria respecto a la lectura en comparación con las de sus alumnos.* [Beliefs of primary education teachers as compared to those of students]. Masters' thesis, Universidad de Las Américas, Asociación Civil, México, Distrito Federal.

Arciniega-Olvera, M. C. (2001). *Enseñanza estratégica de la escritura en el marco de la integración educativa.* [Strategic teaching of writing within a context of educational mainstreaming]. Masters' thesis, Escuela Nacional de Estudios Profesionales de Iztacala, Universidad Nacional Autónoma de México.

Burton, R. R., & Brown, J. S. (1978). Diagnostic models for procedural bugs in basic mathematical skills. *Cognitive Science, 2,* 155–192.

Bruner, J. (1996). *The culture of education.* Cambridge, MA: Harvard University Press.

Berger, B. L., & Luckmann, T. (1967). *The social construction of reality: A treatise in the sociology of knowledge.* New York: Anchor.

Cazden, C. B. (1988). *Classroom discourse: The language of teaching and learning.* Portsmouth, NH: Heinemann.

Cochran-Smith, M., & Lytle, S. (1990). Research on teaching and teacher research: The issues that divide. *Educational Researcher, 19*(2), 2–10.

Cole, M., & Wertsch, J. V. (2001). Beyond the individual–social antimony in discussions of Piaget and Vygotsky. [On line] http://www.massey.ac.nz/-alock/virtual/colevyg.htm

Connelly, F. M., & Clandinin, D. J. (1990). Stories of experience and narrative inquiry. *Educational Researcher, 19*(5), 2–14.

Floden, R. E., & Klinzing, H. G. (1990). What can research on teacher thinking contribute to teacher preparation? A second opinion. *Educational Researcher, 19*(5), 15–20.

Fullan, M., & Miles, M. (1992). Getting reform right: What works and what doesn't. *Phi Delta Kappan, 73*(10), 744–752.

Fullan, M., & Steigelbauer, S. (1991). *The new meaning of educational change.* New York: Teachers College Press.

Gage, N. L. (1989). The paradigm wars and their aftermath: A "historical" sketch of research on teaching since 1989. *Educational Researcher, 18*(7), 4–10.

Gimeno Sacristán, J. (1989). El curriculum: una reflexión sobre la práctica. [Curriculum: A reflection about practice]. Madrid: Morata.

Ginsburg, H. (1977). Children's arithmetic. The learning process. New York: D. Van Nostrand Company.

Heath, S. B. (1991). The sense of being literate: Historical and cross cultural features. In R. Barr, M. L. Kamil, P. B. Mosenthal, & P. D. Pearson (Eds.), *Handbook of reading research II* (pp. 3–25). New York: Longman.

Heller, A. (1977). *Sociología de la vida cotidiana.* [Understanding everyday life]. Barcelona: Ediciones Peninsula, Colección Historia-Ciencia-Sociedad Num. 144.

Hollingsworth, S. (1989). Prior beliefs and cognitive change in learning to teach. *American Education Research Journal, 26*(2), 160–189.

House, E. R., Mathison, S., & McTaggart, R. (1989). Validity and teacher inference. *Educational Researcher, 18*(7), 11–17.

Jackson, Ph. W. (1990). *Life in classrooms.* New York: Teachers College Press.

Jodelet, D. (1988). La representación social: fenómenos, concepto y teoría. [Social representation: phenomena, concepts and theory]. In S. Moscovici (Ed.), *Psicología social II* (pp. 469–494). Barcelona: Paidós.

Knowles, J. G. (1994). Metaphors as windows on a personal history: A beginning teachers' experience. *Teacher Education Quarterly, 21*(1), 37–63.

Lampert, M., & Clark, C. M. (1990). Expert knowledge and expert thinking in teaching: A response to Floden and Klinzing. *Educational Researcher, 19*(5), 21–23.

Lara-Benítez, D. (2000). *Las concepciones sobre la lectura y su aprendizaje en la escuela, en niños de tercer grado de primaria.* [Conceptions of third graders about reading and learning to read]. Tesis de Licenciatura de la Facultad de Psicología, Universidad Nacional Autónoma de México.

Lochhead, J. (1979). On learning to balance perceptions by conceptions: A dialogue between two science students. In J. Lochhead & J. Clement (Eds.), *Cognitive processes instruction* (pp. 147–178). Philadelphia, PA: The Franklin Institute Press.

Lortie, D. (1975). *Schoolteacher: A sociological study.* Chicago: The University of Chicago Press.

Lozada-Martínez, A. R. (2000). *Análisis de las creencias de niños de tercer grado de primaria en relación con la escritura.* [An analysis of third graders beliefs about writing]. Tesis de Licenciatura de la Facultad de Psicología, Universidad Nacional Autónoma de México.

Lytle, S., & Cochran-Smith, M. (1990). Learning from teacher research: A working typology. *Teachers College Record, 92*(1), 83–103.

Macotela, S., Flores, R. C., & Seda, I. (2001). Las creencias de docentes mexicanos sobre el papel de la escuela y del maestro. [The beliefs of Mexican teachers about their role and that of school]. *Revista Iberoamericana de Educacíon.* http://www.oei.es/buscador.htm

Macotela, S., Seda, I., & Flores, R. C. (1997). *Desarrollo y evaluación de un programa de colaboración entre maestros de aula y maestros de apoyo y su relación con el logro académico.* [Development and evaluation of a collaborative program between classroom and resource teachers and its relation to academic achievement]. Proyecto de Facultad de Psicología de la Universidad Nacional Autónoma de México. Consejo Nacional de Ciencia y Tecnología.

Merriam-Webster's collegiate dictionary (10th ed.). (1993). Springfield, MA: Merriam-Webster.

Pajares, M. (1992). Teachers' beliefs and educational research: Cleaning up a messy construct. *Review of Educational Research, 62*(3), 307–332.

Paradise, R. (1979). Socialización para el trabajo: La interacción maestro-alumno en la escuela primaria. [Socialization for work: Interactions teacher-students in elementary school]. *Cuadernos de Investigación Educativa,* vol. 5, México D. F.: Departamento de Investigaciones Educativas del Cinvestav.

Paris, S. G., & Ayres, L. R. (1994). *Becoming reflective students and teachers with portfolios and authentic assessment.* Washington, DC: American Psychological Association.

Pérez-Sánchez, V. (2000). *Creencias de docentes de aula y de apoyo en relación con la enseñanza de la escritura.* Masters' thesis, Facultad de Psicología, Universidad Nacional Autónoma de México.

Popkewitz, T. (1985). Ideology and social formation in teacher education. *Teaching and Teacher Education, 1*(2), 91–107.

Rasinsky, T. V., Padak, N. D., Church, B. W., Fawcett, G., Hendershot, J., Henry, J. M., Moss, B. G., Peck, J. K., Pryor, E., & Roskos, K. A. (Eds.). (2000). *Teaching comprehension and exploring multiple literacies: Strategies from The Reading Teacher.* Newark, DE: International Reading Association.

Richardson, V. (1990). Significant and worthwhile change in teaching practice. *Educational Researcher, 19*(17), 10–18.

Richardson, V. (1996). The role of attitudes and beliefs in learning to teach. In J. Sikula (Ed.), *Handbook of research on teacher education* (pp. 102–119). NY: Macmillan

Rockwell, E. (1991). Los usos escolares de la lengua escrita. [School uses of written language]. In E. Ferreiro & M. Gómez-Palacio (Eds.), *Nuevas perspectivas sobre los procesos de la lecto-escritura,* (pp. 296–320). México, D. F.: Siglo XXI.

Shutz, A. (1974). *El problema de la realidad social.* [The problem of social reality]. Buenos Aires, Argentina: Amorrortu.

Tatto, M. T. (1998). The influence of teacher education on teachers' beliefs. *Journal of Teachers Education, 49*(1), 66–77.

Taylor, D. (1983). *Family literacy: The social context of learning to read and write.* Portsmouth, NH: Heinemann.

11

Lessons From the Reading Clinic

Michael W. Kibby
Debra A. Dechert
The Center for Literacy and Reading Instruction,
University at Buffalo, State University of New York

In this chapter, we present some important lessons about diagnostic teaching learned from our experiences in a university reading clinic. Space requires us to focus on either what children learn in diagnostic teaching or what teachers learn as they become diagnostic teachers; our focus here is the developing reading teacher. We describe what we expect diagnostic teachers to know; how we expect them to design, conduct, assess, evaluate, and reflect on each re-mediation lesson; how their understanding of themselves as teachers changes; and how they should affect not only children's reading performance but also, how they help children change their perception of themselves as instrumental in their own reading improvement. Before delving into the topic of diagnostic teaching, we discuss two important issues that concern reading clinicians: (a) re-mediation and the (b) problem of "has a."

ON THE WORD *RE-MEDIATION*

Among many reading professionals there is growing reluctance to use the term *remedial reader*. Abandoning the word *remedial*, as in *remedial reading* or *remedial reader*, is certainly not a signal to abandon intensive instructional interventions for children who struggle with reading. Klenk and Kibby (2000) pointed out that the word *remedial* derives from *remedy* and means to cure or restore to proper condition. They argued that most children who en-counter difficulty in learning to read have had difficulties with reading from the very beginning of school, and by third grade these children were well below their expected level of reading; indeed, borrowing the term from Merton (1968), Walberg and Tsai (1983) applied the term *Matthew Effects* to describe this scenario, and Keith Stanovich (1986) made the term part of the common vocabulary of reading specialists with his oft-quoted article, "Matthew Effects in Reading ..." (Stanovich, 1986).

The model of Gallimore and Tharp (1990) proposes the development of reading ability as having five major stages with each stage requiring vary-ing forms of assistance—this assistance being called *mediation*. In the first stage, the learner needs the teacher to mediate the initial stages of print rec-ognition by either direct instruction or, more likely, by modeling. "Assisted performance" is required at the second level of learning, where the learner requires direct assistance or mediation from the teacher to accomplish cer-tain forms of a reading task. Some use the term *scaffolding* instead of *assisted performance* (Vygotsky, 1978). Level 3 is guided practice, when the learner is capable of accomplishing this form of reading task with self-assistance or self-mediation, usually seen in self-directed speech as the learner thinks through the learning task. Automaticity in carrying out this reading task in-dependently—without teacher mediation—is level 4. The fifth level is called *recursiveness* (Gallimore & Tharp, 1990), where the learner success-fully accomplishes new versions or forms of this reading task without in-struction or teacher mediation.

Accomplishment of any stage assumes that the learner has active partici-pation in the learning task—as contrasted to the view that children encoun-tering reading difficulties are passive and helpless. The view here is that for children to learn to read, they must mediate the increasingly more complex aspects of reading—from deciphering the nature of the printed word, to monitoring their own gain and retention of knowledge and processes from texts, to transferring what they have learned to new texts—and that most children who encounter difficulty in reading need assisted performance or scaffolding in this transfer process. All children who learn to read must construct their own understanding of the process of using print for infor-mation and enjoyment, and when they learn to read they learn a great deal more than the sum of what their teachers presented to them. In the child's process of mastering the printed form of language—which is not naturally acquired by mere existence in a social environment, as oral language is—teachers must also mediate, by structuring the conditions, materials, forms, and pace of instruction to facilitate the child's progression in read-ing. And because the child will—or must—learn more than the teacher di-rectly teaches, teachers build into their conceptualization of the teaching of reading that learners must also learn to teach themselves a great deal about the reading process. As we point out later in this chapter, it is part of teachers' jobs to monitor and facilitate children's metacognitive awareness of the reading process so that they come to see themselves as learners of reading.

If learning to read is a mediation process for teacher and learner, and this process is not completely successful in what is traditionally called *developmental reading* (note by implication here that the failure is in the process, not in the child or even in the teacher), then both teacher and child must reengage this mediation task—*re-mediation*.

THE PROBLEM OF "HAS A"

In the jargon used by nearly every classroom teacher, re-mediationist, special educator, or school psychologist to describe children encountering difficulties in learning to read, the words "has a" occur, for example, "he has a learning disability," "he has a learning problem," "he has a reading disability," "he has dyslexia." Sometimes, "is," the more pernicious form of "has a," may be used: "He is dyslexic," "He is reading disabled," "He is learning disabled."

Educators and psychologists do a great disservice to children who encounter difficulty in reading by using terms to describe them that imply that the problem or difficulty resides in the child. Whether it is intentional or not, when we say a child "has a reading problem" or a child "is learning disabled," we are saying that the problem is a property of the child. Such language changes our views of what the problem is and where the problem resides. Moreover, perhaps even more important, children so labeled come to believe the problem is theirs, is in them, and is their fault.

As we discuss later, this kind of thinking should have been abandoned well over half a century ago with the work of Marion Monroe (1932) and Helen M. Robinson (1946). We argue that such a view of reading difficulties is perpetuated in part by the language we continually use to describe children for whom the typical reading instructional program has failed. Although we would never recommend such, why is it that we do not say that the school has a "reading program problem" or the classroom teacher "has a teaching disability"?

So, in professional parlance, every effort should be made never to say that a child "has a reading problem." Phrases such as "a child encountering difficulties in reading," "reading is difficult for this child," "this child experiences difficulty in reading," "reading is not a task this child accomplishes easily," "struggling reader" and other similar expressions are more correct and preferred. These terms are longer, and in the beginning, they come off the tongue clumsily, but with increased usage they come forth more fluently. Even more important, however, is that when terms such as these are used instead of "has a reading disability," you know that your portrayal of the child is more positive and more respectful of the child's wholeness. Furthermore, you will feel both more precise and professional in your language. We suggest that all of us adopt such terms and discard the "has a" terminology and thinking. We now turn to the development of our major thesis: what teachers learn as they become diagnostic teachers.

WHAT SKILLED READING TEACHERS OUGHT TO KNOW AND BE ABLE TO DO

Much time, effort, space, and expense go into graduate reading programs for previously certified classroom teachers. These programs require as many as six to eight reading courses and practica. Practica are often, and increasingly (Mosenthal & Evenson, 1999), conducted in university reading centers or reading clinics, requiring a dedication of university space and resources. Such would not be allotted if it were not believed that at the completion of these programs, reading teachers would have gained knowledge, insights, abilities, and techniques beyond those of most classroom teachers. Following are 10 beliefs we have about what it is that reading teachers know and are able to do.

First, skilled reading teachers have adopted or developed a decision-making model of diagnostic assessment and evaluation. Such a model provides an overall perspective, or *gestalt*, of the components and strategies important to successful reading and a sequence for routinely assessing and evaluating those components and strategies in a rational and efficient manner (Kibby, 1995; Kibby & Barr, 1999; Kibby & Scott, 2002; Klenk & Kibby, 2000; O'Flahavan et al., 1992; Polin, 1981: Snow, Burns, & Griffin, 1998, p. 287).

Second, expert reading teachers have knowledge and models of good readers at the various stages of reading development (Chall, 1983). They know what a good reader at a given stage is able to do and not do, and they are able to contrast this model to children they are teaching who find reading difficult in order to build reasonable goals for them (Kibby & Barr, 1999). They also have internalized and used models of effective teaching (Allington & Cunningham, 1996, p. 163). Perhaps most important, an expert reading teacher is an excellent "systematic observer" who "drops all presuppositions about a child ... and listens very carefully and records very precisely what the child can in fact do" (Clay, 1993a, p. 3). As coined by the title of Eisner's (1991) book, these excellent reading teachers had developed the *enlightened eye*.

Third, skilled reading teachers know that in diagnostic assessment, determining what readers know is as important as learning what they do not know. All learning of any form must build on what the learner already knows. The expert reading teacher determines not only what is difficult about reading for the reader but also what reading strengths or knowledge the child possesses. An adage long attributed to George Washington Carver applies here: "You must go forward from where you are with what you have; there is no other way." So too the design of instruction must start with what the reader already knows and can do and go forward from there; there is no other way.

Fourth, for any given intensive intervention reading lesson, good reading teachers substantiate, document, or explain why they are providing that specific instruction, they can explain what the child is able to do and how they know; they can explain what the child needs to learn next; they can explain the important parameters (e.g. methods, materials, pace) of the instruction the child requires to learn and how they know; and they can explain the form of supporting guidance and review that children will need in applying or practicing this new knowledge and how they know (Clay, 1993b; Pinnell, Fried, & Estice, 1990).

Fifth, good reading teachers view all their planned instruction as "responsive instruction" (Shanahan & Barr, 1995, p. 963), "adaptive flexibility" (Spiro, 2001), or "diagnostic teaching" (Kibby, 1995, p. 49). One outcome of this instruction is that teachers presume that every lesson they design requires adjustment while it is being conducted; that is, the lesson as designed is never the same as the lesson conducted, and good reading teachers know that changes to the lesson's design will occur during the lesson (Allington & Cunningham, 1996, p. 164; Clay, 1993b; Pinnell et al., 1990). This in-process-of-instruction adjustment is continual and requires critical analyses of children's responses to the text being read (prior to, while, and after reading), knowledge of the demands of the text, and the ability to implement a wide range of instructional techniques. Another outcome of viewing all instruction as diagnostic teaching is that every individual lesson is a diagnostic assessment, and any one lesson must be based on the results of the previous diagnostic lesson (Clay, 1993b; Morris, Ervin, & Conrad, 1998).

Sixth, reading teachers select text for reading comprehension instruction not so the student learns the content of the text but for the student to apply the reading skills and strategies learned from instruction to process the text such that comprehension results. To elaborate, a science teacher chooses texts specifically for the content they provide, as the science teacher's goal is for the student to gain that specific information. Conversely, processing the text for information gain is the reading teacher's goal, and the nature of the content of that text is not particularly germane. The purpose of student comprehension for the reading teacher is that it determines whether the learner has been able to apply the reading skills and strategies taught well enough for reading comprehension. Therefore, when a reading teacher's students do not comprehend, the teacher knows the reading instruction must be adjusted: that is, that he or she must teach new, or review previously taught, reading skills and strategies; but when the science teacher's students do not learn, that teacher has the option of presenting the content of the text in some other format. This is because gaining the content of the text is the science teacher's goal, whereas for the reading teacher, effective processing of the text for comprehension is the goal.

Seventh, good reading teachers know that solid reading instruction requires a balance of easy (independent, nondirected, or unguided) reading and more difficult (instructional, directed, or guided) reading. They know that learning to read is moving from not knowing; to knowing how; to doing; to doing with ease, accuracy, and speed. Whether a child is still attempting to master the essentials of word recognition or striving to develop the comprehension strategies of analysis and synthesis, fluency is required. Therefore, not all of every instructional session can be devoted entirely to teaching children new strategies, skills, or information. Some of every lesson must be devoted to helping children do what they can already do—but must do more rapidly, with less attention, and with fewer errors, that is, with greater fluency (Clay, 1993b, Snow et al., 1998). It is this fluency-building component of instruction that allows readers to see their success with text, which then facilitates the readers' growing concept of themselves as active readers.

Eighth, the most precious commodity reading teachers are able to give to students, besides their talents, is their time. Teachers of reading do not waste instructional time. Barr (1973–1974) found in first-grade classrooms that the amount learned was highly dependent on *instructional pace*, that is, the rate at which teachers accomplished the lessons. Therefore, expert reading teachers know that they must maintain an instructional pace that keeps the student learning as rapidly as possible.

Ninth, although it is a major goal of re-mediation to help children progress in reading ability, it is equally important when teaching children encountering serious difficulties in reading that the children learn to become active participants in their own learning, not only during instruction but also independently. Perhaps it is the case that no one ever teaches any child to read but rather arranges certain skills, strategies, and texts in such a manner that with teacher mediation or scaffolding (guidance, support, and encouragement), children construct their own understanding of the processes of reading and their own metacognitive awareness of what they need to do to gain comprehension from text. Not only have children who encountered difficulty in reading not learned many reading skills and processes, but also they generally have given up taking responsibility for their own progress in learning to read. Re-mediation must help such children reestablish confidence in their ability to continue to progress in learning to read, as such confidence is necessary to take an active role in learning to read.

Tenth, and finally, good reading teachers realize that the purpose of any lesson is children's learning, not the mere accomplishment of the lesson. This child focus means that the teacher's perception is affixed to what is and is not being learned, not on whether or not such-and-such an instructional activity is completed.

The effective deployment of these skills and abilities in reading re-mediation requires teachers to become skilled in the diagnostic assessment of reading instruction.

BECOMING A DIAGNOSTIC TEACHER OF READING

There is no form of instructional planning that is not directed by decision making. Sometimes, instructional decision making is simple—adopt such-and-such curriculum or instructional materials—and sometimes instructional decision making is much more rigorous: child centered and informed by valid and reliable observations of the child, the child's reading, and the child's response to instruction. The latter view—child-centered instruction based on continual diagnostic assessment during instruction—must be adopted in re-mediation.

DIAGNOSTIC ASSESSMENT:
THE FOUNDATION OF DIAGNOSTIC TEACHING

Making instructional decisions for child-centered instruction is informed by thorough, valid, and reliable observations that result in knowledge of the child as a person, what the child knows and does not know about reading, and the child's learning from diagnostic teaching. From such evaluations and observations, the reading teacher is able to design a complete instructional reading program, including goals, objectives, methods, materials, and evaluation methods specifically tailored for the child.

This process of collecting valid and reliable observations about a child's reading abilities is called *reading diagnostic assessment* or sometimes just *reading diagnosis*. We argue that all re-mediation demands diagnostic assessment procedures, which we call *diagnostic teaching*. (In our clinic, a reading diagnostic assessment always includes some diagnostic teaching—indeed, perhaps 60% of one of our diagnostic assessments is diagnostic teaching.) The view that child-centered instruction is based on assessment for informed decision making by teachers is substantiated by a poll of classroom and reading teachers and reading specialists (O'Flahavan et al., 1992) that found that 68% of those surveyed rated "teacher decision-making in the classroom" as highly important; 52% of this same group also rated "teacher development in assessment" as highly important.

Some in the field of reading automatically associate the word *diagnosis* with the medical model of reading difficulties, in which the purpose of diagnosis is thought to find the "cause" of a child's reading problem. Nothing could be further from the truth: indeed, neither one of us has ever known the cause of any child's reading problem. (Michael W. Kibby once thought he had found the cause of a second-grade girl's reading difficulty when he discovered that in first grade she had 32 different teachers in the 40 weeks of school. But it was found that 11 of the 16 children in that girl's second-grade classroom who had also been in her first-grade classroom were reading at or above average for that city.)

The medical model of diagnosis—that is, searching for a cause of the reading difficulty—should have died long ago, for two major reasons. First, physicians themselves do not define *diagnosis* as a search for the cause of a problem; instead, they define it as "the determination of the nature of a disease" (Stedman & Dirckx, 2001). Why reading people think physicians define diagnosis as a search for the cause of a problem is a curiosity. More important, landmark research in the 1930s and 1940s should have shattered this notion that reading problems have some knowable root cause.

A major research focus between 1920 and 1950 attempted to delineate the cause or causes of reading difficulties. This focus was thought important after the development and use of individual tests of intelligence, during which it was found that many children experiencing reading difficulty were of average or above-average intellect. Some of the potential causes studied were visual acuity, auditory acuity, general physical status, neurological factors, emotional/psychiatric factors, visual perception, and intelligence. The two landmark studies on this topic were by Marion Monroe (1932) and Helen M. Robinson (1946). Robinson first conducted an exhaustive review of the research on each of the hypothesized causes of reading difficulty. This was followed by comprehensive evaluations of 30 children experiencing severe reading problems. Every child was seen individually by a pediatrician, otologist, ophthalmologist, psychiatrist, neurologist, clinical/school psychologist, social worker, and special education teacher. Robinson and Monroe (and others) never found the specific cause of any given child's reading difficulty.

On publication of Robinson's (1946) book (*Why Pupils Fail in Reading*), 30 years of research had been accumulated that concluded the so-called medical model of reading diagnosis—to search for the cause of the reading difficulty—was not valid. It was at that time that reading diagnosis took a major turn. The medical model was abandoned by some; diagnostic assessment moved from the medical model to the intensive instructional intervention model of "a process of gaining a thorough knowledge of a person's reading performance, strategies, skills, and instructional needs through accurate observations for the purpose of modifying instruction" (Kibby, 1995, p. 2). The word *diagnosis* derives from the Greek *dia*, meaning "thorough or through," and *gignoskein*, meaning "to know." Reading diagnostic assessment is an active, problem-solving, decision-making process conducted for the purpose of identifying those instructional milieus, methods, and materials likely to lead to the most rapid reading growth by the student.

Diagnostic assessment incorporates measurement, assessment, and evaluation. *Measurement* is creating a test or scale that numerically quantifies degrees of variation on a human trait; *assessment* is collecting measurements to determine "the degree to which the student has achieved" certain learning (Nitko, 1996, p. 4); and *evaluation* comes after measurement and assessment and is "making a value judgment about the worth of the student's product or performance" on a measurement (Nitko, 1996, p. 8). Scriven (1967) defined the latter form of evaluation as *summative evaluation*. Unfortunately, many today use the term *assessment* when what they are discussing is actually evaluation. Diagnostic assessment requires measurement, assessment, and summative evaluation—but adds to it the components of diagnostic teaching (designing, applying, and evaluating specific instructional methods for a specific child) and uses this information to formulate an instructional program that will maximize the student's learning to read. Scriven called this *formative evaluation*.

Nitko (1996) stated that diagnosis centers on the question "What learning activities will best adapt to this student's individual requirements and thereby maximize the student's opportunities to attain the chosen learning target?" (p. 9). He continued, "Diagnosis implies identifying both the appropriate content and the features of the learning activities in which a student should be engaged to attain the learning target" (p. 9). Diagnostic assessment is the foundation of diagnostic teaching. To be a reading teacher means to be able to measure, assess, and evaluate a child's reading abilities during instruction so as to formulate, implement, and evaluate an instructional program to facilitate the child's most rapid growth in reading—all of this is what we mean by the diagnostic teaching of reading.

DECISION-MAKING MODEL:
THE FOUNDATION OF DIAGNOSTIC ASSESSMENT

Diagnostic assessment is a problem-solving process: identifying the needed information about a child, deciding how to gain that information, interpreting and evaluating that information, integrating the information with previous information, and deciding what further information is needed. Without a decision-making model for this information gathering and interpretation—diagnostic assessment as a problem-solving process often becomes lockstep or hit and miss (Gil, Vinsonhaler, & Wagner, 1979; Gil, Wagner, & Vinsonhaler, 1979; Kibby & Barr, 1999; Sherman, Weinshank, & Brown, 1979; Vinsonhaler, 1979; Wagner & Vinsonhaler, 1978). A comprehensive model of the diagnostic process provides the framework or "a chart of the process of reading diagnosis" (Kibby, 1995, p. vi). Such a diagnostic decision-making model (Kibby, 1995) forms the basis of much of the diagnostic assessment done at our reading center, including the diagnostic assessments that are part of diagnostic teaching.

We have described at length the hallmarks of a skilled diagnostic teacher of reading. We now turn to how it is possible to help a classroom teacher become a diagnostic teacher.

CLASSROOM TEACHERS BECOMING DIAGNOSTIC TEACHERS OF READING

Earlier, we presented a rationale and citations to support our views that certain cognitive knowledge or information is important in becoming a diagnostic teacher, namely, diagnostic assessment and a diagnostic decision-making model. To this list we add knowledge of the normal progress of literacy from early childhood to high school; theories and processes of learning and motivation; the theories of learning to read words, meaning vocabulary acquisition, reading comprehension, reading rates, and reading-study abilities; the psychodynamics of reading difficulties in school, the home, and society; multiple techniques and materials for teaching reading; and the instruments for measuring, methods for assessing, and standards for evaluating reading performance. As important as these are, however, they are just the foundations for becoming a diagnostic teacher.

We argue that it is not enough for skilled reading teachers to have the cognitive awareness that reading is a complex process that involves the rich interplay of prior knowledge, knowledge of orthography and syntax, skills for word recognition and word meaning, and strategies for constructing meaning from a variety of different texts and genre—it also requires an ability to plan and implement instruction with an understanding that before, during, and after any part of the re-mediation lesson the developing reading teacher be capable of adapting instruction to maximize the child's learning and minimize frustration. In facilitating the development of a reading teacher's adaptive flexibility and confidence during instruction, we use the lesson plan as a major tool to promote cognitive awareness, reflection, and insight.

What is essential to underscore here is that we often find that the first step in cultivating the developing reading teacher's ability to mediate learning requires them to learn that instruction and assessment are not separate entities. Our goal is to enhance the ability to observe a child engaged in the process of silent reading "while determining which parts of the process are interrupting the smooth operation of the whole" (Purcell-Gates, 2001, p. 124). This is done as teachers' kid-watching skills are developed and assessment techniques are integrated within the instructional session.

Many times, we find that the developing reading teachers do not avail themselves of the many assessment opportunities inherent in instruction through methods such as retelling, think-alouds, open-ended questions, reciprocal teaching, literature circles, Book Club, language experience activities, and prediction—to name but a few. In this first step, if you will, of the discovery process that transforms the developing reading teachers into diagnostic teachers, it is essential for them to become keenly aware of how they are teaching and how children respond to their instruction. They must learn to be accurate perceivers of their teaching and their students' learning. They must critically analyze children's ability to retell what they have read, critically analyze children's ability to make predictions based on all cueing systems, critically analyze the cognitive processes revealed in children's think alouds, critically analyze interpretations shared during peer discussions at Book Club—indeed, critically analyze and evaluate all aspects of every component of the lesson. We "push their thinking" here by requiring what we call *Diagnostic Reflection and Insights* to be written into the required daily lesson plans.

At the onset, the reflective process of putting into words a critical analysis and evaluation of the teaching and learning of the completed lesson is painstaking, and these first reflections are often barely a paragraph. By semester's end, however, Diagnostic Reflections and Insights have evolved into eloquent statements sometimes two or three pages in length with citations of research, theory, or methods texts. We do this also by requiring teachers to describe their lesson; guiding them to self-question before, during, and after instruction; and to use the resultant answers as the foundations on which they build their Diagnostic Reflections and Insights. These questions are based on their assessments of what they know about the children they are instructing: the strategies they know but do not consistently apply, the background knowledge they have that is relevant to the context of what is read, their interest and motivation for reading, and their ability to monitor for comprehension.

Becoming a diagnostic teacher, then, requires critical analysis and self-questioning of one's own teaching and the impact it has on the learner; it is part of the process that we call discovering the *what, why, how,* and the *"now what?"* of re-mediation. This knowledge leads to adaptive flexibility between and within lessons and culminates in confidence to engage in diagnostic teaching. To chronicle the discovery process that leads to reflective ability as a diagnostic teacher, we offer some further elaboration.

LEARNING TO DESCRIBE A RE-MEDIATION LESSON

In classroom teaching, most teachers focus their attention on the instructional activities, especially in terms of time to be used for the activity, keeping all students attentive during the activity, and managing the activity in such a manner that it is accomplished. It often appears to the observer that the activity of the moment is the purpose of instruction, not the learning that the activity was originally planned to develop (Allington, 1995; Kibby & Barr, 1999). One reason for this might be that the teachers' focus is on the content to be learned, not on the processes used or needed by their learners. Beginning reading teachers are no different. To help them come to focus on the learners, the learning, and the teaching, we require clinicians to write a full description of what occurred in their re-mediation lesson—after they have already written an evaluation of each of the lesson's objectives. We call this section of the lesson plans *Reflections and Insights*—but it takes weeks before what is written progresses from description to reflection—which is why we start by calling this section "Learning to Describe a Re-Mediation Lesson."

In the beginning, the descriptions are generally skimpy and lack detail and, if they do address assessment, it is usually without quantitative data or supportive description. An example of a teacher's early lesson description follows:

> Even though the book I used with Jason today during instruction was more difficult than the book we read during our last session, he was able to read and comprehend successfully with only minimal text preparation. For today's lesson the text preparation included development of sight vocabulary, activation of prior knowledge, and setting purposes for reading through prediction.

This information tells us little about the ways in which the reading teacher used assessment or reflective thinking in drawing conclusions about Jason's learning. She has provided an extremely light description of the learning that occurred and provides none of the quantifiable information on which re-mediation is based. An important tenet of diagnostic teaching is that the teacher not only integrate assessment with instruction but also be able to write her diagnostic insights and reflections in a way that clearly delineates how (a) the assessments were used to evaluate Jason's learning, (b) *how* and *why* she changed her instructional plan during the course of instruction, and (c) how and why assessments of Jason's learning affected her plans for further instruction.

Diagnostic assessment of reading re-mediation is learning to ask questions of yourself regarding all aspects of your instructional planning and implementation and the students' engagement, learning and application—we call this *self-questioning*. Developing specialists in the teaching of reading need direction from a supervisor to learn and apply these strategies and interaction with peers to facilitate the co-construction of knowledge (Vygotsky, 1978).

SELF-QUESTIONING

Recognizing that the developing reading teacher often begins writing Reflections and Insights of the lesson as more of a description, the supervisor guides or scaffolds the reading teacher's self-questioning, usually by directing questions on the lesson plans or during discussions of instruction. We believe it is critical for the diagnostic teacher to provide data that have been gathered during the ongoing assessment integrated with the instruction.

The following questions illustrate the feedback Jason's teacher received in her lesson plan book as her supervisor attempted to scaffold the teacher to use assessment of instruction and instructional outcomes in her evaluations and reflective thinking.

1. *What* made this book more difficult than the one you used during a previous lesson, and why did you make the decision to use it? Did you determine that the book was more difficult based solely on text issues, such as fewer picture cues, longer sentences, more difficult concepts? Did you consider Jason's interest in reading the book or his prior knowledge about the information in the text, and what importance this may have had on his ability to construct meaning from the text?

2. *How* did you determine that only minimal text preparation was needed before Jason began to read the text? Did you use some form of assessment of prior knowledge on the text topic, such as a *quickwrite*, discussion, or anticipation guide?

3. *Why* did you decide that the text preparation for today's lesson required development of sight vocabulary, activation of prior knowledge, and setting purposes for reading through prediction? Based upon information you have gathered about Jason from previous lesson, did you determine that he had limited sight vocabulary, which contributed to difficulties in word recognition and fluency and, therefore, decided to teach sight vocabulary before he read?

4. *How* did you determine that activation of prior knowledge was necessary in preparing Jason to read this text? *What* if you determined that Jason had misconceptions in his prior knowledge that may interfere with his ability to comprehend—in the course of instruction, *now what? How* might you clarify any misconceptions in Jason's prior knowledge?

5. *Why* did you choose to use prediction as a way to set purpose for reading? Elaborate in your Reflections and Insights about the cognitive and metacognitive value placed on using prediction to facilitate comprehension from a theoretical stance.

6. *How* did you use assessment during instruction to determine that "Jason was able to read and comprehend successfully?" On what do you base a determination of successful comprehension? Did you use a rubric for an oral retelling? Did you listen to him read orally to ascertain levels of fluency that improved his ability to read and comprehend? Did you encourage Jason to engage in think-alouds as he read to provide you with knowledge of his metacognitive processes?

We have observed that when clinicians do not use self-questioning, it limits their ability to plan effective instruction that is child centered. What that really means is that instruction may appear to be organized and well presented, but it will not be specific for the strengths and needs of the individual child, that is, not child centered. We repeat, when the planning of instruction is not child centered, it often becomes activity oriented, not learning oriented. Diagnostic teachers know that planning a re-mediation lesson is much more than effective research-based methods—although such methods are important in good diagnostic teaching—it also includes using methods that the clinician determines will be effective based upon insights during close observations and assessments. Learning to self-question in the manner described facilitates the clinician's ability to develop insights that include hypotheses, notions, and understandings about a specific child's ability to construct meaning from a text. We look for evidence in the clinician's writing of the Reflections and Insights that he or she has collected assessment data and analyzed those data in order to monitor the child's reaction to instruction and learning.

ONGOING ASSESSMENT

Assessing reading is easy when everything the learner does is oral (e.g., reading text orally, answering aloud questions presented orally, reading flash cards or lists of sight words orally, and completing isolated phonics tasks orally) or when the lessons consist of worksheets or skill-development activities. This is one of the reasons round-robin reading, workbook pages, and self-correcting comprehension texts are popular and widely used. Perhaps excellent learners are able to stitch together an understanding of the reading process from such piecemeal reading activities, but children who find reading a difficult and puzzling task are not likely to gain insight into what reading is all about by completing dozens of workbook pages on short vowels and consonant digraphs or taking turns to stumble from one word to the next in a round-robin reading session.

If a child is going to learn to read, most especially a child who has already encountered serious difficulties in learning to read in previous instruction, then we believe that child must be engaged in the reading—silent reading—of complete and authentic texts. And if the child is, for the most part, going to read these texts silently, then a teacher must learn to assess and evaluate (diagnostic assessment) that child's reading by means other than listening for reading errors or scoring worksheets. Instructional assessment means that diagnostic teachers must learn to listen and observe during (a) prereading predictions, purpose setting, and background development; (b) students' think-alouds or queries during reading; (c) and students' retellings, peer group conversations, and responses to open-ended questions.

Diagnostic teachers must learn to use instruction as assessment and to use the assessment of instruction to plan further instruction.

A major benefit from gaining an ability to assess learning by attending to the children's responses to instruction and text during a lesson is that diagnostic teachers learn they do not have to hear children read daily or to complete numerous worksheets to know whether their students have or have not learned. A small part of the supervisor's role here is insisting on silent reading being the dominant activity in every lesson. Helping the developing diagnostic teacher learn to self-question—that is, to ask the right questions about the child's learning—is also an important tool of the supervisor. Yet another method to help develop these abilities to observe instruction from an assessment point of view is requiring teachers to evaluate each objective of their lesson. They sit with their lesson plans, anecdotal notes from the lessons, audio- or videotapes of the lesson, and the work products of the lesson and write an evaluation of each and every objective of the lesson.

REFLECTIONS AND INSIGHTS

We stated in an earlier section that when beginning to write reflections or insights from the diagnostic teaching, the product is usually vague and nonspecific. An example of such a description by a teacher in the first week of clinic was given. The recursiveness of writing plans for instruction, assessing instruction, evaluating the goal of each lesson, and self-questioning under the tutelage of a supervisor who watches at least 50% of every lesson, helps lead clinicians to develop the ability to reflect on their lessons.

In actuality, this Reflection and Insights portion of each day's lesson plan is what allows the supervisor to gain a glimpse of the thinking the teacher is using to plan, conduct, assess, and modify instruction. *Reflection* is the process of learning what we know by thinking about what we did (Schön, 1987). When the supervisor reads the Reflections and Insights, what the teacher thinks is revealed. Learning to be a diagnostic teacher of reading is not "hard science"; although learning to be a diagnostic teacher of reading has a core knowledge, much of what is learned in the final stages is learned by apprenticeship with the mentoring of a supervisor and the support of fellow apprentices. Polanyi's (1958) observations about "an art" are germane here in thinking about an apprenticeship in a university reading clinic: "An art which cannot be specified in detail cannot be transmitted by prescription, since no prescription for it exists. It can be passed on only by example from master to apprentice" (p. 53). And this growth does happen, teacher after teacher (although not in every case). Note the growth by Jason's teacher from the loose description she wrote in the first week of remediation to the following Reflections and Insights written after 12 weeks of instruction, a portion of which follows:

There were many parts of today's lesson where my teaching was right on and fit with what Jason needed to learn and was able to learn. I knew he had a strong interest in the book we were reading (even though I selected it for him, with his approval). I had told him it was a bit difficult, so we would have to work extra hard in terms of number of hard words, but that he should be able to understand the book if I helped him to read the words (I did both the Dale–Chall Revised and the Flesch–Kincaid on MSWord.). This actually seemed to motivate him (I think his success lately has made him become less passive about each lesson).

The Distinctive Features Method of teaching sight vocabulary is becoming less necessary for him each week. He learned the 7 sight words I taught him today in about half of the time I allotted for this instruction. It seems as he learns more words, he needs less instruction in order to learn yet more words (he still has a lot of words to learn, however). He seems to have developed the ability to examine and retain words I teach him with relative success—though he still learns words at about 1/3 the rate he should be learning them. It is not necessary to point out the distinguishing characteristics as often as in the past. I wonder if I can step up the number of words I teach him each lesson? Since he needs less instructional time to learn each word, can he learn more words in that time or is the limit on his learning not instructional time, but number of words? I will try this idea out in the next four lessons. I will teach three more sight words per day before each text, and after the lessons compare his retention of these words to his retention of the words taught the two weeks before this experiment.

I was not adequately prepared today, however, for teaching meaning vocabulary to Jason. I need to read about vocabulary instruction this evening (I will re-read Beck, McKeown and Kucan (2002) tonight, and review my notes from 557 [the course preceding clinic]). Jason has a great deal of background information, but for some reason, he has a greater need to be taught the words that label or signify those things he knows than I had thought. There were four words in the first chapter that he could "bark" (I was glad of that, his word recognition strategies are improving), but he did not know what each word signified and I had presumed he did (*rustler*, *rise* [a raised part of the ground], *graze*, and *poker*). I need to be more cognizant of meaning vocabulary for him; as I said, he knew about moving wood in a fire with a piece of metal, he just did not know it is called a *poker*.

He still answers my comprehension questions excellently, even open-ended ones; what he continues to struggle with is retelling. It seems that it is not the process of comprehending that is difficult for him (but, this is in a diagnostic teaching activity and the text is two years below his expected grade level), but rather the process of organizing this information to retell. I will check this notion out in the next lesson by helping him make brief notes of information he reads that he thinks would be important to remember if he had to tell someone about what he had read; then he can use these notes to tell me what he read.

This is only about half of what this clinician wrote. Note how she honed in on where her teaching of meaning vocabulary needed to be redirected based on Jason's difficulty with knowing what words signify concepts he already knows; her cognitive information about various degrees of knowledge of things and words fits hand-in-glove with her assessment of what Jason does and does not know, and both lead to reconceived instructional methods. Her insights about Jason's gradually increasing ease in learning words—juxtaposed to his still being far behind in the number of words he can actually read—are also insightful and useful. Note that after she steps up her teaching of sight vocabulary for the next 2 weeks, not only will she know whether Jason can learn at this pace, but she will have also learned on her own whether Jason's learning is limited by how much he can learn in a given time or on how many words he can learn at once. She forms a second hypothesis in these Reflections and Insights regarding retelling. She notes that she just seemed to expect Jason to be able to retell given that he did comprehend (seen in his ability to answer direct questions). She has seen that the comprehension task consists of more than just "getting what is in the text," but is also dependent on the manner in which the comprehension must be exhibited. Note that she has moved from helping him to comprehend to helping him learn to demonstrate his comprehension.

It can be seen in this Reflections and Insights segment that the teacher is asking questions about her teaching and the learner's learning at almost every turn. We find that both of Vygotsky's (1978) forms of reflection—intermental (social interaction) and intramental (in your own mind)—promote more critical levels of analysis and thinking. So, in addition to the Reflections and Insights portion of every lesson plan, we facilitate self-questioning, analysis, and critical thinking with peer interactions. A portion of this interaction is between supervisor and teacher, but a very important in this growth of reflective ability is interaction with peers who are also engaged in re-mediation. In planned twice-a-week seminars and unplanned bull sessions after the children have gone home there is a constant sharing of insights, concerns, victories, methods, materials, and struggles. We have observed these discussions over the years, but in the future, we need to study these sessions.

ADAPTIVE FLEXIBILITY

Adaptive flexibility (Spiro, 2001) is perhaps the ultimate goal of any university reading clinic's graduate program. One important form of adaptive flexibility has already been demonstrated in the Reflections and Insights of Jason's teacher. She indicates in three places (recall that only about half of her writing was presented) where, why, when, and how she is going to change or adapt her instruction (sight vocabulary, meaning vocabulary, and retelling). As important as it is to reflect on a day's lessons and to determine how to adapt one's methods and materials to enhance even further the student's learning in the next lesson, it is as important to adapt instruction in the process of instruction. No re-mediation lesson is ever completed exactly as planned; if a lesson is completed exactly as it was planned, the lesson has not been conducted by a diagnostic teacher. Together, we have observed more than 1,000 teachers teaching more than 2,000 children—which results in observations of far more than 10,000 or 12,000 re-mediation lessons; any lesson we have ever seen that was accomplished just as the teacher intended it was not a good lesson and always failed to fit the child's responses to instruction, texts, content, skills, or even the teacher. Assessing instruction is not only a postlesson process but occurs time and again during the lesson. And with each assessment, the diagnostic teacher must make a decision as to how to proceed in the next portion of the lesson. Often—even in lessons that have been insightfully planned—this means changing directions, materials, teaching methods, and assessment methods. Sometimes it even means dropping an activity for which the child is not ready or the teacher is not prepared to meet the child's instructional need. This does not necessarily mean poor planning; each new lesson is intended to take the child to new ground, to a yet higher level, to a yet greater challenge. The ability to adapt instruction successfully in the process of instruction is the benchmark toward which we strive to bring every reading teacher, and when they arrive, they are diagnostic teachers of reading.

CONFIDENCE

Directing a university reading clinic has many rewards, not the least of which is participating in the growth and success of a child who once found reading difficult and frustrating. But the major reward is watching teachers who come into your clinic already reasonably competent classroom teachers grow into diagnostic teachers of reading (reading clinicians). They start out competent, but in the process of helping students who are experiencing reading difficulties gain in reading ability and reading confidence over the course of re-mediation, teachers gain confidence. They gain confidence not only in what they know but also in what they can do and what they can learn (adapt) to do if necessary. This is the best reward: seeing diagnostic teachers who look forward to their encounter with the next child they meet who needs a great deal of help in reading. They are eager to begin to work with him; they are confident that they know how to help; they know that if they find they cannot help with what they know at the time, they can read, research, or create a way to help; they know they will help the child grow in reading—even if not to the point of the child's expected level; and their confidence allows them to take risks that will have both a positive impact on the children's learning as well as their own.

CONCLUSION

In recent years, there has been discussion and some debate regarding reading clinics within the university setting (Mosenthal & Evenson, 1999). As stated earlier, clinics use valuable university resources, and some may wonder if they are worth the investment. Another comment on clinics is that they generally provide one-to-one instruction, something that a teacher is not likely to do in the public schools. But it is not one-to-one teaching that is the focus of a university reading clinic; instead, the focus is on providing teachers a milieu in which to maximize their learning about their teaching, assessment, and evaluation abilities.

In a university reading center, teachers are provided the rare experience of teaching in a one-to-one milieu, with guidance and support from an experienced supervisor; interaction with peers similarly engaged; and requirements for extensive planning, assessment, evaluation and reflection. The teacher is able to focus exclusively on the student, the student's learning, and her (or his) impact on that instruction and learning—that is, the teacher has the opportunity, structure, and support to become a fully capable and competent diagnostic teacher of reading.

REFERENCES

Allington, R. L. (1995). Literacy lessons in the elementary schools: Yesterday, today, and tomorrow. In R. L. Allington & S. A. Walmsley (Eds.), *No quick fix: Rethinking literacy programs in America's elementary schools* (pp. 1–15). New York: Teachers College Press.

Allington, R. L., & Cunningham, P. M. (1996). *Schools that work: Where all children read and write.* New York: HarperCollins.

Barr, R. (1973–1974). Instructional pace differences and their effect on reading acquisition. *Reading Research Quarterly, 9,* 526–554.

Beck, I. L., McKeown, M. G., & Kucan, L. (2002). *Bringing words to life: Robust vocabulary instruction.* New York: Guilford.

Chall, J. S. (1983). *Stages of reading development.* New York: McGraw-Hill.

Clay, M. M. (1993a). *An observation schedule of early literacy achievement.* Portsmouth, NH: Heinemann.

Clay, M. M. (1993b). *Reading Recovery: A guidebook for teachers in training.* Portsmouth, NH: Heinemann.

Eisner, E. W. (1991). *The enlightened eye: Qualitative inquiry and the enhancement of educational practice.* New York: Macmillan.

Gallimore, R., & Tharp, R. G. (1990). Teaching mind in society. In L. C. Moll (Ed.), *Vygotsky in education: Instructional implications and applications of sociohistorical psychology* (pp. 175–205). Cambridge, England: Cambridge University Press.

Gil, D., Vinsonhaler, J. F., & Wagner, C. C. (1979). *Studies of clinical problem solving behavior in reading diagnosis* (Research Series No. 42). East Lansing: Institute for Research on Teaching, Michigan State University.

Gil, D., Wagner, C. C., & Vinsonhaler, J. F. (1979). *Simulating the problem solving of reading clinicians* (Research Series No. 30). East Lansing: Institute for Research on Teaching, Michigan State University.

Kibby, M. W. (1995). *Practical steps for informing literacy instruction: A diagnostic decision-making model.* Newark, DE: International Reading Association.

Kibby, M. W., & Barr, R. (1999). The education of reading clinicians. In P. Mosenthal & D. H. Evenson (Eds.), *Advances in reading/language arts: Vol. 6. Future directions for university reading clinics* (pp. 3–40). New York: JAI.

Kibby, M. W., & Scott, L. (2002). Using computer simulations to teach decision-making in reading diagnostic assessment for re-mediation. *Reading Online, 6*(3). Retrieved February 14, 2005 from http://www.readingonline.org/articles/art_index.asp? HREF=/articles/Kibby

Klenk, L. & Kibby, M. W. (2000). Re-mediating reading difficulties: Appraising the past, reconciling the present, constructing the future. In M. Kamil, P. Mosenthal, P. D. Pearson, & R. Barr (Eds.), *Handbook of reading research* (Vol. III, pp. 667–690). New York: Longman.

Merton, R. (1968). The Matthew effect in science. *Science, 159*(3810), 56–63.

Monroe, M. (1932). *Children who cannot read.* Chicago: University of Chicago Press.

Morris, D., Ervin, C., & Conrad, K. (1998). A case study of a middle school reading disability. *Reading Teacher, 49*(5), 368–377.

Mosenthal, P., & Evenson, D. H. (1999). *Advances in reading/language arts: Vol. 6. Future directions for university reading clinics.* New York: JAI.

Nitko, A. J. (1996). *Educational assessment of students* (2nd ed.). Englewood Cliffs, NJ: Merrill.

O'Flahavan, J., Gambrell, L. B., Guthrie, J., Stahl, S. S., Baumann, J. F., & Alvermann, D. E. (1992, August/September). *Reading Today, 10,* 12.

Pinnell, G. S., Fried, M. D., & Estice, R. M. (1990). Reading Recovery: Learning how to make a difference. *Reading Teacher, 43*(5), 282–295.

Polanyi, M. (1958). *Personal knowledge: Towards a post-critical philosophy.* Chicago: University of Chicago Press.

Polin, R. M. (1981). *A study of preceptor training of classroom teachers in reading diagnosis* (Research Series No. 110). East Lansing: Institute for Research on Teaching, Michigan State University.

Purcell-Gates, V. (2001). What we know about readers who struggle. In R. F. Flippo (Ed.), *Reading researchers in search of common ground* (pp. 118–128). Newark, DE: International Reading Association.

Robinson, H. M. (1946). *Why pupils fail in reading.* Chicago: University of Chicago Press.

Schön, D. A. (1987). *Educating the reflective practitioner.* San Francisco: Jossey-Bass.

Scriven, M. (1967). *The methodology of evaluation (AERA monograph series on curriculum evaluation, Publication No. 1).* Chicago: Rand McNally.

Shanahan, T., & Barr, R. (1995). Reading Recovery: An independent evaluation of the effects of an early intervention for at-risk learners. *Reading Research Quarterly, 30,* 958–996.

Sherman, G., Weinshank, A., & Brown, S. (1979). *Training reading specialists in diagnosis* (Research Series No. 31). East Lansing: Institute for Research on Teaching, Michigan State University.

Snow, C. E., Burns, M. S., & Griffin. P. (1998). *Preventing reading difficulties in young children*. Washington, DC: National Academy Press.

Spiro, R. (2001). Principled pluralism for adaptive flexibility in teaching and learning to read. In R. F. Flippo (Ed.), *Reading researchers in search of common ground* (pp. 92–97). Newark, DE: International Reading Association.

Stanovich, K. E. (1986). Matthew effects in reading: Some consequences of individual differences in the acquisition of literacy. *Reading Research Quarterly, 21,* 360–407.

Stedman, T. L., & Dirckx, J. H. (2001). *Stedman's concise medical dictionary for the health professions, illustrated 4th edition*. Philadelphia: Lippincott Williams & Wilkins.

Vinsonhaler, J. F. (1979). *The consistency of reading diagnosis* (Research Series No. 28). East Lansing: Institute for Research on Teaching, Michigan State University.

Vygotsky, L. (1978). *Mind in society: The development of higher psychological processes* (M. Cole, Ed.). Cambridge, MA: Harvard University Press.

Wagner, C. C., & Vinsonhaler, J. F. (1978). *On the conceptualization of clinical problem solving* (Research Series No. 9). East Lansing: Institute for Research on Teaching, Michigan State University.

Walberg, H. J., & Tsai, S. L. (1983). Matthew effects in education. *American Educational Research Journal, 20,* 359–373.

Author Index

Subject Index